PERCEPTIONS OF CUBA:
CANADIAN AND AMERICAN POLICIES
IN COMPARATIVE PERSPECTIVE

In 1976, with the U.S. trade embargo against Cuba under way,
Canada's Prime Minister Pierre Elliott Trudeau visited the island
nation, befriended his counterpart, and exclaimed publicly, 'Long live
Prime Minister Fidel Castro!' During the past half-century of communist rule in Cuba, Canada's policy of engagement with the country has
contrasted sharply with the United States' policy of isolation. Based on
a series of interviews conducted in Havana, Washington, and Ottawa,
Perceptions of Cuba moves beyond traditional economic and political
analyses to show that national identities distinct to each country contributed to the formation of their dissimilar foreign policies.

Lana Wylie argues that Canadians and Americans perceive Cuba
through different lenses rooted in their respective identities: American
exceptionalism made Cuba the polar opposite of the United States,
while Canada's self-image as a good international citizen and as 'not
American' has allowed the country to engage with the Cuban government. By acknowledging that competing national identities, perceptions, and ideas play a major role in foreign policies, *Perceptions of Cuba*
makes a significant contribution to our understanding of international
relations.

LANA WYLIE is an assistant professor in the Department of Political
Science at McMaster University.

LANA WYLIE

Perceptions of Cuba

Canadian and American Policies in Comparative Perspective

UNIVERSITY OF TORONTO PRESS
Toronto Buffalo London

ISBN 978-1-4426-4061-0 (cloth)
ISBN 978-1-4426-1007-1 (paper)

Printed on acid-free, 100% post-consumer recycled paper with vegetable-based inks

Library and Archives Canada Cataloguing in Publication

Wylie, Lana, 1968–
Perceptions of Cuba : Canadian and American policies in comparative
perspective / Lana Wylie.

Includes bibliographical references and index.
ISBN 978-1-4426-4061-0 (bound). – ISBN 978-1-4426-1007-1 (pbk.).

1. Canada – Foreign relations – Cuba.   2. United States – Foreign relations –
Cuba.   3. Cuba – Foreign relations – Canada.   4. Cuba – Foreign relations –
United States.   5. Cuba – Foreign public opinion, Canadian.   6. Cuba –
Foreign public opinion, American.   7. National characteristics, Canadian.
8. National characteristics, American.   I. Title.

FC251.C82W95 2010   327.7107291   C2009-907062-6

This book has been published with the help of a grant from the Canadian
Federation for the Humanities and Social Sciences, through the Aid to
Scholarly Publications Program, using funds provided by the Social
Sciences and Humanities Research Council of Canada.

University of Toronto Press acknowledges the financial assistance to its
publishing program of the Canada Council for the Arts and the Ontario
Arts Council.

 Canada Council   Conseil des Arts
for the Arts   du Canada

 ONTARIO ARTS COUNCIL
CONSEIL DES ARTS DE L'ONTARIO

University of Toronto Press acknowledges the financial support for its
publishing activities of the Government of Canada through the
Book Publishing Industry Development Program (BPIDP).

To my parents, Lloyd and Ferne Wylie

Contents

Preface

Perceptions of Cuba makes the case that foreign policy is constructed by our perceptions which in turn have their origins in our identities. This research began with a research question that was familiar in the literature at the time. I set out to explain why the United States continued to isolate Cuba while Canada followed a policy of engagement. I began by reviewing the standard explanations based on electoral and interest-group politics and economic interests.

Certainly, in the United States, Cuban Americans have become a powerful immigrant group. When they vote as a bloc, they are able to influence election outcomes in Florida, and since Florida is a swing state in presidential elections, Cuban Americans become an important focus of campaigns. Their concerns are well known in Washington and they often have the ear of policy makers. Canada, on the other hand, does not have a significant Cuban immigrant population and Canadians are able to sell many of their products to Cubans without a concern for American competition. In most of the scholarly literature, these explanations have been well accepted as the reasons for the existence of the two policies.

Yet, once I began to conduct my interviews in Washington, Ottawa, and Havana, I was amazed by the differences in the way Canadians and Americans saw the same issues, events, and people in Cuba and even understood the country itself. In Havana, American and Canadian diplomats often reside in the same neighbourhoods, use the same grocery stores, and frequent the same restaurants, yet they told me very different stories about life in Havana and politics and society in Cuba. Electoral politics or economic advantages could not explain these different perceptions, these different ideas of the 'truth.'

This book explores the role of perception in the construction of these two policies. Although perceptions of Cuba have evolved in Canada and the United States over the years, the book makes the case that some perceptions have persisted for many decades. The cover represents a particular view of Cuba that resides in the American imagination. The image portrayed harkens back to a pre-revolutionary era in Cuban history when Cuba was considered within the American imagination as 'America's playground.'

The research for this book first began in the late 1990s as I was completing my PhD. At that time I conducted thirty-five confidential interviews of Cuban, American, and Canadian policy makers and other influential individuals in Washington, D.C., Ottawa, and Havana. Some of these people were in government positions at that time while others had retired or assumed new roles in the private sector. Still others were powerful actors in business, academic, or policy making circles. In subsequent years I had many more discussions with other people in similar roles, and although most of these conversations were not formal interviews, they certainly contributed to my understanding of Canadian and American policy towards Cuba.

This book would not have been possible without the assistance of many colleagues, friends, and family. I am pleased to acknowledge them here. It has been a pleasure to work once again with Daniel Quinlan, a fabulous editor at the University of Toronto Press, and with a highly skilled copy editor, Curtis Fahey. Both of them went above and beyond to help me turn a manuscript into this published book. I appreciate, too, the assistance of Len Husband and Wayne Herrington, also with the University of Toronto Press. The manuscript was greatly improved by the suggestions of the anonymous reviewers. I thank the many research assistants who worked with me on the book. They are Meaghan Willis, Lucy Draper-Chislett, Calum McNeil, Maegan Baird, and Jacqueline Cummings. Thank you also to the late Mary Haslam, who, as a life-long educator, would have been pleased that her gift enabled my first research trip to Cuba.

I am greatly indebted as well to all my colleagues in Canada, Cuba, and the United States who also study Cuba and who provided me with invaluable feedback, support, and advice. Although it is impossible to name everyone here, I would like to acknowledge especially a few people who went above and beyond. Mark Entwistle provided invaluable insight into the Canada-Cuba and U.S.-Cuba relationships and urged me to get the book published when it was in its infancy.

Robert Wright encouraged me from the moment I first told him about the project, freely shared his knowledge of Cuba and the Canadian-Cuban relationship with me, and has given me his friendship and support. My friends and colleagues in the Cuban-Canadian Working Group at the University of Havana, particularly Raúl Rodriguez and Jorge Mario Sanchez, have provided much support and advice. Over the years I have come to think of these people as friends as well as colleagues. I am grateful to everyone, past and present, at the Canadian embassy in Havana for their assistance and hospitality during my many trips to Cuba. In particular, I would like to thank Jean-Pierre Juneau, Alexandra Bugailiskis, Simon Cridland, and Ram Kamineni.

I consider myself fortunate to work with a great group of colleagues at McMaster University who have encouraged the publication of this volume. Similarly, it would have taken me much longer to turn the rough manuscript into a book without the support of the staff of the Department of Political Science. They are often a step or two ahead of any request and in the end they help to make my job a pleasure. I also thank my undergraduate and graduate students at McMaster University and previously Yale University for their insights.

I completed much of the research for this project when I was a graduate student at the University of Massachusetts, Amherst, so I am also indebted to my fellow graduate student colleagues there, the staff of the Political Science Department, and, of course, everyone who provided guidance on my dissertation project. Most important, I owe a large debt to my supervisor, Howard J. Wiarda, who introduced me to his network of contacts in Washington and helped guide the dissertation research. The other members of my dissertation committee, Eric Einhorn and Carmen Diana Deere, were also very supportive of the project. Likewise, I owe a large debt of gratitude to Gregory Huber of Yale University who encouraged my continued research on this project even though it was far removed from the focus of the post-doctoral fellowship I conducted under his guidance.

Although I am unable to thank everyone I interviewed because the interviews were all conducted under the assurance of confidentiality, I would like to say to each of the people who took time to speak with me that I am very grateful for your time and frankness.

I owe the biggest debt of all to my family. Duane Hewitt provided support, advice, and encouragement throughout the project. I am truly grateful for his partnership. My children, Chloe Hewitt and Duncan Wylie, shared their mother with this book and I hope to make up for some lost time now that it is finally in print. Thank you also to my sisters Lynn Rider and Lori Stark. Lynn has graciously read and commented on large sections of the manuscript and both of them have been there for me when I most needed the type of friendship only a sister could give. My parents, Lloyd and Ferne Wylie, actively encouraged a love of education and helped to nurture my curiosity about the world from kindergarten onwards. They were the best kind of parents and for this reason the book is dedicated to them.

PERCEPTIONS OF CUBA:
CANADIAN AND AMERICAN POLICIES
IN COMPARATIVE PERSPECTIVE

1 Introduction

Canadians should be ashamed of themselves.

– U.S. Senator Jesse Helms

[Helms-Burton is] the latest manifestation of the bully in the American psyche.
– Canadian Member of Parliament Bill Blaikie

In 1996 a private member's bill was introduced into the Canadian Parliament to allow descendants of the United Empire Loyalists to claim compensation for the land confiscated by the United States government after the American Revolution in 1776. The Godfrey-Milliken Bill, though never passed, was written in retaliation for an American measure designed to hamper other countries from investing in Cuba. This measure, the Cuban Liberty and Democratic Solidarity (*Libertad*) Act, commonly known as the Helms-Burton Act, outraged Canadians because they interpreted it as Washington trying to dictate Canadian policy. Outrage was directed north as well. U.S. Senator Jesse Helms compared Canada's relationship with Cuba to Britain's appeasement of Hitler at Munich. He declared that Canadians should 'be ashamed of themselves.' A Canadian Member of Parliament shot back by calling the United States a 'bully.' The minister of foreign affairs, Lloyd Axworthy, remarked that 'Helms-Burton is bad legislation.'[1] How did the cross-border rhetoric over this American bill designed to thwart foreign investment in Cuba become an issue of such magnitude in Canadian-American relations?

It certainly wasn't the first time that Canadians and Americans exchanged harsh words over Cuba. Even before the world stood on the brink of nuclear war over Cuba in 1962, the United States and Canada had distinct policies towards Fidel Castro's revolution. These differences persist in the twenty-first century and have, at times, caused considerable tension between the countries flanking the 49th parallel. The American isolationist approach is in many ways antithetical to Canada's policy of constructive engagement.[2] Much of the current literature offers traditional economic or domestic-interest-group explanations for the two policies. This study questions the conventional narratives and proposes another account based on ideational variables.

To most of the world, the differences between Americans and Canadians seem marginal. Indeed, the two societies are closely intertwined. Connections between Canadians and Americans exist at all levels of commerce, government, and civil society. The two countries are the other's largest trading partner. Over 200 million people cross the border each year.[3] People from both countries often work, live, or have friends or relatives in the other country. The American ambassador to Canada, Gordon Giffen, put it this way: 'Maybe it's our sheer proximity, with its famous 5,500 mile unguarded border. Maybe it's our tangled histories. Maybe it's a product of Canadians visiting Florida or Americans skiing at Whistler.' He continued: 'Maybe it's the impact of the ubiquitous presence here of American-owned media with their ubiquitous Canadian-born journalists and entertainers. Or maybe it's the expansion of the NHL to places like North Carolina, Tennessee and Florida. Whatever the reason, our relationship is unlike that between any other two sovereign nations anywhere, anytime.'[4]

Yet, despite these connections, there are important differences between the two societies. This is true of their foreign policies and particularly true when we compare policy towards Cuba. By examining the two countries' policies towards Cuba in tandem, this study will demonstrate that there is far more than domestic political, security, or economic calculations involved in the formulation of these foreign policies.

The reasons put forth to explain American policy towards Cuba have changed over the years. Before the Cuban American community was a force to reckon with in U.S. politics, the most popular explanation advanced for U.S. policy was a security-based argument which asserted that the policy of isolation was a reflection of Cuba's status as a Soviet satellite. After the consolidation of the large, electorally powerful Cuban American community in the 1980s, a domestic-interest-group explanation became the most popular narrative. This explanation argues that the American policy is a direct result of the power of the Cuban American lobby. Claiming that the Cuban American community's strong presence and electoral clout in Florida and New Jersey practically guarantees its ability to dictate policy towards Cuba, this theory continues to be viewed as the main explanation for U.S.-Cuba policy.

The often heard explanation for the Canadian policy of engagement is the national-economic-interest argument. It maintains that the opportunity for Canadians to invest in Cuba, free of American competition, drives Canadian engagement.[5] This study questions these explanations and demonstrates that the policies are distinct because the two countries are different in other ways: they have their own identities and perceptions that contribute to the formation of very distinct approaches towards Cuba.

The Approach

The book adopts a constructivist approach to this question. Rising out of the end of the Cold War, constructivism is now recognized as a useful approach to some of the major problems in international relations. In the 1980s and early 1990s, both the fields of international relations (IR) and comparative politics eschewed studies based on 'soft' explanations like ideas and culture.[6] IR was dominated by varieties of realism, an approach that dealt in hard-power calculations and notions of balance between states. By that time, comparative politics had dismissed most of the early political-culture studies as ethnocentric. The field of comparative foreign policy was focused on behavioral studies that touched on cultural or ideational factors in only a cursory manner.

Yet the end of the Cold War and the failure of realism and other models to explain the seemingly sudden change in Soviet domestic and foreign policy, and the rapid reconfiguration of global politics that followed, forced scholars to take another look at the earlier 'soft' explanations.[7] They found that cultural and ideational factors could help them understand the demise of the Soviet Union and the end of the Cold War. Furthermore, the questions that had dominated the study of world politics for decades – superpower rivalry, the arms race, and bipolarity – became, almost overnight, the relics of an earlier era. Instead, the once often considered secondary, or even irrelevant, issues of international relations drew increasing scholarly attention. The rise in ethnic tensions, questions of nationality, and the spread of democratic values – all by-products of the collapse of the Soviet Union and the break-up of the Warsaw Pact alliance – came to the forefront of political science. Culture and identity variables were at the heart of these now important issues. Political-cultural studies enjoyed a renaissance.

Realizing the relevance of these variables, a greater number of political scientists began to apply norms, beliefs, identity, and cultural factors to other research questions. As the 1990s drew to a close, these variables were being increasingly used both in conjunction with traditional explanations and to provide alternative hypotheses for a wide variety of international behaviour.

In the past two decades, cultural studies have been embraced by a new scholarly tradition in international relations. Known as constructivists, or sometimes as reflectivists, the proponents of this approach posit that culture and identity are integral to a complete understanding of the dynamics of international relations. Unlike other mainstream IR theories (such as neorealism or neoliberalism), constructivism does not treat the identity and interests of international actors as given but instead problematizes them, revealing that they are socially constructed. Constructivists maintain that social structures mould the identity and interests of actors who, in turn, create social structures through their interactions and beliefs. It is a mutually constituting process. These scholars emphasize that our perceptions, beliefs, assumptions, ideas, actions, and interactions create the world we live in.

In 1989 Nicholas Onuf gave rise to the term constructivism in political science.[8] In *World of Our Making*, Onuf argued that people use language to understand the world and also use it to bring their influence to bear on the world itself. Language is used as a tool to influence how others understand the world. Onuf states, 'Fundamental to constructivism is the proposition that human beings are social beings, and we would not be human but for our social relations. In other words, social relations *make* or *construct* people … Conversely, we *make* the world what it is … [and] talking is undoubtedly the most important way that we go about making the world what it is.'[9] However, it is Alexander Wendt's 1992 article 'Anarchy Is What States Make of It: The Social Construction of Power Politics'[10] that has become the seminal work in constructivism. Wendt uses the concept of anarchy to show that many things that are taken as given are actually created by our ideas, perceptions, norms, culture, and interactions: 'People act toward objects, including other actors, on the basis of the meanings that objects have for them.'[11] For example, he explains that 'if a society "forgets" what a university is, the powers and practices of professor and student cease to exist ... It is collective meanings that constitute the structures which organize our actions.'[12] Wendt asserts that, just as people have identities (like daughter, wife, lawyer, activist, nurse), so do states (like superpower, leader of the Western alliance, peacekeeper). He defines identities as 'relatively stable, role-specific understandings and expectations about self.'[13] How others relate to those people (or states) and how those people or states act is often based on those identities. 'Identities are the basis of interests.'[14] Interests will differ based on 'who you are.' It is in the interest of a professor to conduct research, publish, and teach whereas it is in the interest of a student to learn and achieve good grades. This is what students and professors 'do' or at least strive to do. Similarly, it is in the interest of a state that identifies itself as a 'democratic leader' to promote the development of free and fair elections among its neighbours. Another, perhaps even a democratic, country that does not see itself primarily in this fashion will be less insistent that its neighbours conduct their elections in certain ways and consequently have a different relationship with those neighbours.

Contrary to neorealism, Wendt argues that the structure of the system (anarchy) does not produce the identity and interests of the actors; instead, the states themselves (i.e., their interests and identities) have created the structure of the system which in turn influences those very interests and identities. He explains that anarchy as we know it is a creation of social context. States act as if they are in a self-help environment – they believe that other states are threatening and as a consequence engage in activities (building up their own armaments etc.) that appear threatening to others. Other states in turn do the same in response, which creates a security dilemma – and thereby creates anarchy. It becomes a self-fulfilling prophecy. 'Self-help security systems evolve from cycles of interaction in which each party acts in ways that the other feels are threatening to the self, creating expectations that the other is not to be trusted.'[15] In other words, according to constructivists, we make our own reality – in this case an anarchic self-help international system.

Roots of Self-Identity: Domestic and International Contexts

Yet scholars of foreign policy have only recently begun to investigate the relevance of this approach to their own research. The delay in applying an explicitly constructivist approach to foreign policy can be traced in large part to the constructivist focus on systemic-level analyses. This book argues that mainstream constructivist approaches, which stress systemic-level identities, must be supplemented by studies examining national-level identities in order to understand differences in foreign-policy behaviour.

Although they argue that structures and agents are co-constitutive, the most well-known constructivists rely more heavily on structure. For example, Wendt explores identity formation at the systemic level. He examines the formation of collective identities across states to explain international behaviour. Much of this type of constructivist theorizing ignores domestic contexts. However, many of these scholars allude to national-level variables. In passing, Wendt allows that states can have competing knowledge. He explains, 'States know a lot about each other, and important parts of this knowledge are shared – not all, to be sure, but important parts nonetheless. States and scholars alike treat these shared beliefs as the background, taken-for-granted assumptions that any competent player or student of contemporary world politics must understand: what a "state" is, what "sovereignty" implies.'[16]

But what happens when knowledge is not shared at the system level? This study looks at Wendt's 'not all' category – when knowledge is not shared between states, when states have their own, competing, taken-for-granted assumptions. Wendt refers to this knowledge as 'private.' He recognizes that 'private knowledge consists of beliefs that individual actors hold that others do not. In the case of states this kind of knowledge will often stem from domestic or ideological considerations. It can be a key determinant of how states frame international situations and define their national interests.'[17] This study departs from the mainstream constructivism of scholars like Wendt by focusing on such 'private' knowledge. Competing ideas and identities are a major source of tension in the international system and thus consideration of them is important for a complete understanding of international relations.[18]

Another group of constructivists examine the rise of identity at the unit or state level and in this sense explore the very thing that Wendtian constructivists ignore. A number of the chapters in Peter Katzenstein's edited volume *The Culture of National Security* are some of earliest examples of this form of analysis. For example, in that volume Thomas Berger argues that Germany and Japan's anti-militarism has become part of their identity and Robert Hermanin makes the case that the end of the Cold War can be traced to changes in Soviet self-identi-fication and, thus, interests.[19] These and many of the other contribu-tors to the Katzenstein volume see state identity as reflective of domes-tic characteristics.

Unlike these two types of analysis, this study sees identities as con-structed at both the domestic and international levels. In doing so, it borrows from previous research in comparative politics, foreign policy, and international relations. The state is the main actor in the international system, but to understand fully the 'why' of state action it is necessary to open the black box and delve into the domestic-level factors studied in comparative politics and by much of the traditional research in foreign-policy analysis. It is not just international culture that constructs a state's identity and corresponding behaviour but also domestic-level culture, identity, and ideas.

Constructivism can help us understand how states respond differ-ently to the same international situation or issue. This study will demonstrate that the different responses arise from the different iden-tities of the states in question and that these identities and their corre-sponding perceptions are formed by both international- and domestic-level processes.

The Identity-Perception Connection: The Power of Perception

People only see what they are prepared to see.

– Ralph Waldo Emerson

All our knowledge has its origins in our perceptions.

– Leonardo da Vinci

Political and cognitive psychology literature has shown that people interpret situations in ways that reinforce their current opinions.[20] In other words, perceptions, which are understandings of people, things, or situations, are not isolated from prior experience or knowledge. Once formed, perceptions often persist over time. Research in interna-tional relations has borrowed from this literature to demonstrate a link between perception and foreign policy. Robert Jervis's work on per-ception and misperception in the 1970s is the most well known in this genre.[21] Similarly, other research on foreign-policy attitudes links spe-cific opinions about certain foreign policies to more general beliefs. Important work in this genre includes Yaaccov Vertzberger's *The World in Their Minds* and Glenn Chafetz et al.'s 1998 article in *Security Studies*. Consistent with earlier studies, both of these pieces argue that individuals ignore or distort information that is inconsistent with previously held beliefs or conceptions.[22] Thus, individuals, including foreign-policy makers and the people who influence them, are 'cognitive misers' who must make new information fit into their existing perceptions and views.

Identity as the Wellspring of Perceptions

Where do these existing perceptions and views come from? The psychology literature points to how we see ourselves.[23] Self-identity is considered the 'frame of reference in terms of which all other perceptions gain their meaning.'[24] Identity has been defined as 'the state of being similar to some actors and different from others in a particular circumstance. Identity involves the creation of boundaries that separate the self and other.'[25] Each of us defines ourself within large and often abstract social categories or in opposition to these categories.

An idea of who we are then permeates, often unconsciously, almost everything we do. The old adage 'Where you stand depends on where you sit' is relevant here. However, I would argue that 'where we stand,' in other words, our position or opinion on various issues, depends on where we *think* we sit, or, in other words, who we think we are and what we think our role is in society (or family, group, what have you). Thus, where we sit largely takes place within our own heads. This is our self-identity. Our own conception of our identity can be based on factors such as our ideas, values, and culture as well as on how we see ourselves in relation to others. Moreover, our self-image is not static and international actors (like the rest of us) can have multiple and sometimes conflicting identities that vary depending on context. Our self-identity influences our worldview and perceptions. Perceptions are both constructed by identities and can be part of the construction or evolution of identities.

Research in international relations has also tied perceptions to identity factors. Vertzberger states that, when 'information is characterized by high ambiguity and uncertainty, societal and cultural rules of judgment become salient; historical analogies and national conceptions of self-identity (e.g. role, status, belonging) and the appropriate relationships with other nations that they imply are often used in making judgments.'[26] Chafetz argues that 'identity is a mental construct that

both describes and prescribes how the actor should think, feel, evalu-
ate, and ultimately, behave in group relevant situations.'[27] Identity
creates norms that tell us what we should do or usually do in a particular situation and these norms often form patterns of behaviour over
extended periods of time.[28] A state's ideas about itself and its environment influence the state's actions and in turn those actions can reinforce the state's identity, ideas, and perceptions, thus creating 'reality'
as understood within that state.

Differences in identities cause states to view, understand, and interpret situations differently. Wendt acknowledges this connection.
According to him, 'actors need to define the situation before they can
choose a course of action.' He asserts that 'these definitions will be
based on at least two considerations: Their own identities and interests, which reflect beliefs about who they are in such situations; and
what they think others will do, which reflect beliefs about their identities and interests.' Thus, 'when these various beliefs are not shared,
when there is no cultural definition of the situation, then actors are
likely to be surprised by each other's behavior.'[29] The following four
chapters will demonstrate that the United States and Canada have
been continually puzzled by the other's approach to revolutionary
Cuba because both countries are operating on the basis of different
perceptions that ultimately have roots in their different self-identities.
These disparate interpretations (or perceptions) produce different
foreign policies. To lay the foundation for the analysis in the rest of the
book, the remainder of this chapter will introduce the reader to the two
case studies used.

The Cases: A Concise History of the Relationships

From the earliest periods in Canadian and American history, the two
countries have had very different relationships with Cuba. Even prior
to the 1898 war (known in the United States as the Spanish-American
War), the United States was actively involved in domestic Cuban politics and was heavily invested financially in the island. In contrast,
though Canada always had a presence of one sort or another in Cuba,
its involvement was, in comparison, minimal and understated. This
section begins by chronicling the long and tumultuous relationship
between the United States and Cuba. It then reviews the relatively
quiet, yet often celebrated, relationship between Canada and the
island nation.

U.S.-Cuba Relations: A Short History

Extremes of closeness and animosity have characterized U.S.-Cuban relations. The bilateral relationship began when Cuba was a Spanish colony. During the American War of Independence, trade flourished between Cuba and the United States and over the next one hundred years the American people and their government became involved in many sectors of the Cuban economy. By the middle of the nineteenth century, the volume of Cuba's trade with the United States had surpassed trade with Spain.

The United States was also interested in closer political and strategic ties with the Spanish colony and, after various unsuccessful attempts to purchase Cuba from Spain, the interest culminated with American involvement in Cuba's war with Spain in 1898. Many saw annexation as a natural evolution of the relationship between the two countries, but, though the idea was debated, the government of President William McKinley stopped short of outright annexation. The official policy (written in the Teller Amendment to the American declaration of war) was that Cuba would not become a U.S. colony. Before pulling out of Cuba in 1902, however, the United States made sure to promulgate its authority in the region by attaching a rider, later to become known as the Platt Amendment, to the Cuban constitution. This rider, giving Cuba the status of an American protectorate, would come to define and symbolize the future of U.S.-Cuba relations.

Over the next quarter-century, the economic and political influence of the United States on the island became progressively less overt but nonetheless played an instrumental role in defining the paternalistic relationship between the two countries. The rise of Fulgencio Batista as military leader of Cuba in 1933 was the result of extensive American manipulations and pressures.[30] From 1933 to 1959, power in Cuba belonged to General Batista, who was adamantly supported by the United States on account of his unwavering acquiescence to American foreign policy and economic goals. In 1958 the American embassy in Havana reported that the Batista government had 'taken the lead in opposing Communism and in advocating policies and courses of action desired by the United States.'[31]

The year 1959, when Fidel Castro overthrew the Batista regime, marked the beginning of a steadily deteriorating relationship between the United States and Cuba. The initial relationship was not openly antagonistic until the nationalization of American assets in Cuba and the strengthening of Cuban-Soviet relations led to an ideological stand-off in which the United States accused Fidel Castro of communist leanings – an unforgivable sin according to American ideology.

In October 1960 the United States imposed an economic embargo on Cuba, restricting trade on all products except food and medicine. This 'program of economic denial' became the cornerstone of American policy. Its purpose was to demonstrate to Cuba and the world that communism was not a viable option.[32] Two years later, in 1962, the Cuban Missile Crisis further jeopardized bilateral relations and the United States tightened the embargo, preventing Americans from visiting Cuba and forbidding all trade with the island.

Since Washington wanted Fidel Castro overthrown but did not want American troops involved, it assisted Cuban exiles, outraged by Castro's reforms, to plan and execute an invasion at the Bay of Pigs in April 1961. After defeat at the Bay of Pigs, the Central Intelligence Agency (CIA) continued its efforts to oust the Cuban leader from power, replacing outright military force with covert measures including numerous assassination attempts.

Despite some efforts to normalize relations in the mid-1970s, a mass migration in 1980 of over one hundred thousand Cubans to the United States (the Mariel exodus) once again increased tensions between Havana and Washington.[33] The U.S. government used the affair as further evidence of the political and economic failures of the Cuban system.

The next major milestone in U.S.-Cuban relations came in 1992 with the passage of the Cuban Democracy Act (CDA). On the one hand, it tightened the trade embargo; however, on the other hand, it contained provisions to increase 'people-to-people' contact between Americans and Cubans and to strengthen Cuban civil society. The following years under President William Clinton were mixed for the bilateral relationship, with policies and agreements that at times further constrained the relationship, such as the passing of the 1996 Helms-Burton Act, and at other times ameliorated relations, such as the 1998 easing of restrictions to promote humanitarian development in Cuba and the 2000 decision to permit the limited sale of food and medicine to Cuba on a cash basis.[34] The custody battle over Elían Gonzalez, a six-year-old Cuban boy who was the sole survivor of a boat wreck off the coast of Florida, became the focus of the bilateral relationship, dominating headlines in the United States and Cuba for months in 2000.

Despite some variance in U.S. foreign policy towards Cuba, the bilateral relationship under the presidency of George W. Bush could be best characterized as one of rhetorical hostility. In 2001 President Bush announced that his administration would 'oppose any attempt to weaken sanctions against Cuba's government' and then gave key positions to Cuban Americans who supported his views on the relationship. He increased support for dissidents on the island and imposed additional restrictions on family visits there. In addition, the Bush administration's pre-emptive approach to rogue regimes and its jingoism towards Cuba added to the tension in the relationship. The election of Barack Obama in 2008 had a moderating effect on the relationship, as Obama reversed some his predecessor's restrictions on family visits and remittances. The recent history will be explored further in Chapter 5.

Canada-Cuba Relations: A Short History

Canada's initial interests in Cuba prior to Fidel Castro's revolution were defined by economic exchanges despite some limited Canadian involvement in the Ten Years' War of 1868–78 (the first of Cuba's three wars of liberation against Spain) and in the 1895–8 Cuban War of Independence. Canadians were among the many farmers who settled in Cuba in the early nineteenth century and in 1915 one of the largest sugar production and distribution hubs was formed by a union of Canadian planters.[35] Canadian financial institutions were also active in Cuba prior to the revolution. Both the Royal Bank and the Bank of Nova Scotia had many branches in Cuba. By 1950, the Royal Bank was the largest commercial bank in Cuba and Canadian insurance companies held a majority of Cuban insurance policies.[36] Trade considerations also dominated the budding Canadian-Cuban relationship. In 1902 Canada exported US$265,000 worth of goods to Cuba, creating a trade relationship that increased steadily in the first half of the twentieth century, with Canada's exports to Cuba reaching Cnd$17.5 million by 1950.[37]

Canada established diplomatic relations with Cuba in 1945.[38] In 1959, when revolutionaries overthrew the Batista regime, the Canadian government, though sceptical, recognized the new government as legitimate and continued normal relations. Government documents reveal that, in private, members of the Canadian government were critical of Fidel Castro and were hesitant to extend an invitation to him to visit Ottawa in 1959.[39] However, although Canadian officials initially thought that the revolution was a 'mere change of guard at the top, as is so common in Latin America,' the government fairly quickly began to see the possibility that the revolution 'may be a deeply popular revolution.' Ottawa thus instructed the embassy officials: 'As the representatives in Cuba of a friendly country, you and the members of your mission will, therefore, display as much patience and understanding as are compatible with your functions and seek ways to reconcile Canadian political and economic interests with a revolution which cannot be stabilized until the deep grievances that produced it have been redressed.'[40] This decision would mark the beginning of a somewhat rocky but overall respectful and open relationship between Ottawa and Havana.

Despite declared allegiance to the United States, Ottawa's relatively unwavering open policy towards Cuba placed tensions on the Canada-U.S. relationship. The strain came to a head during the Cuban Missile Crisis when President John F. Kennedy requested full Canadian support in the affair and Prime Minister John Diefenbaker refused to comply fully, claiming that if Canada agreed to this U.S. request then Canadians would 'be their vassals forever.'[41] At this time, Canada and Mexico were the only countries in the Americas that did not acquiesce to U.S. demands to sever relations with Cuba.

Yet, in spite of differing viewpoints in regard to the degree to which Canada should engage Cuba and thus defy the United States, Canadian leaders have been careful not to alter significantly Canada's official relationship with Cuba. The policy of Prime Minister Lester Pearson (1963–8) towards Cuba was characterized as 'coldly correct.'[42] In contrast, Prime Minister Pierre Trudeau (1968–84) was very interested in warming relations between Havana and Ottawa. He was the first leader of a U.S. ally to make an official visit to Castro's Cuba.[43] Trudeau was instrumental in expanding trade with the island because he strongly believed that the transition to democracy in Cuba could best be furthered through trade not isolation. Prime Minister Brian Mulroney (1984–93), considered one of the most pro-American leaders in Canadian history, maintained diplomatic and trade ties with Cuba while very carefully sending the message to Havana that Canada was foremost an American ally. Under Jean Chrétien (1993–2003), relations once again warmed. In addition to the reinstatement of official development assistance and diplomatic visits, Canadian-Cuban trade and investment increased under the Liberal governments of Chrétien and

Paul Martin (2003–6). Today Canada remains one of the top sources of foreign investment in Cuba.[44] It bears noting, too, that the Chrétien government strongly advocated 'constructive engagement' as the most effective way to foster change in Cuba. This policy attempts to create linkages between Cuban and Canadian people and their governments in order to influence Cuba to open its economy, to give greater respect to human rights, and to encourage the development of representative government.[45] Under Prime Minister Stephen Harper (2006–), Canadian 'constructive engagement' began to show some signs of strain although fundamentally Canada's policy towards the island followed the pattern first established by Diefenbaker – to treat Cuba as a 'normal' state.

Overview

Though each country's relationship with Cuba stretches back hundreds of years, to the period when all three were mere colonial holdings, it is possible to see harbingers of the policies now in place. Though this section has mainly served to provide a historical backdrop to the rest of the study, it also demonstrates that parts of the contemporary policies have historical roots.

Both countries have similar goals and would like to see greater respect for human rights and democracy on the island, but they have chosen very different means to that end. The United States has used its economic and military power to attempt to force the end of Fidel Castro's 'socialist experiment.' In contrast, Canada has maintained a working relationship with the Cuban state while attempting to encourage the hoped-for changes. It has long been Canada's policy to maintain diplomatic relations with Cuba whether or not the country is led by Fidel or Raúl Castro or someone else. These respective decisions are a testament to the distinctive identities of each nation.

The Structure of the Book

This volume uses the constructivist framework popular in IR but studies a topic more frequently addressed in the comparative foreign-policy scholarship, the interplay between domestic factors and foreign policy. It also borrows from previous work in comparative politics. By combining the ideas and methods used in three subdisciplines of political science, the book provides an alternative explanation for Canadian and American policies towards Cuba. It shows that the traditional explanations behind the two policies do not offer complete accounts of the reasons *for* each policy nor can they explain the *difference* in the two approaches. This alternative view of both policies reveals the importance of perceptions and identities. The book demonstrates that Canadian and American publics and policy makers rely on certain conceptions about the Cuban state and their country's role in relation to Cuba that are rooted in the identities of the two nations. Not only can these variables provide explanations for each approach but they can also explain why Canadian and American policies continued to diverge, even well after the end of the Cold War.

The following chapters examine Canadian and American policies towards Cuba in detail, highlighting the socially constructed elements. Chapter 2 explores the connection between identity, perception, and American foreign policy and analyses the U.S. approach towards the island, demonstrating the relevance of ideational factors and the failings of other paradigms to offer complete explanations. Chapter 3 similarly ties identities, values, and perceptions to Canadian foreign policy. It then examines the Canadian approach towards Cuba, revealing that Canadian identity, norms, and ideas have greater explanatory power in this case than the traditional accounts. Chapter 4 directly compares the Canadian and American reactions to, first, the shooting down of a Brothers to the Rescue plane, and, second, the possibility that the Cuban state supports bioterrorism. Chapter 5 reviews recent developments in the bilateral relationships and concludes by exploring the connection between identity, perception, and policy change.

Conclusion

When I began this project I was fairly certain I was going to arrive at an answer to my research question that would fit nicely into established foreign-policy theories. Yet, a few days into my interviews with Canadian and American officials stationed in Cuba, I realized that I had uncovered something much more interesting – indeed, I could not believe what I was hearing as I made my way across Havana. U.S. and Canadian officials' descriptions of the events, people, and issues I asked about were remarkably different. At the American Interests Section, I listened to a high-level official describe what he saw as the utter failure of the Cuban system. Then, at the Canadian embassy, I was taken aback when an official chided me for asking what Canada was doing to assist Cuba to democratize. Why did I assume that Cubans needed any assistance at all in this realm? Clearly, these different interpretations were the views of two individuals, and, even though they occupied positions representing their two governments, I could not be sure that their views reflected wider perceptions. However, after further interviews and research into official and unofficial statements, policies, and literature, I realized that, though there was variation among individuals, there were fundamental differences in the way Canadians and Americans understood all things Cuban. What follows is my account of these perceptions and where I think they come from. Given the obvious similarities in Canadian and American worldviews, this study is far from an ideal way to showcase this phenomenon. Yet, for the same reasons, it serves as an excellent test case. Attention to different perceptions and the roots of those perceptions in each country's self-identity should be easily transferred to other cases. What is true for differences in Canadian and American perceptions should certainly be applicable to other countries with less similar baselines.

2 The Exceptionalist and the Cuban Other

The Cold War is but a distant memory yet the American relationship with Cuba appears to be one of the last vestiges of this bygone era. Despite the much diminished security threat posed by Cuba, this island country continues to be thought of as an enemy of the United States and relations between the two countries remain tense. Although it has gone through various modifications since the early 1990s, including some relaxation of trade in food and medicines, American policy towards Cuba remains, in its essence, the same as that adopted by President Kennedy at the height of the Cold War.

This chapter explores the reasons why the U.S. policy towards Cuba has developed in this way. To understand the policy fully, it is necessary to question many elements of the U.S.-Cuba relationship, including Cuba's status as a threat and the power of the Cuban American community. In doing so, I will demonstrate that the power of the Cuban American community cannot be understood as a separate factor influencing the continuation of the current policy. The chapter asks how is it possible not only that relations evolved in this fashion but that the policy towards Cuba has remained hostile despite the end of the Cold War and the more recent moderation of the Cuban American position.

American citizens and policy makers rely on certain conceptions about their own identity as Americans, perceptions of the rule of Fidel and Raúl Castro, and views of their country's role in relation to Cuba to inform policy towards the island. This chapter will highlight how these conceptions of self-identity and related perceptions play a significant part in the development and continuation of American policies towards Cuba.

The U.S. Identity

No country, state, or nation has a single self-image. Identities by their very nature are socially constructed and constantly in flux. There are many American identities and many of them are in conflict with one another. Yet at the centre of many of these identities lies a core self-image of exceptionalism that has been continuously reinforced for much of U.S. history. In relation to the domestic environment, exceptionalism is understood as the combination of values and beliefs born out of the Enlightenment's emphasis on individual liberty and the influence of Puritan morality.[1] These beliefs translate at the international level into a set of assumptions about what the United States stands for and what is appropriate international behaviour given these beliefs and values. The discourse of exceptionalism asserts that the United States is not only special but also is politically, socially, economically, and morally superior to other states. This self-image portrays a United States that is not only the best country in the world but also the embodiment of democracy, the champion of freedom and human rights, and the leader of the West. Exceptionalism contains a missionary norm as well. It asserts that, since the United States is superior in these ways, it has special rights and duties associated with promoting its values internationally and especially within the hemisphere. These representations are accepted as obvious and natural in American foreign-policy circles.

The belief that the United States is an exceptional nation has contributed to the development of U.S. foreign policy. One of the best articulations of exceptionalism in relation to foreign policy is that of John O'Sullivan, a journalist and the author of *Manifest Destiny*. The following, written in 1845, encapsulates the most accepted ideas of exceptionalism:

> Yes, we are the nation of progress, of individual freedom, of universal enfranchisement. Equality of rights is the cynosure of our union of States, the grand exemplar of the correlative equality of individuals; and while truth sheds its effulgence, we cannot retrograde, without dissolving the one and subverting the other. We must onward to the fulfilment of our mission – to the entire development of the principle of our organization – freedom of conscience, freedom of person, freedom of trade and business pursuits, universality of freedom and equality. This is our high destiny, and in nature's eternal, inevitable decree of cause and effect we

must accomplish it. All this will be our future history, to establish on earth the moral dignity and salvation of man – the immutable truth and beneficence of God. For this blessed mission to the nations of the world, which are shut out from the life-giving light of truth, has America been chosen; and her high example shall smite unto death the tyranny of kings, hierarchs, and oligarchs, and carry the glad tidings of peace and good will where myriads now endure an existence scarcely more enviable than that of beasts of the field. Who, then, can doubt that our country is destined to be *the great nation* of futurity?[2]

To O'Sullivan and many Americans since, the United States represents the best of what a nation can aspire to be and is destined to play an international leadership role.

Over a century after O'Sullivan tied American identity to foreign policy, these same thoughts continued to be echoed in foreign-policy doctrines and discourse. The 1950 statement of U.S. Cold War policy, the then top secret NSC 68, declared that the United States has 'the responsibility of world leadership. It demands that we make the attempt, and accept the risks inherent in it, to bring about order and justice by means consistent with the principles of freedom and democracy.'[3] Fifty years later, Secretary of State Madeleine Albright reaffirmed that the United States had a 'responsibility, as the world's leading democracy ... to work in partnership with others to help nations in transition move to a higher stage of democratic development.'[4] In 2003 President George W. Bush told the American public: 'America's duty is familiar ... Once again, this nation and all our friends are all that stand between a world at peace, and a world of chaos and constant alarm. Once again, we are called to defend the safety of our people, and the hopes of all mankind. And we accept this responsibility.'[5]

The belief that the United States is exceptional has continued to construct foreign policy in the western hemisphere and beyond. However, it has particular relevance for U.S. policy towards Cuba.

Exceptionalism and Cuba Policy

American policy towards Cuba is an interesting example of the interplay between this identity and foreign policy. Cuba policy emerges from the way American officials and, more generally, American society understand what it means to be 'American.' This identity influences their worldview, their understanding of Cuba, and their perception of the American-Cuban relationship. Officially, Cuba policy is constructed by foreign-policy officials in the State Department, White House, Congress, and the various other agencies involved in making foreign-policy decisions.[6] It is also heavily influenced by the large and electorally powerful Cuban American community, based primarily in Miami and represented by the Cuban American National Foundation (CANF) and the more recent Cuban Liberty Council (CLC). Each of these decision makers makes sense of the Cuban-American relationship within a context that contains certain assumptions and worldviews. One of these worldviews revolves around the notion of what it means to be American. By positioning the United States as exceptional, this identity thereby establishes a context wherein 'othering' of Cuba becomes not only natural but necessary for the continuation of the U.S. self-image. It is natural because conceptualizing the United States as exceptional automatically puts all other states in an inferior category. States that are understood to be similar to the United States are seen as less inferior than those conceptualized as very different from the American model. Cuba has been understood as different and thus inferior since the earliest point in the bilateral relationship. But there is more to it than that. Since 1959, Cuba has been seen as not just different and inferior but as anathema to U.S. values and characteristics.

Cuba became the political epitome of the 'other.' The American self-identification as the guardian of freedom and democracy and the contrasting images of Cuba helped to construct American policy. Furthermore, Cuba, under the leadership of Fidel Castro, presented a direct challenge to the U.S. identity as exceptional. Cuba's very existence as a state challenges the U.S. self-image as exceptional, for this is a country that publicly seeks not to emulate the United States, that is highly critical of the U.S. political system and values, and that makes the case that American attempts to dominate the hemisphere are not only morally wrong but have failed. Americans ask a series of questions about this state of affairs. How is it possible that the regime established by Fidel Castro in 1959 remains in control of Cuba despite the efforts of ten American presidents to oust him from power and restore Cuba to its pro-American position? How has revolutionary Cuba been able to resist the sheer attraction of the obviously superior U.S. model? How has the Cuban state been able to resist American political, diplomatic, and even military might? The way Americans have been able to maintain their belief in the exceptionalist character of the United States and still answer these questions to their satisfaction is to conceptualize Fidel Castro as not only a dictator but an inherently evil tyrant. In this line of reasoning, Cuba has remained immune to the U.S. model because the Cuban state is solely focused on repressing its populace and undermining American efforts in the region.

This understanding of the United States as an exceptional nation has produced and reproduced certain ways of 'seeing' Cuba which naturally lead to the favouring of some policy options over others. These perceptions of Cuba and the United States are social constructions that are often presented as objective 'facts.' By examining these 'facts,' the rest of this chapter will explore how the particular ways that American policy makers understand 'the United States' and 'Cuba' have constructed American policy.

Historical Representations: Cuba as the Other

Even in the early days of the U.S.-Cuba relationship, American exceptionalism influenced the U.S. approach towards the island. In the nineteenth century, Cubans were caricaturized as well-meaning children or gendered as female. These representations appeared in American cartoons, official rhetoric, and popular discourse. Cuban inferiority and the necessity of American tutelage were inherent in all representations.[7] Prior to the revolution, Cubans (and other Latin Americans) were portrayed as a naive, uncivilized, and childlike people who required American guidance. President McKinley said that Cuba, the Philippines, and Puerto Rico were a 'great trust' that the United States had taken on 'under the providence of God and in the name of human progress and civilization.'[8] Senator Albert Beveridge justified American involvement in the 1898 Spanish American War over Cuba because God has made Americans 'the master organizers of the world to establish system where chaos reigns ... He has made us adept in government that we may administer government among savage and senile peoples ... He has marked the American people as His Chosen nation finally to lead in the regeneration of the world.'[9] In 1902 a future president, Woodrow Wilson, echoed these sentiments in a speech about the Spanish American War and American responsibilities in Cuba and the Philippines, referring to Americans as 'apostles of liberty and self-government' and to the Filipinos and Cubans as children.[10]

Cubans were understood as incapable of taking care of themselves. The Platt Amendment to the Cuban constitution asserted that 'the United States may exercise the right to intervene for the preservation of Cuban independence, the maintenance of a government adequate for the protection of life, property, and individual liberty.' As late as the 1950s, American cartoons portrayed Cubans as children in need of American guardianship. Even as Castro assumed power, this image was alive and well, with senior Washington officials viewing Cuba's leader as a wayward child. Nixon talked about needing to lead Fidel Castro 'in the right direction.' More recently, Vicki Huddleston, the chief of the American mission in Havana from 1999 until 2002, remarked that 'it is fundamental that Cubans begin to learn how to govern themselves.'

Likewise, the American view of life in Cuba has not changed a great deal since the early 1900s. The Platt Amendment declared that Cuba needed to follow American instructions regarding the sanitation of the cities of the island, to the end that a recurrence of epidemic and infectious diseases might be prevented, thereby assuring protection to the people and commerce of Cuba. The 2006 report of the Commission for Assistance to a Free Cuba made a similar statement: 'The U.S. Government stands ready to help the Cuban Transition Government begin to address the immediate water, sanitation, health, food, shelter and education needs of the Cuban people.'[11] This representation of Cuba ignores the well-known evidence that Cuba has achieved results in many of these areas that rival American ones. For example, according to the United Nations, Cubans and Americans share the same life expectancy (seventy-seven years in 2005).

Surveys reveal that the American public also believes that Cuba is inferior. A 2000 poll asked: 'Generally speaking, is the U.S. system of economics and government morally superior to the Cuban system of economics and government?' Sixty-three per cent said yes, another 28 per cent answered that they were not sure, and only 9 per cent said no.[12] This contributes to the sense that the United States knows what is best for the island and the corresponding policies that attempt to dictate Cuba's future.

The American sense of superiority is often associated with the political character of the United States, a particular belief that the United States represents the embodiment of democracy and freedom. Cuba is represented as an enemy of democracy and freedom in U.S. legislation, official speeches, and most media reports. President George W. Bush emphasized these images in a 13 July 2001 speech. He stated that the Cuban government 'routinely stifles all the freedoms that make us human. The United States stands opposed to such tyranny and will oppose any attempt to weaken sanctions against the Castro regime until it respects the basic human rights of its citizens, frees political prisoners, holds democratic free elections, and allows free speech.'[13] How the United States sees itself and how the United States sees Cuba go hand in hand, each reinforcing the other identity.

Policy towards the island is constructed in a large part by these images and identities that are taken for granted.[14] Most foreign embassies in Havana operate under the assumption that human rights are not fully respected in Cuba but they disagree with each other on the extent of the violations. The American comments on this matter are almost always more vehement than those of other countries. Helms-Burton describes the human-rights abuses in Cuba as 'massive, systematic, and extraordinary.'[15] Similar language frames Fidel Castro as a tyrant, categorizing him together with Saddam Hussein, Slobodan Milosevic, Josef Stalin, or Adolf Hitler in the American imagination. In contrast, most other countries in the world take a much more moderate position towards Cuban human-rights violations and focus their critiques mainly on violations of political rights such as freedom of expression, freedom of assembly, and freedom of the press. Speaking to the House of Commons in 2003, a British government representative simply referred to Cuban politics as 'out-of-date' and belonging to the Cold War era.[16] Although the United Kingdom explicitly states that entirely normal relations between it and Cuba are not currently possible because human-rights violations do indeed occur in Cuba, the general rhetoric is relatively passive. The official position of the United Kingdom towards Cuba is that it 'urge an end to arbitrary detention, intimidation and imprisonment on political grounds.'[17] Furthermore, unlike American rhetoric which acts to demonize almost every aspect of the Cuban state, European Union (EU) members are willing to acknowledge the significant advances that have been made in Cuba, even though they may impose temporary sanctions in response to particular events.

Cuba is often represented in contrast to the United States in American discourse. Specifically, the American view of human rights and democracy in Cuba is reinforced by the comparison between the United States and Cuba. For example, in 1984 the chairman of the House of Representatives Committee on Foreign Relations, Dante

Fascell, asserted: 'Just come to my State and look at the smiling, happy faces of almost 1 million people who came from Cuba to the land of freedom, and I'm sure many others in Cuba would like to do the same thing if they had the opportunity.'[18] The 2006 report of the Commission for Assistance to a Free Cuba declares: 'Cubans continue to be imprisoned for activities that Americans take for granted each and every day.'[19]

The United States is focused on changing the political face of Cuba. Historically, this included not only the removal of Fidel Castro (and later, Raúl Castro) from power but also the stipulation that Cuba adopt a democratic political system and market economy modelled on the United States. The end of the isolationist policy is firmly tied to these changes. A January 1997 government document declares: 'Once Cuba has a transition government – that is, a government committed to the establishment of a fully democratic, pluralistic society – the United States will be prepared to begin normalizing relations and provide assistance to support Cuba's transition.'[20] The Americas Free Trade Act introduced in the Senate on 22 January 2001 states that Cuba will remain an exception to free trade until:

> freedom has been restored in Cuba, for purpose of subsection (a), unless the President determines that –
> (1) a constitutionally guaranteed democratic government has been established in Cuba with leaders chosen through free and fair elections;
> (2) the rights of individuals to private property have been restored and are effectively protected and broadly exercised in Cuba;
> (3) Cuba has a currency that is fully convertible domestically and internationally;
> (4) all political prisoners have been released in Cuba; and
> (5) the rights of free speech and freedom of the press in Cuba are effectively guaranteed.[21]

According to American policy, political and economic life on the island must change in these ways before the United States will reinstate full diplomatic and normal economic relations.

The U.S. foreign-policy establishment considers it a *duty* to ensure that Cuba democratizes. The Helms-Burton Act declares: 'The United States has shown a deep commitment, and considers it a moral obligation, to promote and protect human rights and fundamental freedoms as expressed in the Charter of the United Nations and in the Universal

Declaration of Human Rights.'[22] Helms-Burton also states: 'The Cuban people deserve to be assisted in a decisive manner to end the tyranny that has oppressed them for 36 years, and the continued failure to do so constitutes ethically improper conduct by the international community.'[23] Daniel W. Fisk, a senior staff member of the Senate Foreign Relations Committee that drafted the 1996 Helms-Burton Act, explains U.S. policy towards Cuba this way. He says that many accounts of the policy totally miss 'an essential element of American foreign policy, that is, the views of a significant segment of the foreign policy elite of America's mission in the world and how this "mission" is played out through the structure and interaction of the policy-making institutions.'[24] The United States considers itself to be on a moral mission in Cuba.

Policy towards Cuba is also constructed by the idea within American exceptionalism that the United States has special rights and duties within the hemisphere. The states in the region are considered to be not just close neighbours but part of the 'American family.' While this negates some of the 'othering' of states in the western hemisphere, it also reinforces American hostility towards Cuba.

Nearness Narratives: From Sphere of Influence to Family Ties

Cuba is considered to be both an extreme 'other' and yet at the same time part of the 'American family.' American foreign policy makers have historically conceptualized the western hemisphere as being within their own 'sphere of influence.' American behaviour that would be considered inappropriate in other areas of the globe is considered normal within the western hemisphere. Similarly, references to Latin America and the Caribbean as 'America's backyard' reflect the perception that these countries are not wholly independent. Consequently, the U.S. government believes that it has latitude to intervene in the internal affairs of the countries in the region. This attitude was officially expressed in 1823 when President James Monroe warned European powers that Latin America and the Caribbean were the exclusive concern of the United States. This policy, known as the Monroe Doctrine, marked the beginning of an historical pattern that has characterized U.S. policy towards the region ever since. The American annexation of the territories now known as Texas, New Mexico, and California, from Mexico in the first half of the nineteenth century, and the confrontation with the British over the Venezuelan border after the American Civil War were early examples of the Monroe Doctrine in action.

In 1904 President Theodore Roosevelt reinterpreted Monroe's message, giving the United States an enforcement role in the hemisphere. The Roosevelt Corollary described the United States as 'a self-respecting, just, and far-seeing nation' that should 'take action which in a more advanced stage of international relations would come under the head of the exercise of the international police' because 'a great free people owes it to itself and to all mankind not to sink into helplessness before the powers of evil.'[25] Under the Corollary, the United States set itself up as the judge responsible for overseeing other nations' conduct:

> [If] a nation shows that it knows how to act with reasonable efficiency and decency in social and political matters, if it keeps order and pays its obligations, it need fear no interference from the United States. Chronic wrongdoing, or an impotence which results in a general loosening of the ties of civilized society, may in America, as elsewhere, ultimately require intervention by some civilized nation, and in the Western Hemisphere the adherence of the United States to the Monroe Doctrine may force the United States, however reluctantly, in flagrant cases of such wrongdoing or impotence, to the exercise of an international police power.[26]

The Roosevelt Corollary rearticulated the exceptional identity of the United States and reinforced the connection between that identity and the country's pre-eminent role in the western hemisphere.

Cuba, by virtue of its proximity and historically close ties to the United States, is perceived to be even more within the American sphere of influence and in need of American guidance.[27] In fact, a former senior U.S. government official asserted that 'geography was the most important factor determining U.S.-Cuban relations.'[28] Americans were interested in the island as early as the colonial period, when they traded with Cubans. Once Florida was purchased from Spain in 1819, American leaders became even more aware of their island neighbour. Strategic concerns over Cuba were complemented by the growing perception that Cuba could not function independently and that, because of its proximity, the island would one day become part of the United States. President Martin Van Buren thought that Cuba should be tied to Spain or to the United States because

Cubans were incapable of governing the island themselves.[29] Consequently, the United States made repeated attempts to purchase Cuba
from Spain.[30]

When the United States intervened in Cuba's war with Spain in
1898, President McKinley declared that the country was carrying out
its duty because the island 'is right at our door.'[31] American intervention ended the war that same year, but the United States continued to
occupy Cuba until 1902. The Platt Amendment listed numerous conditions under which the Cuban government should operate and stated
that the United States had a right to intervene in Cuban affairs.[32]
American leaders fully believed in this right and continued to exercise
immense influence on the island. By 1906, the U.S. military was once
again in control of Cuba. This second intervention lasted only three
years, but it reinforced the American attitude that the United States
had a duty to take care of the island because of Cubans' innate inca-
pacity for self-government.[33] In the years that followed, Americans
continued to view Cuban sovereignty as pliable. For example, in 1933
the United States refused to recognize the new nationalist government
that declared the Platt Amendment invalid and initiated reforms that
would reduce American influence and holdings on the island.[34] The
next year, the United States assisted the more conservative and pro-
American faction in the revolutionary coalition, led by Fulgencio
Batista, to assume power.

During the first half of the twentieth century, American economic
and political influence in Cuba was enormous. At this time, Americans controlled all of the oil refineries, 90 per cent of the mines, and
80 per cent of the public utilities.[35] Although investment in Cuba was
on the decline from its height in the early 1920s, by 1959, Americans
still had one billion dollars invested in Cuba.[36] A statement made by
American Secretary of War Elihu Root in 1902 remained relevant in
Batista's Cuba, fifty years later. He said: 'Although [Cuba] is technically a foreign country, practically and morally it occupies an inter-
mediate position.'[37] José Martí, the revered father of Cuban independence, observed that the United States is 'a nation that, due to
geographic morality, has proclaimed its right to crown itself ruler of
the continent and has announced ... that it is entitled to all of North
America and that its imperial right should be acknowledged.'[38]
Cuba, by virtue of its location and its history of ties to the United
States, was seen to be intimately connected to the United States. Since
the end of Spanish domination, the United States had looked upon

Cuba as a parent would an irrational child, in need of U.S. control for its own good.

The American norm that Cuba was in its sphere of influence continued to influence U.S. policy even after the Cuban Revolution tore the island away from the U.S. fold in the early 1960s. When Fidel Castro challenged American domination of Cuba, it was natural for the United States to assume that it could buy Castro off and, when that failed, to oppose him. Castro came to power touting Cuban sovereignty and denouncing American interference. The perception that Cuba was not wholly independent from the United States is revealed by the language used to describe Cuba and U.S.-Cuba relations at the time. Government officials frequently spoke of the 'loss' of Cuba. Consequently, tension characterized even the early relations between the United States and the revolutionary government.

Fidel Castro's challenge to the U.S. perception that Cuba was firmly within the American sphere of influence intensified the growing animosity between Havana and Washington. In 1960 Congressman Mendel Rivers (D-SC) told Congress: 'We should assert the Monroe Doctrine. We should threaten Castro with Blockade. We should, if necessary, and, if conditions demand it, occupy Cuba.'[39] The U.S. government was not shocked by such language; on the contrary, it shared its underlying values. During the Cuban Missile Crisis, the United States policy makers turned back to the Monroe Doctrine, asserting that it 'is just as valid in 1962 as it was in 1823.'[40]

Not understanding the strong support within Cuba for independence from their northern neighbours, American leaders thought that the Cuban people would welcome a U.S. invasion. Relying on their own perceptions of the attraction and superiority of the American model, President Kennedy and his advisers were shocked when Cubans supported their new leaders during the ill-fated Bay of Pigs invasion. Yet, even after the Bay of Pigs, American policy makers still believed that they had a special relationship with Cuba which entitled them to intervene in Cuban affairs. All the while, Fidel Castro remained ardently protective of Cuban sovereignty and continued to challenge the American perception of U.S.-Cuba relations. These different perceptions go to the heart of the U.S.-Cuba hostility.

The belief that Cuba should be under American protection, that it did not have a legitimate right to complete sovereignty, continued to shape the American approach towards Cuba after the end of the Cold War. To this day, Cuba is considered to be within the American sphere of influence. Daniel Fisk has explained: 'US foreign policy contains a "democracy agenda," especially in its relations towards the Western Hemisphere.'[41] The end of the Cold War has done nothing to erase this long-held perception of Cuba within the United States.

Cuba's physical and psychological location, and all that it implies, continues to mould policy. The Helms-Burton Act, more strongly than any American document of the Cold War era, demonstrates that the United States still believes it has a right to dictate Cuban affairs. Section 205 states that Cuba will have a transitional government when the Cuban government releases all political prisoners, makes all political activity legal, and establishes free and fair elections. In addition, Helms-Burton states that both Fidel and Raúl Castro must be absent from the new Cuban government.[42] Essentially, if the Cuban people were to choose Fidel or Raúl Castro as their leader in a free and fair election, the United States, under Helms-Burton, would automatically declare the election invalid. According to Helms-Burton, too, any new Cuban government must also allow for the unfettered transmission of U.S. government-sponsored broadcasts to Cuba in the guise of Radio and TV Martí. Furthermore, this act dictates that Cuba give up its socialist system and return property to American citizens.[43] In many respects, Helms-Burton attempts to take the U.S.-Cuba relationship back to the pre-Castro days when the United States openly violated Cuban sovereignty.

In 2003 George W. Bush created a commission to devise a plan to 'assist Cuba's transition to democracy and free market economy.' The goals of the Commission for Assistance for a Free Cuba are to 'bring about a peaceful, near-term end to the dictatorship; establish democratic institutions, respect for human rights, and the rule of law; create the core institutions of a free economy; modernize infrastructure; and meet basic needs in the areas of health, education, housing, and human services.'[44] The then secretary of state, Colin L. Powell, opened the report with: 'Over the past two decades, the Western Hemisphere has seen dramatic advances in the institutionalization of democracy and the spread of free market economies. Today, the nations of the Americas are working in close partnership to build a hemisphere based on political and economic freedom where dictators, traffickers and terrorists cannot thrive.' He continued: 'We want to help the Cuban people put Castro and Castroism behind them forever. Any post-Castro succession that perpetuates the regime's hold on power would be completely contrary to the hemisphere's commitment to freedom. There can be no reconciliation between the United States and Cuba until far-reaching steps are taken to ensure political and economic liberty on the island.'[45] In July 2006 the commission released another report that made additional recommendations 'to hasten the end of the Castro dictatorship.'[46] The American perception that the United States has a right to be involved in Cuban affairs has greatly influenced the course of policy towards Cuba. Fidel Castro's challenge to these elements inherent in American identity is one of the reasons behind the American view of Cuba.

The commission's reports are a good example of how perceptions play out in policy. Both these reports express an understanding of Cuba that is contested by contrary evidence. Specifically, the reports are critical of the Cuban health-care system and assert that the United States will endeavour to assist the transitional government to improve health care on the island in order 'to meet the basic needs of the Cuban people' and ensure 'that adequate health and social services are provided.' This ignores the fact that the Cuban health-care system is regarded as excellent by international standards. After the World Bank's 2001 edition of 'World Development Indicators' (WDI) reported that Cuba had achieved excellent health and education results, World Bank President James Wolfensohn said the Cuban government was doing 'a great job.'[47] Despite much evidence to the contrary, the American reports dismiss Cuba's international reputation and health statistics as clever 'manipulation' by the state.

Likewise, the 2006 report asserted that 'Fidel Castro and his inner circle have begun a gradual but intrinsically unstable process of succession.' In fact, the same month the report was issued, Fidel Castro transferred power to his brother after announcing that he was to undergo intestinal surgery. Yet life in Cuba continued as it had before. The success of the leadership transfer was reinforced in 2008 when Fidel Castro permanently gave up the presidency of Cuba, demonstrating that, contrary to American perceptions, the Cuban government had devised a stable process of succession.

Cuba's physical and psychological location within the American worldview, and all that it entails, continues to influence U.S. perceptions of Cuba and the Cuban-American relationship. Yet these perceptions are further intensified by the emotions that are generated when the logics underlying the different perceptions collide.

The Emotional Factor: Squaring the Reaction

In 2000 Neta Crawford wrote that scholars of international relations have given insufficient attention to the role of emotion in world politics. She noted that we should begin 'to examine the ways that emotion and emotional relationships affect individuals' and groups' ways of perceiving, thinking, and acting.'[48] Emotional references characterize the rhetoric, policy statements, and official speeches about Cuba that emanate from Washington. Why is it that policy towards Cuba seems to be so emotionally laden? I suggest that the emotional component evolves from a fundamental clash of images and perceptions. The American identity as exceptional is fundamentally at odds with revolutionary Cuba. In particular, Fidel Castro's revolutionary message and Cuba's apparent ability to resist the United States contradict the American self-image as exceptional and the various images of Cuba that have been held in the American imagination for hundreds of years. The multiple schisms and contrary conceptions operating at once challenge the American self-image and its understanding of its role in relation to other countries of the western hemisphere and consequently evoke emotional reactions.

Fidel Castro came to power with a nationalist message that directly challenged Cuba's ties to the United States and the American role in the region. In 1959 Castro explained: 'We have been historically the victims of the powerful influence of the United States in the destinies of our country.'[49] In 1960 he stated that, in the past, Cuba was not an 'independent republic; there was only a colony where orders were given by the Ambassador of the United States. We are not ashamed to have to declare this. On the contrary: we are proud to say that today no embassy rules our country; our country is ruled by its people!'[50]

This nationalist message created a sense of betrayal within the United States, for various reasons. First, the popular narrative that the United States and Cuba are, or at least should be, intimately connected has a long history in the U.S. imagination, dating back to the days when Cuba was expected to join the American union. This vision of the relationship was reinforced in the decades leading up to the 1959 revolution. At that time many Americans not only invested heavily in Cuba but also vacationed on the island or even made Cuba their second home, creating a sense that Cuba was intimately part of the

American family. The exodus of Cubans to Miami in the months following the revolution added to the sense that the two societies were connected by family ties. The family metaphor still resonates with many Americans. In 1997 the person then in charge of the State Department's policy towards the western hemisphere, Jeffrey Davidow, told an audience that the 'repression and hardship is happening just 90 miles from our shores to, among others, the parents, brothers, and sisters of U.S. citizens in a country of 11 million people.'[51] American diplomats continue to espouse 'solidarity' with the Cuban populace and are at the same time indignant that the revolution has 'forced' Cubans to betray the United States.

Second, revolutionary Cuba presents a direct challenge to the American self-image as exceptional. The challenge to a core identity of the United States from a country that was often thought of as an American 'child' intensifies the emotional component of the policy. Fidel Castro created a Cuba that attacked representations of the U.S. role in the hemisphere and Cuba's 'natural' inferiority. In the early years of the Castro reign, the United States fought the Cuban challenge to its identity with military might, covert actions, economic isolation, international condemnation, and other means, yet nothing worked. Cuba in this era continued to challenge the United States successfully by simply existing. The failure of a succession of U.S. governments to oust Castro added insult to injury since this fact further served to defy the U.S. belief in its exceptional character.

This has helped to produce the emotional reactions often witnessed in Washington on the subject of Cuba and partly explains why the United States has been able to repair relationships with other Cold War enemies like Vietnam and Russia while being unable to dispense with the Cold War-style rhetoric and tensions in the American-Cuban relationship. Fidel Castro is often vilified by American leaders; for example, President Dwight Eisenhower called Fidel Castro a 'little Hitler' in his diary.[52] Such representations are well accepted by the American public. When Americans were asked in 2001 to compare Fidel Castro to 'Adolph Hitler, when he was dictator in Germany during World War II,' over 43 per cent of those surveyed said that Castro was as bad as Hitler and an additional 12.5 per cent said he was worse.[53] A few years later, in 2006, Gallup reported that 82 per cent of Americans had an unfavourable opinion of Fidel Castro.[54]

Given the fundamental self-images and perceptions involved in constructing this policy and the resulting emotions they elicit, it is relatively easy to see how it has become possible for U.S. policy towards the island to have remained hostile for over half a century. However, the very fact that identities and perceptions are socially constructed means that they are always either in flux or at least open to change. The next section will demonstrate that this particular approach towards Cuba is more entrenched than the identities and perceptions that have constructed it. This is because the norms that have arisen from the performance of these particular identities and perceptions have become internalized, thereby promoting the longevity of the approach.

Internalized Norms and the Role of the Cuban American Lobby Groups

The norms that govern U.S.-Cuba relations have become internalized as legitimate. They appear as taken-for-granted assumptions in American discourse on Cuba. The norms have also become well institutionalized since they are embedded in organizations that are given access to the highest levels of the U.S. government and have become incorporated into legislation.

The Cuban American Community

Most of the current scholarship that examines the U.S.-Cuba relationship stresses the importance of the Cuban American community in the development and continuation of the embargo. Susan Eckstein, author of numerous books and articles on U.S.-Cuba relations, emphatically states: 'Foreign policy toward Cuba is a domestic political issue.'[55] Indeed, this large ethnic group has become one of the most electorally powerful groups in American politics, consistently voting as a bloc and even managing to sway the outcomes of elections in Florida, which, as the 2000 presidential contest proved, is a crucial swing state in national elections. Furthermore, the continual election of Cuban Americans to Congress since Ileana Ros-Lehtinen was first elected to the House of Representatives in 1989 has aided the entrenchment of these perceptions. In 2008 there were four Cuban American members in the House of Representatives and two Cuban American senators. They actively reinforce uncompromising perceptions of Cuba and advocate the continuation of the isolationist position.

For many years, Cuban American representatives in Congress worked closely with what was then the most powerful Cuban American lobby group in Washington, the Cuban American National Foundation. This well-connected interest group had access to many prominent Washington officials of both political parties, including the president and other members of Congress, and consistently out-manoeuvred many other powerful groups that wanted to establish normal relations with Cuba.

Yet the situation is more complicated than it appears. Once we ask a fundamental question – How have hard-line elements of the Cuban American community and their interest groups been able to wield so much power? – we can see how perceptions and norms have become internalized as common sense.[56] This chapter contends that it became possible for the community, represented from the late 1980s through to the early 2000s by CANF, to influence policy because its understanding of the transformation of Cuba under Castro and the role of the United States in relation to Cuba was consistent with the American understanding. The anti-Castro wing of the Cuban American community and American officials agreed on the discursive constitution of revolutionary Cuba.

From 1959, the shared narrative created an environment that excluded other understandings of Cuba and U.S.-Cuba relations. Immediately following the revolution, Cuban exiles were given preferential treatment by the U.S. government because their ideas resonated with, and reinforced, the U.S. approach towards the Cuban state. The contrasting identities of Cuba and the United States constructed the American perception of Cuban immigrants and consequently have had a significant influence over policy.

The first wave of Cuban immigrants that arrived in the United States just after Fidel Castro assumed control of the island were characterized as political refugees or exiles who fled Cuba because they were persecuted for their political opinions. They were engaged in a fight for freedom. In fact, many of the Cubans who left after the revolution were likely motivated by fear of political persecution. Yet the American image of these 'refugees from communism' or 'freedom fighters' obscured their other reasons for leaving the island. They were the wealthiest Cubans and lost the most financially when Fidel Castro set his socialist plan in motion.

The later arrivals have proven to be even less politically motivated. María de los Angeles Torres, in her analysis of Cuban exile politics in the United States, reports that the exiles who arrived during the 1980s, the Marielitos, 'generally held a more balanced view of Castro's programs, often praising its systems of healthcare and education, its sports programs, and its gutsy nationalism ... they parted ways with Cuba's leadership because of its inefficient governance and poor economic performance ... They wanted more – more economic and educational opportunities, more consumer goods, more sexual freedom, more liberty to travel.'[57]

Furthermore, the search for a better economic future continues to motivate the most recent arrivals. The increase in the number of rafters during the 'the special period' after Soviet subsidies dried up and the Cuban standard of living plummeted indicates that, in general, the latest Cubans to reach American shores are not as much fleeing political persecution as they are chasing better economic possibilities. However, for decades their economic motives for leaving were downplayed by a political image which influenced and then reinforced the American response to the revolutionary government.

The American perception of Cubans as political refugees was one of the main sources of their influence over U.S. foreign policy. It gave the community credibility and access to the highest levels of policy makers. Angeles Torres asserts: 'In the first instance the political incorporation of postrevolution Cuban émigrés into the United States resulted from their symbolic and political utility ... the political development of Cuban exiles has not followed the typical path of other immigrant communities that first obtained political power at the local level in order to gain access to resources such as jobs and service ... Cuban exiles acquired political significance in the foreign policy realm first and in the domestic realm only later.'[58] Jorge Dominguez elaborates that 'the U.S. government promoted virtually unrestricted migration from Cuba, suspending parts of the U.S. immigration statutes because these were "refugees from communism."'[59] Because the Cuban exiles and American policy makers had the same or similar views of the Cuban Revolution and because the exiles were perceived to be united with the Americans (on the side of democracy and freedom and against Fidel Castro), they were admitted to the United States as political refugees, not immigrants, allowing them to bypass many of the normal restrictions placed on other immigrants. As a result, Cubans became permanent residents and then citizens faster than other immigrant groups, facilitating the rapid growth of the Cuban American population in Florida and their subsequent ability to wield major influence over election results. The American perception of Cuba as an enemy in their backyard and the Cubans as exiles, freedom fighters, or political refugees led to the special status accorded Cuban migrants and, consequently, contributed to their political power.

The U.S. government also facilitated the organization of the Cuban population into a focused and powerful group. After Fidel Castro assumed power, the Cuban exiles in Florida believed that he was a short-term dictator who lacked the support of the general populace. They were eager to push him out of Cuba. This view was also the accepted wisdom on Capitol Hill and within government agencies. The Eisenhower and Kennedy administrations, believing that the revolutionary government did not have the support of the Cuban people, authorized the training and organization of Cuban exiles in Florida to take part in the Bay of Pigs invasion. This shared perception led directly to the invasion and gave the Cuban exiles access to the highest levels of government for the first time.

The influence of Cuban Americans increased significantly under President Ronald Reagan, who encouraged the establishment of the Cuban American National Foundation.[60] Reagan understood that Cuban American perceptions and ideas complemented his own view of Cuba. According to Patrick Haney and Walt Vanderbush, 'the Reagan administration's approach to Latin America coincided almost perfectly with their [the CANF leadership] own worldview.'[61] Reagan wanted to give further credibility to the ideas espoused by his inner circle and also saw Cuban Americans and the newly created lobby group as an ally in his war against communism and Fidel Castro.

At this time, the leadership of the Cuban American community became closely aligned with the Reagan administration. For example, Jeanne Kirkpatrick, Reagan's top adviser on Latin America, became a close friend of the first leader of CANF, Jorge Mas Canosa. In 1985 she was honoured by CANF.[62] Over a quarter of a century later, the Reagan administration is still held in high esteem for its views on Cuba by hard-line elements of the Cuban American community. For instance, Lincoln Diaz-Balart, a Cuban American who was elected to Congress in 1992, has praised Kirkpatrick, stating that her ideas were nearly identical to his own and calling her his 'soulmate.'[63]

The decision of the Reagan administration to accept CANF as an 'expert' in U.S.-Cuba relations entrenched the lobby group's perspective on revolutionary Cuba on Capitol Hill. According to an analysis of the effectiveness of exile organizations, exile 'experts' who have been given preferential access to policy makers via their relationship with key governmental actors 'are able to ally with elected officials to over-whelm potential policy opposition.'[64] CANF, and, consequently, the norms and ideas it espoused, was able to gain and wield influence in some ways similar to how 'epistemic communities' extend their influ-ence. Peter Haas and Emanuel Alder explain that epistemic communi-ties wield influence by 'diffusing ideas and influencing the positions adopted by a wide range of actors, including domestic and interna-tional agencies, government bureaucrats and decision makers, legisla-tive and corporate bodies, and the public.'[65] While CANF is an Amer-ican lobby group and epistemic communities are normally thought of as international in nature, it has been able to sway policy formulation in a similar fashion.

CANF became accepted as the expert on Cuban affairs in Washing-ton from the mid-1980s through to 2001 when those favouring an even harder line towards Fidel Castro's Cuba broke away from the organi-zation and formed the rival Cuban Liberty Council. According to CANF's website:

> For two decades CANF has worked tirelessly to forge a broad bipartisan consensus on U.S. policy toward Cuba and has built bridges of close com-munication with the executive and legislative branches. Our influence extends internationally, where we raise awareness of Cuba's plight with world leaders and in capitals around the globe. CANF's research, educa-tion, and information efforts are designed to enlighten the media, acade-mia, policy makers, and public opinion – domestically and abroad – on Cuban issues. These efforts have led *Hispanic Business* magazine to call CANF 'the leading clearinghouse for information devoted solely to Cuba.'[66]

CANF also received federal funding, through the National Endow-ment for Democracy and other programs, to assist its work, as well as funding to help Cuban Americans resettle in Florida.

Described as the most powerful lobby group in the country, CANF penetrated a number of key institutions involved in formulating Cuba policy. For example, CANF officials were frequently given the floor during congressional hearings to present its opinions and counter opposing testimony. The long-time chairman of CANF, Jorge Mas Canosa, served as chairman of the president's Advisory Board for

Cuba Broadcasting under presidents Ronald Reagan, George H.W. Bush, and Bill Clinton.[67] CANF was given almost total control over the U.S. government's broadcasts to Cuba through Radio and TV Martí. A former director of Radio Martí, Ernesto Betcancourt, claimed that 'Mas Canosa, his projects, his politics are presented as if they were American policy.'[68] The organization's version of events was often accepted without question.[69]

The Cuban lobby has also directly advised congressional leaders on drafting legislation. This has been especially the case when the legislation is being drafted by Cuban American members of Congress. The current president of CANF, Francisco 'Pepe' Hernandez, describes how he and his predecessor helped draft what would become known as the Helms-Burton legislation. He reflects:

> In 1995, Jorge Mas Canosa and I sat in the office of then Congressman Bob Menendez discussing the drafting of the Cuban Liberty and Democratic Solidarity Act, what is commonly referred to as the Helms-Burton bill. In addition to stepping up economic and international pressure on the Castro regime, we recognized the importance of including measures to assist Cuba's internal opposition. We felt that the United States had a critical role to play in bolstering their efforts; much like it had done with Solidarity in Poland, offering material and direct financial support while helping to legitimize their cause internationally. We hoped, through what eventually became Section 109(a) of that landmark legislation, that the United States government could extend the same level of support and commitment to the Cuban people.[70]

Thus, the Cuban American hard-line position has become institutionalized in legislation. The Cuban Democracy Act and the Cuban Liberty and Democracy and Solidarity (*Libertad*) Act embody these ideas and norms about the U.S.-Cuba relationship. Helms-Burton itself furthers the longevity of this approach by removing the president's power to lift the embargo. The perceptions of Cuba and the norms that spur the isolationist approach have become well institutionalized in Washington.

CANF's influence waned after the group's perceptions and policy preferences began to diverge from Washington's. When the more hard-line members of the lobby split off in 2001 to form the Cuban Liberty Council, the new group was given the ear of the administration and Congress. As CANF became more moderate and began to promote limited engagement, the more hard-line CLC began to take centre stage in Washington. For example, members of the CLC, not CANF, were invited to the White House when President George W. Bush announced tightened restrictions on travel to Cuba in October 2003. This new Cuban American lobby group gained influence because its ideas and perceptions aligned with Washington's.

Even though these lobby groups have a large base of support in the Miami area and has been able to mobilize votes, there continues to be a significant element within the Cuban community that opposes these right-wing lobbying efforts. They are represented by other Cuban American groups, such as the Cuban-American Committee, the Cuban-American Pro-Family Reunification Committee, and the Cuban-American Coalition, which advocate dialogue with Cuba. Yet these groups have not garnered much influence despite having at times significant bases of support within the Cuban American community. As Angeles Torres points out, three thousand people attended a breakfast meeting during the 1988 presidential race held by the Pro-Family Reunification Committee. She argues that Clinton would have gained a greater percentage of the Cuban American vote in Florida in the 1992 presidential election if he had altered his policy vis-à-vis Cuba and came down solidly for improved relations.[71]

In spite of the potential number of votes available, presidential candidates have not attempted to tap into the pro-dialogue segments of the community nor have those Cuban Americans been given a voice in policy decisions. That being so, the conservative lobby groups' influence must derive from more than their electoral base. Their influence has been institutionalized and will remain so as long as policy makers and the lobby groups share the same perceptions of the U.S.-Cuba relationship.

Furthermore, even though these elements of the community through their lobby groups have a comparatively large influence over policy formation, many of the government officials I interviewed in Washington and in Havana said that the community's influence is often exaggerated, that the power over U.S.-Cuba policy remains firmly in the hands of Washington policy makers. They stated that elements within the government have used the Cuban American lobby to push for policies that they want to see enacted. When former Cubans attest to the atrocities in Cuba and push for certain policies, they make it difficult for opponents of those policies. The Cubans automatically have more credibility and thus are valuable to pro-embargo policy makers. In short, Cuban Americans who advocate iso-lation do have a voice but not because they have demanded that power or wield electoral clout. To a great degree, they are influential because a significant number of policy makers want this view to be heard.

Richard Allen, President Reagan's national security adviser, claimed that CANF was created by Reagan's people to be used 'as an effective tool to promote the President's aggressive Latin American policy.'[72] Haney and Vanderbush point out that 'the Reagan team and some Cuban-Americans ... were both faced with the need to shift public per-ceptions on related issues at a similar period of time. From the begin-ning, the role of Cuba was an integral part of the Reagan explanation of security threats in Central America and the Caribbean.'[73] Angeles Torres explains that the exiles 'fulfilled the ideological functions of providing evidence that communism is a repressive system; they had shown that they preferred to flee to a free country.'[74] One senior offi-cial put it this way: 'The influence of the Cuban-American lobby is overblown. Their job is one of reminding the government of the reason for their policy toward Cuba.'[75]

Another senior official explained that the government chooses when to consult with the community. This was especially true before CANF was created by the Reagan administration. An official who had worked in the Jimmy Carter administration noted that, although the Cuban Americans were regularly consulted by the administration before decisions were made, Carter's people did not consult with the community when they knew that it would oppose their decision. For example, the administration did not confer with the community in advance of an important meeting with the Cuban government over maritime issues. Only after an agreement was reached between the two countries did the administration inform the Cuban American community. Carter knew that the community would be opposed and wanted to present the agreement to it as a fait accompli.[76] The Clinton administration's return of Elían Gonzalez, the Cuban boy who was the centre of an international incident for months, is a more public example of the government going against the expressed wishes of the lobby.[77]

Thus, although the Cuban American lobby is powerful and does hold some sway over policy towards Cuba, its influence is a product of shared ideas and agreement on policy towards Cuba. The Cuban

American community gained preferential treatment and access to the upper echelons of the government because it reinforced the perceptions, beliefs, and ideas of a significant segment of the government. Its power was most dramatically increased under Reagan, the president whose view of Cuba most closely matched its own. The Reagan administration was instrumental in the creation and rise of the Cuban American National Foundation and successive administrations have frequently used the lobby as a tool to advance their policy goals.

The continued power of the anti-Castro elements of the community is a direct result of the ideas that were held in common by influential Cuban Americans and the policy community. The hard-line segment of the community would not have the power or the ability to sway policy if they did not share ideas and perceptions about Cuba and the United States with the foreign-policy establishment. Contrary to popular belief, the Cuban lobby has not held the U.S. government hostage. The scholarship that purports to explain policy towards Cuba solely on the basis of the effectiveness of the Cuban American lobby not only exaggerates the lobby's power but often neglects to explain why and how it is able to exert influence. By asking how it became possible for the lobby groups to be seen as wielding this power, we reveal important dynamics that are missed by taking their status for granted.

The acceptance of these ideas for so many decades has constrained policy debate. One senior American official admitted that 'there was a fair amount of inertia' involved in the continuation of the current policy.[78] The perception of Castro's Cuba as an enemy to the values of democracy and freedom and the United States itself has become institutionalized. The hardliners' approach, including their support for the embargo, has likewise become institutionalized in legislation, thereby making it more difficult to change policy.

International Norms

The strength of these domestic ideational factors has enabled the United States to resist strong international norms that favour open relations with Cuba. The embargo is seen as violating norms concerning the sovereign equality of states and non-interference in domestic affairs as well as norms regarding free trade, extraterritoriality, and international law. The United States has also been accused of defying less clearly defined humanitarian norms, such as those concerning the imposition of suffering on civilian populations. It has felt the pressure, especially since it claims to support enthusiastically many of the very same norms in other circumstances.

Furthermore, the United States has been accused of violating these norms by an overwhelming majority of the international community. Opposition to American policy is voiced within international forums like the United Nations, the Organization of American States (OAS), and the World Trade Organization (WTO), among others. The United Nations has frequently condemned the U.S. approach towards Cuba. In 1992 the UN General Assembly adopted a resolution that called for an end to the embargo against Cuba. That year, fifty-nine states, including major U.S. allies such as Canada, France, and Spain, voted for the resolution, three (Romania, Israel, and the United States) voted against it, and seventy-four abstained.[79] Each year since, the UN has passed a similar resolution calling for the lifting of the American embargo. In 2009, 187 nations voted in favour of the resolution, three voted against it, and two abstained.[80] Each year representatives from all regions of the globe speak out against the embargo during this vote. In 2000 the EU representative to the General Assembly declared: 'The European Union noted with concern the findings of United Nations agencies and programs in situ, and deplored the adverse and often dramatic effects of the United States economic embargo on Cuba's population, in particular, on women and children. Members of the Union would unanimously vote in favour of the draft resolution.'[81] Other friends and allies of the United States have voiced their opposition to the policy in this and other international forums as well.

Protest is not confined to the UN or other international organizations. Though Cuba policy is generally not a top priority of heads of states visiting Washington, many senior officials have subtly, and sometimes not so subtly, raised their opposition to the embargo and especially to the Helms-Burton Act with American policy makers.[82] For example, Lloyd Axworthy, the Canadian foreign minister, was especially critical of the U.S. embargo. He stated: 'The whole embargo and the Helms-Burton bill is totally counterproductive … It just doesn't work.'[83]

Furthermore, the moral issues raised by Pope John Paul II during his visit to Cuba in 1998, and since then by other religious leaders as well, have come to bear on the American ideational factors that influence the continuation of the embargo. Unlike the numerous UN resolutions, pressure from religious leaders had some temporary impact on American policy towards Cuba. An American foreign policy so closely tied to the notion of a 'moral mission' could not completely ignore calls from the pope. Consequently, there was some change in American policy, most specifically resulting in the series of measures enacted in March 1998.[84] Yet these measures were not lasting. For example, in 2003 President George W. Bush tightened restrictions on travel to the island.

Overall, U.S. policy has resisted international pressures. American officials assert that the sanctions will continue until they see considerable change in Cuba's political, social, and economic systems. Thus, despite international norms and some domestic pressures to relax tensions with Cuba, the embargo remains the cornerstone of U.S. policy, a reflection of the degree to which the domestic norms and ideas have been embedded in American foreign policy.

Conclusion

The United States approaches Cuba policy with a number of ingrained perceptions, norms, and images. These are not simply by-products of the relationship but are fundamental to the development of the relationship itself. Furthermore, how the United States understands its own role in the world is no less important to the relationship. Just as our identity moulds everything we do and influences how we see the world, the identity of states does the same. These factors can explain why the United States did not fundamentally change its policy towards Cuba at the end of the Cold War and still demonizes Cuba despite the recognition that the island is no longer a threat. Not only do ideational variables explain the anomalies not accounted for by realism and other similar gaps in the 'Cuba story,' but the variables examined here also illuminate the 'how possible' questions hidden by the narrative. For example, they offer a coherent account of how the Cuban American National Foundation came to be regarded as one of the most powerful interest groups in the country. In short, to understand the U.S. approach to Cuba from the time of the Monroe Doctrine to the enactment of Helms-Burton, we need to turn to the power of perceptions, images, ideas, norms, and identities.

3 The Independent International Citizen and the Other Cuba

'Viva le Primer Ministro Fidel Castro!' shouted Pierre Trudeau during his 1976 state visit to Cuba.[1] This cheer to the crowd in Havana has taken on an almost mythical status in Canadian understandings of Cuba. Although that moment or even one like it has not been repeated, it is frequently accepted as representative of the closeness of the bilateral relationship. To many Canadians, Cuba represents more than a possible vacation spot. It has a special place in the Canadian psyche that frequently plays out in the world of high politics and international relations.

In the decades since 1959, when Fidel Castro's rebel movement changed the course of Cuban history, Ottawa has maintained diplomatic ties and, when possible, economic, educational, and cultural connections with the Castro government. Yet this approach has engendered controversy because pressure to take a very different stance towards the island has come from many quarters, most seriously from Canada's primary trading partner and closest neighbour, the United States. During the height of the Cold War, Canada was only one of two countries in the hemisphere (the other was Mexico) that refused to follow the American dictate to isolate Cuba.

This chapter explores the reasons why Canada's policy towards Cuba has taken the particular form it has. To understand this policy fully, it is necessary to examine closely the accepted wisdom of the Canadian-Cuban relationship including the role of economic interests. Accordingly, I ask how it is possible not only that relations evolved in the way they did but also that policy towards Cuba has remained relatively unchanged despite developments within Cuba and pressure by the United States. In addressing this question, I suggest that Canadian citizens and policy makers rely on certain conceptions about their own identity as Canadians that influence foreign-policy formation. Canadians like to think of themselves as good international citizens and at the same time want to be seen as charting their own course through the choppy waters of international relations, especially taking a route that is different from the American one. These self-images produce and reproduce perceptions of the Cuban Revolution and views of Canada's role in relation to Cuba that inform policy towards the island. This chapter will highlight how these conceptions of self-identity and related perceptions of Cuba play a significant part in the development and continuation of Canadian policies towards Cuba.

The Highs and Lows of Canada's Cuba Policy

Canada's relationship with Cuba has a long history, and until 1959 this history was rather unremarkable. The trading relationship that began in the nineteenth century was cemented by the establishment of a diplomatic relationship in 1945. At this time, Canada did not have another diplomatic mission in the Caribbean.

When Fidel Castro's rebel movement overthrew the government of Fulgencio Batista in 1959, Ottawa officially recognized his revolution as legitimate and consequently maintained normal relations with the new government. In contrast to the American approach of treating Cuban immigrants as 'refugees from communism,' Canada made a concerted effort to discourage disaffected Cubans from establishing a base in Canada. The minister of citizenship and immigration explained: 'We were concerned over the fact that a number of Cubans had obtained entry into Canada for short periods of time as visitors and subsequently caused us embarrassment through the fact that they began to organize from a base in Montreal activities directed against the Castro régime in Cuba. This led us to review the means by which we might more effectively control the entry of similar persons from Cuba in the future.'[2]

The policy of conducting normal relations with the Cuban state continued throughout Fidel Castro's reign and shows no signs of change now that Cuba is under the leadership of his brother Raúl. Though generally warm, relations between Canada and Cuba have not always been especially friendly as a number of issues, including those as serious as Havana's involvement in African conflicts and as seemingly insignificant as the jibes exchanged after Canada hosted the 1999 Pan-

American Games, have come between the two countries. However, formal diplomatic relations have never been severed.

Economic and diplomatic ties were maintained throughout the ebb and flow of the Cold War period and despite pressure from the Americans to follow their lead on Cuba and institute an economic embargo. Officially, Ottawa asserts that trade, investment, and aid are not only good for the Canadian and Cuban economies but will encourage a movement towards democratization and improved civil and political rights in Cuba. According to the Department of Foreign Affairs and International Trade (DFAIT), the policy, frequently termed constructive engagement, 'means a determined attempt to work with the Cuban government and Cuban society in order to encourage institutional change and political and economic opening.'[3] This includes raising human-rights issues with the Cuban government and in multilateral forums like the United Nations. In 1997 Ottawa and Havana signed a fourteen-point Joint Declaration, which established cooperation between the two governments in a number of areas, including human rights and standards of good governance.[4] This once celebrated document instituted collaboration between Canadians and Cubans on legal and judicial matters and in counter-narcotics, while also enhancing communication between the Cuban and Canadian parliaments, ministries of health, and non-governmental organizations (NGOs). Additionally, various Canadian organizations such as universities and cultural groups maintain links with Cuban counterparts, Canada remains the top source of tourists for Cuba, and the Canadian embassy in Havana keeps in quiet contact with human-rights activists and NGOs active on the island.[5]

The bilateral relationship has weathered some difficult periods. For example, in the late 1990s a series of events created a palpable strain between Havana and Ottawa. During Prime Minister Jean Chrétien's 1998 visit to Havana, he made a personal plea on behalf of four dissidents who were scheduled to be tried in Cuba. Yet the trials went forward as planned.[6] Relations worsened during the 1999 Pan-American Games that were held in Winnipeg. Fidel Castro charged that Canada allowed sports scouts to promote the defection of Cuban athletes, withdrew medals from Cuban winners under false charges, and tried to disadvantage Cuban teams.[7] In addition, a number of Cuban students attending Canadian universities defected while in Canada, adding to the tension between the two countries. At the same time, Canadian businesses were becoming more disillusioned with Cuba.[8]

John Manley, who replaced Lloyd Axworthy as minister of foreign affairs in 2000, took a much harder line with Cuba. Cuba was not invited to the Summit of the Americas meeting in Quebec City. As a result of these problems, official high-level visits to Cuba were suspended and a number of joint projects were reconsidered. Yet, on the whole, the repercussions were few and short-lived. On the ground, relations between the two countries remained essentially unchanged.[9]

Economic Interests

Ottawa's approach towards the island, and Canada's role in world affairs generally, is often attributed to the broad influence of economic interests on foreign policy. In 1999 Axworthy told an audience in Princeton, New Jersey, that Canada's involvement in Kosovo was tied to Canada's national economic interest because 'in an increasingly interconnected world, where we are travellers, exporters and importers, investors and donors, we cannot afford to ignore the problems of others – even if we wanted to.'[10] Yet, as scholars of Canadian foreign policy have pointed out, in the Kosovo case, 'few Canadians travel there, export to or from there, or invest money there. The same can be said of virtually all the other places where the Canadian Forces recently have been deployed on peacekeeping or peace enforcement missions.'[11] Thus, the economic-interest thesis is not always enough to explain Canadian foreign policy. In fact, some would argue that the thesis has validity only in rare instances.

A variant on this argument is most often put forward as the explanation for Canada's Cuba policy. Many critics and supporters of Canada's policy towards Cuba emphasize the role of trade in Ottawa's decision to engage with the Cuban government. For example, it was argued that the Diefenbaker government welcomed the American embargo as a potential windfall for Canadian business. The visit of the Cuban trade mission to Canada that occurred very shortly after the U.S. embargo was initiated is cited as evidence that Canada attempted to profit from the tension in U.S.-Cuba relations. Yet, according to the Canadian-American Committee, a group representing business interests, and official documents, the Canadian government did not invite the mission and was embarrassed by the visit.[12] Government documents from the period reveal that Ottawa was very concerned about the appearance that Canada might be trying to take advantage of the embargo.[13] At the time, Prime Minister Diefenbaker asserted that it is 'not our purpose to exploit the situation arising from the United States embargo, and we have no intention of encouraging what in effect would amount to the bootlegging of goods of United States origin.'[14]

To this day, the economic narrative continues to inform our thinking about Canadian-Cuban relations. As well as being frequently cited by policy makers, it appears as one of the primary explanations, and often the most important one, for the relationship in both press and academic accounts.[15] The popular magazine *Maclean's* refers to Canada's 'lucrative friendship with Cuba.'[16] In a letter to the editor written in response to Chrétien's visit to Cuba, Canadian academic Irving Brecher expressed a similar sentiment. He commented, 'The saddest point of all is that the Cuba trip accurately reflects a Canadian foreign policy in which, by and large, human rights are long on rhetoric, short on substance and routinely overridden by trade and investment goals.'[17] Though much more nuanced than journalist accounts, academic scholarship also emphasizes the economic benefits of the Canadian-Cuban relationship. In her article 'Trading with the "Enemy": Canadian-Cuban Relations in the 1990s,' Gillian McGillivray weighs the economic and political motivations behind Canada's policy. In stressing the economic component, she explains that 'Cuba is an increasingly open market in which Canadian companies do not have to compete with Americans.'[18] In their widely read book on Canadian-Cuban relations, John Kirk and Peter McKenna write: 'Foremost, of course, is the trade-commercial factor ... It was important for Canada to solidify political relations at the top as a means of further cementing economic linkages between the countries to shore up Canadian business connections with the island.'[19]

Trade Benefits

The lack of American competition in many areas (though no longer all) would certainly seem beneficial from the Canadian perspective. Indeed, it is easy to see why trade considerations are often viewed as a major reason Canada has maintained relations with Cuba. Canada has sustained a trading relationship with the island for centuries. In the nineteenth and early twentieth centuries, Cuban rum and sugar were traded for Canadian lumber and other natural resources. Canadian financial institutions were also active in Cuba prior to the revolution. During the Cold War, Canadian exports to Cuba continued, rising fairly steadily throughout the 1970s, reaching Cdn$452 million in 1981,

Table 1
Foreign direct investment in Cuba, 1990–9, in U.S. dollars

Country	Foreign Direct Investment in Cuba
Canada	1,807,000,000
Mexico	1,806,000,000
Italy	599,000,000
Australia	500,000,000
South Africa	400,000,000
Spain	350,000,000

Source: U.S. Cuba Trade and Economic Council, 'Foreign
Investment and Cuba,' http://www.cubatrade.org/.

and then declining during Cuba's period of economic crisis after the collapse of the USSR. However, once Cuba began to recover, Canadian trade began to rise again, partly replacing Cuba's trade with Eastern Europe as the former Soviet bloc disintegrated. As Table 1 shows, Canada was the largest foreign investor in Cuba during the 1990s. In addition, between 2001 and 2006, Canada was Cuba's fourth-largest trading partner, after China, Venezuela, and Spain, as seen in Figure 1.

Once Cuba was permitted to purchase food on a cash-sale basis from the United States, Canadian exports, especially in the agricultural sector, faced more competition. However, Canada still remains one of Cuba's top exchange partners, accounting for approximately 7.3 per cent of Cuba's overall trade.[20] Aid is another important facet of the economic relationship. Official Canadian development assistance was re-established in 1994, and, between that year and 2006, the Canadian International Development Agency (CIDA) directed $85 million to Cuban development projects.[21]

However, to understand Ottawa's approach to Cuba more fully, it necessary to look again at this economic narrative. A closer examination of the trade figures calls into question the emphasis placed on the economic benefits. While Canadian exports to Cuba did increase after the introduction of American embargo, so did Canadian exports to other Latin American countries. Exports to Cuba rose from $17.5 million in 1955 to $52.6 million in 1965, a threefold increase. But, in the same ten years, exports to Argentina went from $6.8 million to $32.7 million, an almost fivefold increase, and exports to Venezuela increased from $30.8 million to $73 million. Even after the collapse of

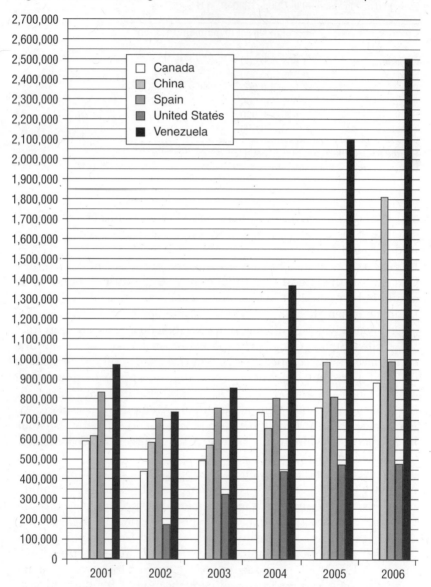

Figure 1: Trade exchange with Cuba in thousands of Cuban pesos

the Soviet Union, Canadian-Cuban trade comprised a relatively small percentage of Canada's overall trade, a mere 5 per cent of total Canadian exports to Latin America.[22] Excluding Mexico, in 2008 Cuba was Canada's fifth-largest trading partner in Latin America and the Caribbean. Moreover, Canada's total trade with Latin American remains to this day relatively minor, given that approximately 80 per cent of Canada's trade is with the United States.

Additionally, many Canadian companies are hesitant about investing in Cuba because of the special difficulties related to Cuba's economic system. Both Cuba's monetary system and the state's control over employees, wages, and other labour matters complicates doing business on the island. Furthermore, rumours of bureaucratic difficulties are rife in the business community. Since foreign-investment decisions are made in a fairly ad hoc manner, companies have been known to spend much time and money exploring agreements with the Cuban government only to have them fall through at the last minute. Contributing further to the business community's unease were Fidel Castro's speeches against the evils of globalization made near the end of his reign as president.[23] In light of all of this, the Canadian government counsels caution. The government publication *Cuba: A Guide for Canadian Business* warns potential investors that 'Cuba is not for the timid or the unprepared. The risks are substantial.'[24] Thus, though trade is important to Canada, Cuba represents a relatively minor and risky market for Canadian businesses.

If trade considerations were one of Canada's main priorities vis-à-vis Cuba, it would seem likely that, given American attempts to discourage Canadian-Cuban trade and the importance of American trade to the Canadian economy, Canada would bow to American pressure. Canada's trading relationship with the United States is much more important than any benefits accrued from trade with Cuba. Trade with the United States represents 79 per cent of Canadian exports and accounts for 24 per cent of Canadian GDP.[25] The Canadian Department of Foreign Affairs asserts: 'We are each other's largest trading partner, with U.S.$1.2 billion in trade now crossing the Canada-US border every single day.'[26] In 2007 Canada's total exports to Cuba were $563 million. In comparison, Canada's total exports to the United States were $355.9 billion. Import figures are similar: Canada's total imports from Cuba in 2007 amounted to $1 billion while imports from the United States reached a total of $220.4 billion.[27]

The rest of this chapter will show that the Canadian approach towards Cuba has more to do with the type of emotional connection to the island nation that drove Prime Minister Trudeau, in the midst of the Cold War, to shout 'Viva Fidel' than it does with any cold calculation of trade figures. In its essence, Canadian policy towards Cuba is intimately tied to the Canadian identity and particular understandings of the interrelationship between the Canadian sense of self and representations of Cuba.

Canadian Identity and Cuba

Canada has many and often competing identities and worldviews. Yet the range of identities that construct behaviour narrows when it comes to foreign policy. When asked to describe 'Canada's role in the world,' most Canadians use similar adjectives.

Cuba policy is informed by two interactive processes of identity construction. One has its roots in the international environment and the other originates in Canada's domestic experience. Typically, national identity is constructed by imagining how we differ from others and in that sense is a reflection of the international environment. David Campbell makes the case that identity is created by difference. In this way, identity is not some idea of ourselves that is separate from the ideas we have about others, but is actually constituted by our thinking about how we are different from others.[28] Identity is fluid and depends on context. We think of ourselves as professors, students, or researchers in the university context but at home we may be children, wives, or husbands. When that identity is constructed by difference, we put the othering in terms of the person, group, or entity under discussion or the focus of attention. As such, in the context of Cuban-Canadian relations, it would be natural for Canadians to define themselves mainly by the ways they think they are different from Cubans. However, in the case of Canada's relationship with Cuba, Canada is 'othering' the United States rather than Cuba. Canadians like to demonstrate to the world that they are 'distinct from the United States.' This identity has had an intense impact on Canadian-Cuban relations.

Even though a country's self-image often emphasizes differences from other international actors, this self-image also has origins that are removed from international experiences. In this sense, identity is less about seeing ourselves in contrast to others and more about reflecting domestic experiences, and, in the Canadian case, it is related to the importance Canadians place on certain values. Canadians identify with those values domestically and want to be seen as promoting them abroad. They believe this makes Canada a good international citizen.

Yet the domestic and international roots of identity cannot always be neatly separated. In the case of Canada's policy towards Cuba, the two processes interact to produce a third effect. Since Canadians 'other' the United States instead of Cuba (the international component), and since they see themselves as a good international citizen (related to domestic-value projection), they end up drawing similarities between Canada and Cuba that reinforce both the international and domestic sources of identity and reproduce the patterns that construct Canadian policy towards the island. We will look at each of these processes in turn, beginning with an exploration of the role that Canada's self-image as a good global citizen plays in the formation of policy.

The 'Good Citizen' and Cuba

Canada's approach towards Cuba is constructed by its self-image as a good international citizen. Canadians believe that their country is a society dominated by the values of peace, order, moderation, compromise, and social justice. The importance of these values to Canadians has been well documented by scholars who trace the Canadian identity to Canada's historical experience.[29] Canadian political culture has been understood to be primarily influenced by a combination of Lockean liberalism and Tory conservatism. Scholars such as Gad Horowitz maintain that, when the Loyalists rejected the American Revolution and fled north, they brought an emphasis on the common good with them to Canada, which today manifests itself in a greater acceptance of socialist ideas and values such as peace, order, and stability.[30] Whether or not Canadians actually live in a society dominated by these values is arguable; indeed, there is much evidence to the contrary. Yet the point is that Canadians see themselves as enlightened along these lines and want their foreign policy to reflect their values.

The connection between such values and foreign policy is acknowledged in the scholarly literature and often trumpeted by the government. Cranford Pratt writes that there is 'a close link between domestic social values and the ethical component of foreign policy. If Canada's liberal humanitarian values are not also reflected in Canada's foreign policy, then popular attachment to them domestically will likely itself decline.'[31] The Liberal government's self-congratulatory 1994–5 foreign-policy review articulated this linkage:

'Foreign policy matters to Canadians. They have deep-rooted values that they carry over into the role they want Canada to play – nurturing dialogue and compromise; promoting democracy, human rights, economic and social justice; caring for the environment; safeguarding peace; and easing poverty. And they can offer corresponding skills – mediating disputes; counselling good governance in a diverse society; helping the less fortunate; and peacekeeping.'[32] Accordingly, Canadians think that their foreign policy should advocate dialogue over estrangement, support international law, and promote social justice.

Likewise, Canadians see their country as one that resolves rather than contributes to international conflict. This is often expressed through the idea that Canadians are peacekeepers. According to a 2008 poll, 'Canadians see peacekeeping as their country's most important contribution to the world.'[33] This idea is a pervasive part of the country's political culture. Though Canadians have nothing to match the scale of the Statue of Liberty, the monument to Canadian peacekeepers near the Parliament Buildings certainly represents the Canadian self-identity. Engraved with the words 'Reconciliation' and 'At the Service of Peace,' this monument is the site of many national ceremonies and services honouring veterans. In addition, the image of a Canadian peacekeeper appears on the Canadian ten-dollar bill. Likewise, the Canadian self-identity is celebrated in Canadian school textbooks. Learning about peacekeeping is a required part of the Canadian high school curriculum. For example, in Ontario, students in the mandated grade ten history and civics course are required to learn about Canada's role as a peacekeeper. Canadian students can also participate in a simulated peacekeeping operation or in peacekeeping essay-writing or poster contests.[34] They can also take part in celebrations organized in many provinces on Peacekeeping Day. The first sentence of DFAIT's introduction to peacekeeping reads: 'For Canada, peacekeeping is an important aspect of our national heritage, and a reflection of our fundamental beliefs.'[35] A former MP and cabinet minister, David Kilgour, calls peacekeeping 'an integral part of our national identity or "national DNA."'[36]

Policy makers believe that Canadians are especially skilled at bringing together disparate groups through dialogue. A recent DFAIT document, *Dialogue on Foreign Policy*, maintains that 'we have been called on by other countries to share our experience with dialogue and the peaceful resolution of differences; many opportunities exist for us to serve a mediating role.'[37] The same document proclaims: 'Amid current international tensions, Canadians may be able to play an important global role in fostering dialogue among different cultural communities.'[38]

When articulated in policy towards Cuba, this identity contributes to a certain perception of the Cuban situation and to the rise of a set of corresponding norms. An element of Canada's positive representation of its self-identity as a good international citizen involves an emphasis on international law. The fourteen-point Joint Declaration signed by the Canadian and Cuban foreign ministers in 1997 outlined how the two countries would strengthen the bilateral ties. It reiterated that 'the Ministers emphasized their mutual commitment and their right to conduct international relations on the basis of the defense of International Law.'

Similarly, the emphasis on dialogue, on opening rather than closing avenues of communication, is evident in the construction of policy towards Cuba. Despite considerable pressure from Washington, Ottawa has consistently advocated dialogue with Havana. The Department of Foreign Affairs and International Trade explains that 'Canada's hope for Cuba is a peaceful evolution to a society with full respect for human rights, genuinely representative institutions and an open economy. *Canada has sought to do this through engagement and dialogue, rather than isolation.*'[39] During Prime Minister Chrétien's visit to Cuba in 1998, he told a Cuban television audience that their two countries 'have always chosen dialogue over confrontation, engagement over isolation, exchange over estrangement.'[40]

The representatives from the Canadian embassy in Cuba and officials representing the Cuban government meet regularly in Havana. Senior Canadian officials including Prime Minister Trudeau, Lloyd Axworthy, and Prime Minister Chrétien have met at length with Fidel Castro. Axworthy said that the purpose of the 1997 Joint Declaration 'was primarily to open up a dialogue.'[41] In this document, 'both Ministers reaffirmed the high value of the longstanding and uninterrupted bilateral relationship between Canada and Cuba.' They then 'underscored the fact that Canada-Cuba relations have always emphasized the importance of maintaining a frank and open dialogue in a spirit of mutual respect, not only on issues in which both sides agree, but as well on issues on which they differ.'[42]

Canada has attempted to facilitate Cuba's communication with the international community. Ottawa has been one of the most vocal proponents of Cuba's re-entry into hemispheric bodies including the

OAS.[43] In 1998 Lloyd Axworthy told the OAS that 'surely the time has come for all OAS members to consider when the suspended 35th member of the organization, Cuba, could once again be seated at the table.'[44] In 1996 the secretary of state for Latin America and Africa, Christine Stewart, urged the members of the hemisphere to 'consider the question of the Organization's 35th member, Cuba, which is not present with us today. Canada shares the hope of many that this situation will one day change, and we urge the Organization to consider renewed forms of contact with Cuba, which would bring us closer to the day of Cuba's eventual re-integration into the inter-American family.' She went on to explain that 'isolationism is not the answer' and that Canada was against isolation because 'it only give[s] rise to the hardening of militant policies and reinforce[s] the wrong kind of nationalism and political rigidity.'[45] To Canadians, encouraging dialogue that would lead to the resolution of international tensions is key to being a good international citizen. This identity creates a preference for engagement over isolation and contributes to the development of policies such as the 1997 Joint Declaration.

The mediating role arising from the self-image of the good international citizen has influenced the Canadian approach towards Cuba. Ottawa has, at various times, attempted to mediate between the United States and Cuba. For example, Joe Clark, as secretary of state for external affairs (1989–91), attempted to bring the two sides closer together. He asserted in 1990 that 'Canada can't solve the contest between Cuba and the United States, but we may well be able to create some conditions ... to create some room where the principle actors might move.'[46] Ottawa repeatedly stresses its willingness to work with the governments of Cuba and the United States. Canada tries to maintain its credibility with each side, usually by offering sympathy and support to both while encouraging policy change.[47] For example, when speaking to Americans, Canadian officials emphasize that Ottawa and Washington have the same goals, while highlighting the benefits of engagement over isolation. When asked about the different approaches to Cuba during a joint press briefing with Madeleine Albright, Lloyd Axworthy said that 'we share the end objective, which is to see a transition in Cuba into a democratic society. We have chosen different methods. We don't think an embargo works ... Our approach to Cuba has been through a form of engagement. We made some progress over the past year. We think it's worth continuing that kind of engagement.'[48] In 2007 Canada's ambassador in Washington, Michael

Wilson, said: 'We have a dialogue, and that is different from the United States because they have nothing like this type of dialogue.' He explained, 'Because of that dialogue, we have an understanding of how Cuba thinks. We also have an understanding of how Washington thinks. Cuba sees us as a North American country with which they can have some sort of dialogue.'[49]

In advocating these policies, Canadian policy makers are not operating on assumptions divorced from Canadian civil society. Many Canadian citizens and NGOs interested in foreign policy also want their government to act as a mediator between the United States and Cuba. In 2001 the Anglican Church of Canada 'urged the Canadian Government, through the Department of External Affairs, to offer to mediate between Cuba and the United States with a view to a normalization of relations between the two countries and the reintegration of Cuba into the Organization of American States.'[50] Policy towards Cuba is clearly influenced by the importance placed on mediation by both the government and citizens of Canada.

Canada's 'good citizen' identity in world affairs has played an important role in the design and development of policy towards the Cuban state. The emphasis on mediation, dialogue, and international law produces a norm that extols the virtues of engagement and thus contributes to the Canadian decision not to isolate Cuba even during times when not doing so has put Canada in an uncomfortable or even disadvantaged situation internationally, especially with regard to its relationship with the United States.

The Influence of Othering:
Canada as 'Not American' and Cuba Policy

Another element of the Canadian self-image, which often has a significant influence on Canadian foreign policy, is an intense desire to be distinct from the United States. Being 'not American' has become an inherent element of the Canadian identity. Othering of the United States has become so much a part of the Canadian identity that it is used to sell everything from beer to military service.[51] When asked for a description of what it means to be Canadian, many Canadians will emphasize how Canada differs from the United States. For example, a member of the Canadian Armed Forces described a Canadian peacekeeper by contrasting the Canadian and American military experiences. He wrote: 'I wear combats, not fatigues and I work for a "leftenant," not a "loo-tenant." I drive an Iltis, not a Jeep or a Humvee and the weapon I carry for my protection is a C7, not an M16. I observe from, or take cover in, a trench and not a foxhole.' He continued: 'Although I am trained to fight in a war, I don't cause them ... I try not to take sides and believe in treating all humanity equally. I don't just go on patrols; I also clear landmines to make the area safe for everyone. In my off-duty hours while deployed, I occupy myself by rebuilding schools or playgrounds and I teach children in a war-torn country about peace and harmony.' He concludes: 'I am my country's best ambassador and I am respected the world over for what I do best.'[52]

Canada's policy of 'constructive engagement' towards Cuba has been held up as an example of independence vis-à-vis the United States since the early 1960s. Protecting Canada's image as an independent country was an important factor in the country's initial decision not to join the American embargo against Cuba. When the United States imposed the embargo, the Department of External Affairs requested feedback from Canada's embassies in Latin America. The Canadian ambassador to Argentina replied in a top-secret telegram in which he stated: 'I need not enlarge on the adverse effect which Canadian support of the United States embargo at this time would have upon our image as an independent state, or upon our influence particularly among the under-developed nations.'[53]

Cuba became a public symbol of Canada's independence during the Diefenbaker administration. The personalities of Prime Minister John Diefenbaker and President John F. Kennedy shaped the two countries' policies towards revolutionary Cuba. The prime minister was known for his nationalism and tended to react strongly against any real or perceived American pressure. This perception was greatly reinforced by what has become widely known among Canadians as the Rostow memo. Diefenbaker's relationship with President Kennedy, and his belief that the Kennedy administration was attempting to 'bully' him, worsened after the Canadian leader found a memo accidentally left by Kennedy's staff following a meeting between the two men. The memo stated that Kennedy should 'push' Diefenbaker on a number of issues.[54] Forgoing polite diplomacy, Diefenbaker did not return the memo but instead kept it, which infuriated the president. This animosity intensified Diefenbaker's desire to forge an independent Canadian foreign policy, particularly over Cuba, since Kennedy seemed focused on moving Canada on this issue.[55] The Americans pressed the matter of Canada's policy towards Cuba in a number of forums at this time. For example, the American ambassador to the United Nations,

Adlai Stevenson, told a Toronto audience in 1960 that Ottawa should follow the American lead on Cuba.[56] Furthermore, tending to see Kennedy as a bully, Diefenbaker sympathized with Castro's determination to chart a course independent of American influence.[57]

Tension between Canada and the United States over Cuba came to a head during the Cuban Missile Crisis, when Diefenbaker refused to put Canadian forces on full alert and implied that the American version of events was possibly unreliable. Kennedy once again voiced his anger, and Diefenbaker in turn became more determined to take an independent path on this issue. At this point, the issue of Cuba became closely tied to concerns over sovereignty and the looming presence of the United States. Charles Ritchie, the Canadian ambassador to Washington during the Diefenbaker era, wrote: 'Do we consider what has happened in Cuba as a popular social revolution and not a Russian-inspired Communist take-over? ... It is unthinkable that anything similar to the developments in Cuba should occur in Canada, but if it did, should we not regard this as our own business and resent intervention?'[58] The stage was thus set. Canada would not follow the American lead on Cuba. Cuba had become a symbol of Canadian independence in foreign affairs.

Every prime minister since has been concerned about this element in the Canadian self-image and has taken steps to avoid appearing too pro-American. Policy towards Cuba has been highlighted by each administration as an example of their determination to chart an independent foreign policy for Canada. However, Prime Minister Pierre Trudeau was especially concerned about Canadian dependence on the United States. Of the United States, Trudeau said, 'Canada has increasingly found it important to diversify channels of communication because of the overpowering presence of the United States of America and that is reflected in a growing consciousness amongst Canadians of the danger to our national identity from a cultural, economic, and perhaps even military point of view.'[59] This view was manifested in the Trudeau government's promotion of the 'Third Option,' a policy that attempted to reduce Canada's vulnerability to the United States by diversifying Canadian trade. A feature of that policy was to increase Canada's ties to Cuba because Cuba not only served as an additional trading partner but, more important, represented another way for the Trudeau government to distinguish Canada from the United States. Trudeau, as we have seen, was the first leader of an American ally to pay an official visit to Fidel Castro in Cuba.[60]

Even Prime Minister Brian Mulroney, widely recognized as being pro-American, did not commit Canada to support of the embargo during his period in office in the mid-1980s to early 1990s. In fact, in the spring of 1990, he sent Louise Frechette, the then assistant deputy minister for Latin America and the Caribbean, to Cuba, where she stressed the importance of Canadian-Cuban cooperation. A senior official at the Canadian embassy in Havana during the Mulroney years told the author that the prime minister's desire to demonstrate to Canadians that he was not an American 'lapdog' was an important reason behind the continuation of Canada's policy towards Cuba in those years.[61] Fifteen years later, these considerations also appear to motivate Stephen Harper. Like Mulroney, he has brought Canadian policy closer to the United States on a number of international issues and certainly cooled relations with Havana but has not altered the foundation of Canada's engagement with Cuba.

Jean Chrétien, prime minister from 1993 to 2003, was adamant that Canada's Cuba policy remain distinct from American policy towards the island. André Ouellet, Chrétien's first minister of foreign affairs, said that he took a firm stance with the U.S. secretary of state, making it plain to 'Mr. [Warren] Christopher that this government was determined to set its own independent course in foreign policy. By being independent I do not mean that we are opposed to the American policy but that we want to see action being taken with a Canadian point of view in mind. Our hope to see the end of the American commercial embargo against Cuba is a clear affirmation of our wish.'[62] A senior official with the Canadian government during this period told the author that, as during the Mulroney years, the need to be distinct from the United States was one of the main reasons for Canada's policy of engagement.[63]

The enactment of Helms-Burton in 1996 incensed Canadians and reinforced the opposition to American policy on Cuba. The federal government's 'Cuba: Trade and Economic Overview' has a section devoted to the Canadian response to Helms-Burton. It states: 'Canada does not tolerate the extra-territorial application of foreign laws contrary to our laws and policy and accordingly expects Canadian companies to carry out business under the laws and regulations of Canada, not those of a foreign country.'[64] A 1996 poll revealed that, in response to Helms-Burton, only 5 per cent of Canadians felt that the Canadian government should ban trade with Cuba and almost half wanted to institute retaliatory trade sanctions against the United States.[65] A majority of senior Canadian officials told the author that Ottawa's reaction to Helms-Burton was first and foremost an issue of Canadian sovereignty vis-à-vis the United States, and much less so about Canada's relationship with Cuba.

Canadian policy towards Cuba was heavily promoted and defended by Ouellet's successor as foreign minister, Lloyd Axworthy, who actively sought to strengthen Canada's ties to other countries in an effort to refocus policy away from the United States. In 1991, while the Liberals were in opposition, Axworthy and Roy MacLaren, the then Liberal critic for international trade, outlined this foreign-policy approach in *Part of the Americas: A Liberal Policy for Canada in the Western Hemisphere*, which stressed that Canada needed to diversify its ties to the rest of the hemisphere. Axworthy's policy on Cuba was clearly influenced by his position on Canadian-American relations. More so than past foreign ministers, Axworthy was known for his outspoken opposition to the U.S. embargo of Cuba. In 1998 Axworthy and American Senator Jesse Helms had a heated exchange of words over Cuba, during which Axworthy declared: 'The whole embargo and the Helms-Burton bill is totally counterproductive. It just doesn't work ... Cuba is facing a form of economic victimization through the embargo.'[66] A senior Canadian diplomat with the United Nations in the early 1990s told the author that Cuba was a 'cheap way for them [the Liberal Party] to distinguish Canada from the U.S.'[67]

Canada's self-image as 'not American' has infiltrated most areas of Canadian foreign policy, and policy towards Cuba stands out as a particularly relevant example of this dynamic. Since Diefenbaker angrily said of Kennedy during the Cuban Missile Crisis that 'that young man has got to learn that he is not running the Canadian government,' Canadian prime ministers, the foreign-policy establishment, and the public have all held Cuba up as an example of Canadian independence.[68] A former Canadian ambassador to Cuba, Mark Entwistle, describes the Canada-Cuba relationship as 'an indispensable instrument in the sovereignty tool-kit.'[69] For Canada to reverse policy over Cuba would involve much more than a recalculation of Canadian-Cuban relations – among other things, it would require a fundamental adjustment in Canadian thinking about their relationship with their largest neighbour, or a very creative spin on the trilateral story that would allow Canada to keep its pride and maintain every appearance of not 'bowing to the Americans.'

Yet Canadian policy towards Cuba is constructed of more than the process of othering. As Canadians 'other' the United States by drawing sharp contrast between the two countries, they also use 'likeness' to reinforce their identity and construct policy. Stressing the similarities between Cuban and Canadian societies leads to sympathetic renderings of the Cuba narrative, reproduces the Canadian identity as a good international citizen and as 'not American,' and leads to the construction of a policy based on engagement.

Combining the International and Domestic Determinants of Identity: Perceiving Cuba as Similar

Canadians identify themselves as a progressive society that values social justice and economic rights. This narrative produces a sympathetic understanding of Fidel Castro and Cuba generally. For instance, the view of Cuba held by the progressive church movement (PCM) in Canada in the 1970s and 1980s is instructive. This broad-based, multidenominational movement in Canada was focused on bringing attention to the abuses of human rights taking place in Latin America, with the goal of influencing Canadian foreign policy to take action on these issues in the region. Yet, according to David Sheinin, 'Cuba simply never registered as a problem for members of the PCM' despite the Cuban government's official opposition to organized religion.[70] 'In church-sponsored events, in dozens of pamphlets, newsletters, and other publications, and in other ways, church progressives made no reference to Cuba when pressing Canadians to define human rights through abuses in Latin America.'[71] In fact, often in private and occasionally publicly, various leaders within the movement would praise the benefits of the Marxist model in Cuba.[72]

Likewise, the Canadian perception of Fidel Castro – or, as he was simply known by many who were sympathetic to his rule, Fidel – was generally positive. Many Canadians admired him when he overthrew Batista. He was widely referred to the 'revolutionary hero' by the Canadian media at the time.[73] The young Jean Chrétien was one of those who held him in great esteem. Chrétien told a reporter that Castro 'was a very popular person, a young man taking on the Batista regime ... He had been in jail, he had risked his life, he wanted to change society ... he was a star for a lot of us.'[74] When Castro visited Montreal in 1959, he was greeted by cheering crowds,[75] his 'star power,' as Robert Wright explains, then being 'in full force.'[76] Prime

Minister Diefenbaker identified with Fidel Castro because he saw him as the leader of another state that must contend with the overwhelming presence of the United States. Similarly, Canadians saw Cuban-style communism as somehow better than the communism of Eastern Europe. Prime Minister Trudeau's foreign policy adviser, Ivan Head, said that Cuba represented 'a departure from classical Communism. There is an opportunity to work with these guys in the multilateral field.'[77]

Today, many Canadians still perceive Fidel Castro as having been somewhat of a lone ranger, struggling against a much larger force in order to establish a better society. The Canadian public, with its sometimes romanticized visions of an intimate connection between Canada and Cuba, tend to be sympathetic to Fidel Castro and the revolution as well as support the maintenance of a close relationship between the two countries. A 2007 poll showed that, while 66 per cent of Americans thought that Fidel Castro's rule was bad for Cuba, only 36 per cent of Canadians did so.[78]

The idea that Cubans and Canadians share a 'special bond' is reflected in the initial growth and continued sustainability of Cuban solidarity groups in Canada. Cynthia Wright describes the early growth in Canada of Fair Play for Cuba Committees (FPCCs), a network of groups across the country that was dedicated to supporting the Cuban Revolution. Wright argues that, in comparison to their American counterparts, 'the Canadian FPCCs were much more long-lasting, surviving well into the late 1960s and beyond. Moreover, they were arguably far more influential than their U.S. counterparts in making space for debate about Cuba.' She also describes the broad base of support for the Cuban Revolution in Canada. She explains that 'the FPCCs enjoyed the support of some CCF-NDP members, some of whom were elected politicians, as well as liberals, revolutionary socialists, independent leftists, university professors, students, housewives, church people, writers, and others.'[79] Although the FPCCs in Canada were diluted by the attention given to opposing the Vietnam War and the growth of other Cuban solidarity groups in Canada, and eventually disbanded, the project they articulated in the earliest years of the Cuban Revolution continues to this day.

Today, most major Canadian cities have a version of a Canadian-Cuban Friendship Association. The Canadian Network on Cuba (CNC) lists fourteen Cuban Friendship organizations in Ontario alone.[80] According to its website, the association in Toronto 'promotes friendship, understanding and co-operation between the peoples of Canada and Cuba. Our activities include exchanges in various areas (i.e. health, education, culture, etc.) as well as the gathering of material aid to Cuba.'[81] The Hamilton Friendship Association with Cuba declares: 'We are founding the Hamilton Friendship Association with Cuba to further strengthen the ties of friendship between the peoples of Canada and Cuba ... At all times we will uphold and respect Cuba's right to national sovereignty and to determine its own way of life. We will oppose any outside interference in Cuba's internal affairs.'[82] The Nova Scotia-Cuba Association (NSCUBA) similarly declares that they 'stand united against the U.S. embargo/blockade. We believe Cuba has the right to sovereignty and self determination.'[83]

Since the collapse of the USSR, the American-dominated discussions of Cuba have moved away from a focus on communism and instead have concentrated on human rights. Certainly, many Canadians perceive Cuba as having a troublesome record on human rights and governance issues, but they normally qualify criticisms of Cuba's political system by emphasizing the social and economic benefits of the revolution. This sympathy with the goals of the revolution is an outcome of the Canadian self-image as a society that cares about social justice and economic rights. Favourable renderings of Cuba continue to reproduce Canadian policy in the post-Cold War period. Canadian discourse still demarcates civil and political rights from the economic and social goals of the Cuban Revolution. Foreign-policy officials emphasize that economic and social rights are respected.[84] Officials stress that 'Cubans continue to enjoy widely accessible systems of health, education, and social security.'[85] Prime Minister Chrétien said that Fidel Castro 'still wants to use communism; I don't believe in it ... I'm a practical politician – that doesn't mean I don't have goals, that I don't want to have social justice. I'm just not doctrinaire on the means. My view is we have to have growth in the world so there will be more money for governments to give to people who are suffering in society. I'm not in politics to make the rich richer. *Castro wants the same thing. He has a different technique.*'[86] The Canadian public shares this view. *Globe and Mail* columnist Marcus Gee is critical of Castro's Cuba but he recognizes that most Canadians do not share his opinion. He complained: 'It's a sure-fire rule. When human rights are trampled in China or Indonesia or Iran, concerned Canadians bombard me with faxes and e-mails denouncing the government involved. When human rights are trampled in Cuba, concerned Canadians bombard me with faxes and e-mails condemning the government of the U.S.' Gee concludes: 'All sorts of intelligent and influential Canadians seem to believe that Mr. Castro and his dictatorship are simply misunderstood.'[87]

Certainly, Canadians and Americans disagree over whether the Cuban state has any democratic features even though support for democracy is very high in both North American countries.[88] Most American policy makers assume that Cuba is a totally undemocratic state, the antithesis of democracy. In interviews, American policy makers emphasized what they saw as the undemocratic nature of the Cuban government to a greater degree than their Canadian counterparts. This became especially clear during interviews conducted in Havana. When asked about Canada's role in promoting democratic development in Cuba, a senior officer at the Canadian embassy in Havana sternly replied that Canadians did not presume that the Cuban form of government was undemocratic, that there were 'many forms of democracy.'[89] Similar statements are heard in Ottawa. For example, in 1998 the speaker of the House of Commons, Gilbert Parent, compared the Cuban system of government to Premier Frank McKenna's one-party government in New Brunswick, where in 1987 the Liberal Party had won all fifty-eight seats in the provincial legislature. Parent said: 'You know, we do have some of our provinces where they only elected one party – I'm thinking of New Brunswick ... I've never heard anyone say that they weren't carrying out the wishes of their people down there.' Parent went on to criticize implicitly the American approach towards Cuba, noting: 'Besides, I don't think it's for us to dictate or tell other people how to run their countries.'[90] Parent also referred to Cubans as 'fellow parliamentarians' and discussed their 'so-called political prisoners.'[91] Though Parent's remarks did encounter considerable criticism from other members of the House of Commons, they do represent the construction of a more favourable perception of the Cuban government in Canada and a tendency to draw sympathetic comparisons,[92] illustrated by a 2005 statement by former Manitoba premier Howard Pawley: 'What Canadians want is to ensure that Cubans have the right to self-determination and to determine their own destinies and to arrive at their own sovereignty and not be fenced in by our powerful neighbour to the south.'[93] While most Canadian officials believe that Cuba does not have fair and free national elections and that there are considerable restrictions on press freedoms, they also maintain that ordinary Cubans play a considerable role in local affairs and participate in their governance in other ways. They are also sympathetic to Fidel Castro's argument about the failings of Western democracies.[94]

These same ideas are voiced by civil-society groups. The Nova Scotia-Cuba Association explains: 'The Cuban electoral system is different than ours, but not any less valid. It is true that Cubans do not directly elect the country's president (Fidel Castro has been the country's leader since the 1959 Revolution). But think about this; neither do Canadians directly elect their Prime Minister. Whoever heads up the national party which wins the most seats becomes leader of our country.'[95] The idea that Canada is a society that values economic and social rights (at least when Canadians compare themselves to the United States) produces affinity for the economic and social goals of the Cuban Revolution and relatively sympathetic renderings of Cuba's human-rights record.

Canada's policy of engagement assumes that it is possible to realize change within the current Cuban government. Improvements in civil and political rights in Cuba are seen as very possible, and thus Canadian officials are easily encouraged by signs of potential change in these areas. Ottawa often attributes such changes to Canada's policy of engagement, thereby highlighting, it is thought, the country's crucial role in improving human rights in Cuba. In the early 1990s Ottawa was confident that the state of human rights in Cuba was improving. In 1996 Secretary of State Christine Stewart told an audience in Ottawa: 'This constant dialogue that Cuba has had with Canada and other countries has helped lead to reform. Cuba is moving ahead with changes to economic policy. There are changes, too, in human rights areas.'[96] The 1997 Joint Declaration, which was chiefly concerned with increasing the dialogue between Canada and Cuba, was based on that assumption. In 1998 Prime Minister Chrétien told a reporter after his visit to Cuba that 'I think he [Fidel Castro] is changing. The fact that my speech was on the air is a large change; the fact that I met the Cardinal in public.'[97] Similarly, Lloyd Axworthy told reporters in 1998: 'We made some progress over the past year. We think it's worth continuing that kind of engagement. We have for example, just recently, as a follow-up to the Pope's visit, agreed to accept a number of political prisoners, who will be coming directly to Canada.'[98] In 1999 Axworthy described the changes then under way in Cuba as 'major.'[99]

Although Canadian officials were more disillusioned with Cuba's potential for human-rights improvement at the turn of the millennium than they were in the 1990s, they remained positive. A 2001 government document stated that, though Canada remained concerned about the 'continued lack of respect in Cuba for civil and political rights,' it stressed that 'on the other hand, systematic violations of the integrity of the person (torture, forced disappearances, summary executions) have not occurred since the early 1960s. Despite a deterioration in services due to the state of the economy, Cubans continue to enjoy widely accessible systems of health, education and social security.'[100] Canadians believe that their policy of engagement will encourage more changes than a policy based on isolation. According to the same 2001 document: 'The Prime Minister and the Foreign Minister continue to raise human rights concerns directly with the Cuban government, and provide leadership to other Western counterparts who are only now beginning to engage with Cuba. Canada is also working hard to support the creation of practical space for non-governmental actors in Cuban society, including improved practices with regard to tolerance of dissent. Canada provides moral support to human rights and political activists, has assisted with penal code reform, and encourages the unconditional release of political prisoners.'[101] Although the Canadian government publicly chided Cuba for its 2003 crackdown on dissidents, relations remained essentially unchanged following this move by the Cuban government. To this day, Canadians are hopeful that revolutionary Cuba will move towards a greater respect for human rights and believe that their policy of engagement will play a role in this evolution. Thus, Ottawa works within the assumption that change within the current Cuban government is possible whereas Washington has thus far assumed that such change is impossible.

The way that Canadians perceive human rights in Cuba is socially constructed by way of the Canadian identity. The emphasis on social welfare in Canadian political culture leads Canadians to conceptualize the human-rights situation in Cuba differently from their American counterparts. Economic and social rights are considered key 'human rights' by many Canadians, and, as a result, they incline to a favourable evaluation of Cuba's human-rights record. Since Canadians perceive the revolution and its goals in this way, they are also more likely, in comparison with Americans, to be less critical of Cuba and to favour less drastic measures to encourage change. Engagement thus becomes the preferred policy.

Conclusion

The 'good citizen' and 'not-American' identities construct a perception of Cuba that emphasizes the similarities and even friendship between Canada and Cuba. These identities and perceptions not only create boundaries on possible actions but also work to construct certain policies. Consequently, the norm that 'engagement is the best approach towards Cuba' is a reflection of the Canadian self-image.

By examining these identities, related worldviews, and perceptions, we can see how Canada's approach towards Cuba has become ingrained. Though other countries have had similar relationships with Cuba, Canada has stood out as one of Cuba's closest friends in the West, even though, as a close ally of the United States, Ottawa has at times been under pressure to 'get in line' with U.S. policy.

Canadian foreign policy is a complex reflection of many variables. Without a doubt, Canadian leaders have sometimes used popular self-images to hide other, more self-interest-based policy objectives such as furthering trade. However, this is more than simple rhetoric. Identity and perceptions play a leading role in most Canadian actions on the world stage. The motto 'peace, order and good government,' which encompasses values such as mediation, dialogue, respect for international law, and social justice, among others, is seen as important by both the foreign-policy establishment and the Canadian public. The Canadian identity as a 'good international citizen' and as 'distinct from the United States' is also deeply interwoven into foreign-policy decisions. Everything from the Canadian perception of Fidel Castro to the decision to negotiate the historic Joint Declaration in the late 1990s is a product of these socially constructed identities and resulting perceptions. And so, while the traditional economic explanation for Canada's Cuba policy is not without weight, we cannot afford to ignore the reality that this policy is driven by more fundamental variables. Cuba is clearly an example of the degree to which Canadian foreign policy can be identity-driven.

4 Exploring Cuba Policy in Tandem

Canadian and American perceptions of Cuba have differed for many decades. At a 1960 meeting between representatives of the Canadian and American governments, the differences in perceptions of Cuba were clearly evident. A senior Canadian diplomat, Basil Robinson, reported: 'The Canadians spoke with such force and candor that the Americans present were shocked at the extent of the division between the Canadian analysis and their own.'[1] The differences caused some tension between the normally friendly neighbours. Americans protested in front of the Canadian embassy in Washington and were discouraged from vacationing north of the border; Canadian tourists in Florida noticed a colder reception.[2]

Almost half a century later, Canadian and American perceptions of Cuba remain, in many ways, antithetical. In 2008 Canadians were asked which countries stand out as a negative force in today's world. Iran, Iraq, China, North Korea, and others figured prominently on the list but Cuba was not mentioned.[3] Although the same poll was not asked of Americans, in 2009 Americans were asked about their overall opinions of various countries. Cuba ranked among the most disliked countries, with 67 per cent of respondents answering that they had an unfavourable opinion of it.[4] Both the State Department and the Department of Foreign Affairs and International Trade provide fact sheets on all countries. The two descriptions of Cuba are telling. The DFAIT sheet on Cuba states the following under the heading *Type of Government*: 'Republic. 14 provinces and 1 special municipality (Isle of Youth). Unicameral National Assembly of the People's Power. Assembly sits twice a year; representatives of the Assembly serve 5 year terms.'[5] In contrast, the State Department's Background sheet on Cuba states the following under *Government Type*: 'Communist state; current government assumed power by force January 1, 1959. Independence: May 20, 1902. Political party: Cuban Communist Party (CCP); only one party allowed. Administrative subdivisions: 14 provinces, including the city of Havana, and one special municipality (Isle of Youth).'6 Both descriptions are presented as fact and neither is technically wrong. Each reflects a different perception of the Cuban government.

The rest of this chapter will explore the connections between perceptions and policy by examining the Canadian and American responses to two prominent post-Cold War Cuba issues – the 1996 Brother to the Rescue incident and the speculation in 2002 that Cuba was engaged in bioweapons research. By analysing the American and Canadian reactions to these high-profile issues that captured the attention of the public and officials in both countries, this chapter will illustrate how much Canadian and American perceptions of Cuba-related events can differ and how these unique perceptions help to construct disparate policies.

Brothers to the Rescue and Helms-Burton

On that fateful afternoon, the ruthless nature of the Castro regime was clearly revealed. Like vultures awaiting their prey, Cuban MiGs circled and hovered until they locked on to the frail Cessna planes.

– U.S. House of Representatives

Although the shooting down of these two planes was quite rightly condemned by the international community, the dead pilots were not exactly on a quixoitic mission. They ... were committed to overthrowing the regime of Fidel Castro by whatever means necessary.

– Canadian Parliament

On 24 February 1996 the Cuban government shot down two planes flown by the Cuban American group Brothers to the Rescue. This group, founded in 1991, was initially formed to assist Cubans who ventured out in often unseaworthy vessels, across the Florida Straits, headed for American shores. The Brothers to the Rescue planes would spot these rafts and alert the U.S. Coast Guard. The Coast Guard ships would then pick up the rafters and bring them to the United States to be processed by Immigration. However, by the mid-1990s, the group was reportedly using these flights for an additional purpose. They would fly over the Cuban mainland, dropping leaflets critical of the Cuban state from their planes. On 9 and 13 January 1996, the planes distributed thousands of these flyers in flights over Havana, obviously embarrassing and angering the Cuban government. As a result, the Cuban Air Force received instructions not to tolerate further incursions into Cuban airspace. Thus, when the Brothers to the Rescue planes approached Cuba on 24 February, the Air Force went after them and downed two.

The international community largely condemned this action by a government against unarmed civilian aircraft. However, the interpretation of the events and the degree of condemnation varied considerably among nations. In particular, countries disagreed about whether the airplanes were over international or Cuban waters when they were shot down and the degree to which the Brothers to the Rescue provoked the Cuban response. The American motion to condemn the attack in the United Nations was passed only after it had been watered down, reflecting the different interpretations of the circumstances among the member states.[7] Reactions in Canada and the United States differed significantly and illustrate the distinct approaches towards Cuba and the importance of the underlying identities.

The American Response

Condemnation was strong and swift in the United States. The American government maintained that the planes were in international airspace at the time and that there was no possible justification for the shoot-down. On 26 February 1996 President Clinton began a speech announcing new sanctions against Cuba with: 'Two days ago, in broad daylight and without justification, Cuban military aircraft shot down two civilian planes in international airspace ... The planes were unarmed and clearly so ... They posed no credible threat to Cuba's security.'[8] Even members of Congress who were vocal opponents of the embargo did not challenge the administration's interpretation of events. For example, though he had argued for normalization of relations for years, Democratic Senator Christopher Dodd stated: 'It is inexcusable for a heavily armed plane to attack unarmed commercial private planes under any circumstances.'[9]

Given this interpretation and the ensuing outrage directed towards the island, the administration decided that a significant response was in order. Though eventually rejected, military action against Cuba was seriously considered in the White House.[10] In the end, intensifying the embargo was deemed to be the appropriate response. The Clinton administration, which until then had been opposing a bill sponsored by lawmakers Jesse Helms and Dan Burton that would tighten the embargo, acted to sign it into law. This bill reflected the official American perception of the events. It stated that 'Brothers to the Rescue is a Miami-based humanitarian organization engaged in searching for and aiding Cuban refugees in the Straits of Florida, and was engaged in such a mission on Saturday, February 24, 1996.'[11] Most American policy makers on both sides of the embargo debate adopted similar interpretations of the incident. Not everyone was supportive of Helms-Burton but most felt that the government had to take significant action against Cuba.

Washington's reaction was constructed by fundamental aspects of the American identity. Americans have long believed that their country is a special nation, above all others, and as such is obliged to assist less fortunate nations to follow the U.S. example. This American exceptionalism, with its American-centric worldview and American moral messianism, helped to construct the U.S. response to the shoot-down. Stuart Eizenstat, Clinton's spokesperson on Cuba, explained to an international audience that the American reaction to the downing could be traced to the fact that there is 'a moral core to our foreign policies.'[12] The passage of Helms-Burton showed that the United States still saw itself as the 'city on the hill' whose responsibility was to demonstrate to the rest of the world how to respond, correctly and morally, to the latest incident in U.S.-Cuba relations. Helms-Burton declares: 'The Cuban people deserve to be assisted in a decisive manner to end the tyranny that has oppressed them for 36 years, and the continued failure to do so constitutes ethically improper conduct by the international community.'[13] As such, Helms-Burton builds upon the 1992 Cuban Democracy Act, which 'calls upon the President to encourage the governments of countries that conduct trade with Cuba to restrict their trade and credit relations with Cuba in a manner consistent with the purposes of that Act.'[14] Title III of Helms-Burton allows for citizens of other countries to be punished in American courts for 'trafficking' in property previously owned by U.S. nationals and confiscated by the Cuban state. Title IV bars those people from entering the United States. In accordance with Title IV, the State Department has informed executives of Canadian and Mexican companies engaged in such activity in Cuba that they will be prevented

from gaining entry into the United States. These extra-territorial provisions are designed to pressure other countries into adopting similar
policies towards the island nation. They demonstrate that the United
States, still acting as the 'city on the hill,' believes it needs to guide
other wayward states like Canada or Mexico into doing the right
thing.

Underpinning Helms-Burton is the century-old belief that Cuba is
the most errant state in the hemisphere, as well as one of the least
capable, and is thus in need of American guidance. This perception
emanates from the American view that the western hemisphere is part
of the U.S. sphere of influence.[15] Since Cuba is located 'only ninety
miles from the United States,' it is understood to be naturally within
the American sphere of influence and hence not fully sovereign.
Helms-Burton, in part, justifies its embargo-tightening measures by
arguing that the United States led an embargo against Haiti, and since
Haiti is 'a neighbor of Cuba not as close to the United States as Cuba,'
it follows that the United States should have a tighter embargo against
Cuba.[16]

Cuba's 'special status' in relation to the United States is described in
many ways. Often Cuba is referred to as part of the 'American family.'
For example, Michael Ranneberger, the coordinator for Cuban affairs
at the State Department, explained U.S. policy this way: 'We do not
react to repression and hardship in Cuba as we would to the plight of
a stranger, but rather as we would to a crisis that befalls a close family
member.'[17] From this belief flows the American policy makers'
assumption that the United States is within its rights to 'bend' Cuban
sovereignty. Helms-Burton, in particular, illustrates the degree to
which the United States believes it has a natural right to intervene in
Cuban affairs. The act assumes that the United States has a responsibility to oversee, if not direct, any transition to democracy in Cuba. It
states that, in order to achieve normalization of its relationship with
the United States, Cuba must undergo a fundamental reorganization
of its political, economic, and social structure.[18] For example, it stipu-
lates that a legitimate Cuban government could not include either
Fidel or Raúl Castro. It also dictates that Cuba give up its socialist
system. Among its many provisions, Helms-Burton requires that the
new Cuban government permit the broadcast of Radio and TV Martí.[19]
Jorge Dominguez argues that these requirements well surpass any
accepted OAS or UN requirements for determining what is a democ-
ratizing government and that 'mandating them in US legislation as

defining characteristics of a democratic or transitional Cuban government makes a mockery of the pledge to respect Cuban sovereignty.'[20]
The perception that the United States is naturally entitled to intervene
in this way because Cuba is, more than any other country, within its
sphere of influence has greatly influenced the course of American-
Cuban relations.

In addition, the metaphors and symbolic references used in the discourse about the Brothers to the Rescue shoot-down reflect and reinforce the emotionally laden good-versus-evil comparisons and moral
reasoning characteristic of discussions of U.S.-Cuba relations. For
instance, in his opening statement at the House of Representatives
hearing about the shoot-down, the chairman declared: 'We are here
because we, as Americans, are a Nation of freedom and independence,
because we believe in liberty, and we certainly believe in human rights
and human dignity.'[21] In contrast, Cuba and Cuban actions are demonized: 'On that fateful afternoon, the ruthless nature of the Castro
regime was clearly revealed. Like vultures awaiting their prey, Cuban
MiGs circled and hovered until they locked on to the frail Cessna
planes.'[22] By reinforcing the intense emotions about U.S.-Cuba relations and influencing how those listening think about the incident,
these representations greatly affect the American response.

Thus, the American reaction to the 24 February downing was a
product of deeply entrenched identities and perceptions. American
exceptionalism and the long-standing perception of the scope of
Cuba's sovereignty within the American sphere of influence helped to
construct the U.S. response to the shoot-down of the Brothers to the
Rescue planes.

Yet, as the next section will demonstrate, other interpretations of the
downing were possible. By reviewing the Canadian reaction to this
same international incident, the following will reveal how a different
set of perceptions rooted in and reinforced by the Canadian identity
constructed a distinctive response.

The Canadian Response

The Canadian response to the incident was a reflection of the Canadian sense of itself and corresponding perceptions. Reaction in
Canada, though critical of the Cuban action, was more mixed and
muted than in the United States. The Cuban justification for the shoot-
down was given greater consideration in Ottawa. Canadians, always

sympathetic to Cuban claims of American interference in their sovereignty, tended to emphasize the previous incursions by the Brothers'
planes. For example, Keith Martin, a Canadian Member of Parliament,
wrote the following about the incident:

> As is often the case, all is not what it seems to be. Although the shooting
> down of these two planes was quite rightly condemned by the interna-
> tional community, the dead pilots were not exactly on a quixotic mission.
> They ... were committed to overthrowing the regime of Fidel Castro by
> whatever means necessary. This organization was flying up to thirty-two
> missions per week, ostensibly to look for Cubans fleeing their homeland
> so they could guide them safely to U.S. shores. However, their activities
> have often taken on a much more invasive role ... dropping leaflets over
> Cuba encouraging the people to insurrect and depose Mr. Castro ... These
> activities can hardly be looked upon favourably by Mr. Castro. In fact, the
> Brotherhood has been repeatedly warned to stay away from Cuba air-
> space but has refused.[23]

Martin goes on to state that many members of Brothers to the Rescue
'are CIA trained and some even took part in the failed 1961 Bay of Pigs
invasion of Cuba.'[24] While his interpretation was not accepted by all
Members of Parliament, most of the points he made were not widely
disputed in Canada. In fact, high-level Canadian officials told the
author in interviews that the Brothers to the Rescue planes were inside
Cuban airspace on a mission to drop leaflets and that the Cuban military warned the planes to leave before they were shot down.[25] This
understanding of the events of 24 February 1996 differs considerably
from the perception voiced by Americans, and reflected in Helms-
Burton, that the planes were engaged in a solely humanitarian mission
to rescue rafters and were shot down without warning.

The shadow of Canadian sovereignty and perceptions of American
encroachment loom large over a great deal of Ottawa's foreign-policy
calculations. The Canadian reaction to the shoot-down became princi-
pally focused on the American decision to pass Helms-Burton, which
Canadians saw as a direct challenge to their identity as an independent actor in world politics. The following was heard on the floor of the
Senate and typifies the reaction in Ottawa: 'Canada, of course, strongly
condemned the shooting down of two civilian aircraft by the Cuban air
force on February 24, the incident which helped the passage of the
Helms-Burton Act, and we were active in the consideration of the inci-

dent by the International Civil Aviation Organization, ICAO. *However, we do not think Helms-Burton is the way to deal with the Cuban problem.'*[26] Similarly, Reform Party MP Darrel Stinson explained Ottawa's reaction: 'I do not appreciate another country's telling Canada how to run our foreign policies. I may not agree with Canadian foreign policy but that is for us, this House and the other place representing the Canadian people to decide. Canadian foreign policy toward Cuba or any other nation must not be dictated by another country.'[27] James Blanchard, the American ambassador to Canada during this period, recalled that in Canada 'Helms-Burton was a headline story in all the newspapers and TV reports, because it looked as though Canadian companies and their executives were being told what to do by the American government. It became a sovereignty issue.'[28]

Another MP, Bill Blaikie of the New Democratic Party, illustrates how the concern over American encroachment draws Canada and Cuba together and influences the Canadian response to related international events. During a discussion about the Brothers to the Rescue downing and subsequent passage of Helms-Burton, he stated: 'Cuba, like Canada, is in the so-called American sphere of influence and is supposed to behave like a good little neighbour. However, when it comes to Cuba, Canada has shown a streak of independence that we do not always show on other issues.' Blaikie went on to urge the minister of foreign affairs to continue to resist 'this latest manifestation of the bully in the American psyche.'[29] Canadians are quick to identify themselves with Cubans, especially when it comes to Canadian and Cuban bilateral relations with the United States. This perception clearly had an influence on their response to the Brothers to the Rescue incident as Canadians empathized with the Cuban position.

The discourse about Helms-Burton reflects not only the emphasis Canadians place on protecting their sovereignty from the United States and their corresponding identification with the Cuban predicament, but also the 'good citizen' identity. For example, in an attempt to defuse tensions, Canadian diplomats, officially and unofficially, raised the issue with their Cuban and American counterparts. During a 1996 visit by a group of parliamentarians from Cuba, Senator Jerry Grafstein asked of the Cuban delegation:

> Please do not take this as being undiplomatic, but it was a question that we, as Canadians, could not answer in our private conversations with senators and congressmen. It is the theory of the Americans – which we do not

accept, but I pass it on – that Cuba provoked the Americans by overreacting to the planes that were flying over Cuba. The suggestion is that there were other means, other forceful means, available to Cuba to remove those planes from the airspace over Cuba if, indeed, those airplanes had invaded Cuban airspace. During the Cold War in Canada we were used to this. The Russians invaded our space, the Americans invaded our space, and we tried to kick them out as gently as we could. That is a rather long prologue to a very short question. We hope that conflicts can be kept to a minimum between now and next year, when we hope that we can reduce the impact of this terrible [Helms-Burton] bill. What is your opinion of this?[30]

Another Canadian senator told the Cubans in this same meeting:

We have a dispute between two countries, Cuba and the United States. It has always been my experience that, in a dispute, nobody is 100 percent right and nobody is 100 percent wrong. Each side has responsibility to try and resolve the dispute. I am not blaming either side here, but I want to know what efforts, if any, Cuba is taking to resolve this dispute. There are other ways to resolve disputes than speaking directly to the person with whom you are having the dispute. There are what are known as – and you will know this – diplomatic initiative. You can go through third parties; you can ask other people to try to broker a deal.[31]

As Senator Grafstein alluded above, Canadians held similar conversations with American politicians. Interviews confirmed that officials at a number of levels discussed the shoot-down with their American counterparts.[32] As Chapter 3 demonstrated, the support for mediation is entrenched in the Canadian identity, and so the attempt to mediate this dispute was a natural reaction for Canadian policy makers.

Since Canadians believe they give great weight to peaceful and orderly resolutions of international incidents and international law, they pushed for the dispute to be deliberated by the International Court. Warren Allmand, a Liberal Member of Parliament, argued: 'The shooting down of the two U.S. planes was indeed a deplorable incident. Both sides claim to be right. Consequently, that is a matter for the International Court and not one for unilateral action.'[33] Similarly, one objection to Helms-Burton was that this legislation was contrary to international law and 'proper' behaviour. Charlie Penson, a Reform Party MP, voiced this opinion: 'I make the point that the United States has every right to challenge Cuba and to put trade sanctions of a binational nature in place. However, it is simply not within the international parameters of good citizenship or international trade to take that outside its borders and apply it to countries such as Canada.'[34] Art Eggleton, the minister for international trade, told Parliament: 'Helms-Burton is unacceptable because it flouts long established international legal practices for settling disputes between nations regarding claims by foreign investors who have had their property expropriated ... By choosing to ignore them now, Helms-Burton sets a dangerous precedent.'[35] On Helms-Burton, Canada sought recourse against the United States in international law. MP Charlie Penson declared: 'Nowadays when a bully bullies us we do not have to put our tail between our legs and run. We do not have to get bloodied in the fight either. We can take that bully to international court. Let us take the Americans to court to see if we can get the Helms-Burton bill overturned.'[36]

Canadians' self-image as both 'not American' and 'good international citizens' constructed their perceptions of the Brothers to the Rescue incident and thus largely determined their response to the ensuing Helms-Burton legislation enacted by the American government. Speaking about Helms-Burton, Roger Simmons, a Liberal MP, rather bluntly summarized the influences on the Canadian perception: 'Apart from the fact that it flies in the face of everything we understand about the rule of law, about the territorial integrity of sovereign nations, it [Helms-Burton] also says volumes about the arrogance of the people who would advance that kind of legislation.'[37] Always fiercely protective of any American encroachment on Canadian sovereignty, and perceiving that Cuba is, to a certain degree, also on constant guard against American infringement, Ottawa, naturally enough, first gave the Cuban 'story' of the events more credence and then reacted strongly against the American decision to pass Helms-Burton. However, invariably focused on being a good citizen, Canada also attempted to resolve the dispute by calling on the involvement of the International Court.

The Canadian and American interpretations of and reactions to that fateful incident of 24 February 1996 illustrates the crucial role played by identities and their related perceptions in foreign policy. The American response was constructed by the long-established perceptions of Cuba's place within the U.S. sphere of influence and related norms rooted in American exceptionalism. The Canadian reaction was a natural outgrowth of the country's identity as both non-American and an international good citizen.

This was not a unique case. The interplay between identity, perceptions, and foreign policy is also revealed in the ways in which the Canadian and American governments approached the issue of Cuba's biomedical success.

Biomedical Researcher or Bioterrorist?

The United States believes that Cuba has at least a limited offensive biological warfare research and development effort. Cuba has provided dual-use biotechnology to other rogue states.
> – John R. Bolton, under-secretary of state for arms control
> and international security, 6 May 2002

This charge, coming less than a year after the 9/11 attacks on Washington and New York, fuelled a discussion in the United States about whether Cuba posed a terrorist threat. Although Canadians were still quite caught up in the discourse of fear that followed the attacks, this particular discussion did not occur in Canada. Canadians did not seem to be worried about such charges and those who were at all interested in Cuban biotechnology continued to discuss the sector within the aid or economic frame of reference used before the 9/11 attacks. The Canadian discourse about terrorism did not single out Cuba.

This section will explore how these two discourses were possible and make the case that the Canadian and American identities ultimately narrowed how each state could perceive Cuban biotechnology. First, to place the two discourses in context, this section will review the Cuban biotechnology sector and look at previous charges about Cuba's ties to terrorism. It will then position Canadian and American responses to the possibility that Cuba presents a terrorist threat.

Cuba's Biotech Industry

In 1959 Cuba's biomedical research and development efforts were basically non-existent. Under Batista, very little government attention had been devoted to medical facilities. In 1958 a person living in Havana had access to medical personnel and hospitals but there was only one hospital in the countryside.[38] Moreover, there were very few scientists in Cuba and the research efforts of those few were dedicated to improving the sugar-cane crops.[39]

Following the Cuban Revolution, the place of health science within Cuban society was fundamentally altered. A massive literacy and education campaign swept the nation. The illiteracy rate fell from 23.6 per cent in 1953 to 12.9 per cent in 1970 and under 4 per cent by the 1990s. By the early 2000s, Cuba could boast that its universities had turned out 700,000 graduates, many of them in science and related fields.[40]At the same time, Cuba's health system underwent a complete overhaul, creating a large demand for trained medical personnel. Consequently, the burgeoning numbers of educated youth were directed into the medical and engineering fields. By the early 1990s, there were 850 students each year studying biology, biochemistry, and microbiology at the University of Havana.[41]

The number of doctors and other medical staff, hospitals, and primary-care facilities proliferated as the government instituted a system of free comprehensive health care. The health of the Cuban populace has significantly improved as a result. According to the World Health Organization, Cuba has achieved health indictors comparable to those of countries in the Organization for Economic Co-operation and Development (OECD). For example, life expectancy at birth for males is seventy-five years and for females seventy-nine years, while child mortality for males is 8/1000 and 6/1000 for females.[42] The government emphasizes primary and preventative health care but also has the facilities to treat advanced illness. Thus, within a few years, Cuba had a well-educated population and a large medical infrastructure, both able to lend support to, and benefit from, the development of a homegrown biomedical research and development effort.

Fidel Castro argued that science was one of the most important keys to successful economic development. He told Cubans: 'The future of our nation is necessarily the future of men of science.'[43] The Cuban state became focused on turning Cuba into a world-renowned health-science leader.[44] Biological science, with its potential to improve the health of Cubans, received special emphasis. José Ferández Alvarez, Cuba's minister of education, explained: 'We think the next century is the century of biology. Microbiology and biochemistry will be used to solve problems, achieve higher production, feed humans, and improve health.'[45]

The number of people employed in scientific research and development expanded dramatically after the revolution. In the late 1990s, over 30,000 Cubans were employed in the scientific research community in Cuba.[46] Most of these individuals worked in one of Cuba's many scientific institutes. In 1965 the Centro Nacional de Investigaciones Cientificas (CNIC) was established. Many other research and development efforts have been created since the early days of the revolution. In 1981 the government established a policy organization called the Biological Front to ensure that Cuba's biological research and development efforts would have access to the necessary investment and state support. At this time the emphasis was on interferons (IFNs) and their applicability to cancer research. In 1982 the Centro de Investigaciones Biologicos (CIB) was established to conduct this IFN research.[47] Even at this early stage, Cuban research received international recognition. In 1985 the Harvard scientist Jon Beckwith described Cuban scientists as 'amazingly *au courant*, sophisticated and creative in the field of genetic engineering.'[48]

The heart of Cuban biotechnology was created in 1986. Costing US$100 million, the Centro de Ingeniería Genética y Biotechnologia (CIGB) was established with the most-up-to date equipment and technology available at the time.[49] The institute hired more than 800 people to work at this complex in Havana, many of them engaged in research on vaccines, therapeutics, and, more recently, bioinformatics and proteomics. By the late 1990s, more than 1,100 people were working at this complex.[50] They have 112 products in their pipeline and have succeeded in producing a recombinant hepatitis B vaccine as well as many other therapeutics. Over half of the scientific papers published by Cubans in international, peer-reviewed journals come from scientists at the CIGB.[51]

Cuban research has produced many successful products. Scientists have been especially successful in developing vaccines, and, as a result, the Cuban populace is one of the most well-vaccinated groups in the world. The Cuban population is vaccinated against thirteen diseases including polio, typhoid, tetanus, measles, mumps, diphtheria, pertussis, rubella, tuberculosis, hepatitis B, haemophilus influenza B, meningitis B, and meningitis C.[52] Cuba's most internationally recognized achievement is the influenza (Hib) vaccine. Since it is synthetic, it is less expensive and of a better quality than the vaccines currently available. According to an American immunologist with the U.S. National Institute of Child Health and Human Development, John Robbins, this advancement in Cuba is 'a pivotal step' that 'is going to pave the way for a new generation of vaccines.'[53]

One reason Cuba has been so successful in biotechnology is that research in Cuba is centrally directed. Ironically, the management of Cuban science most closely resembles the structure of a corporate research company in the capitalist world. The research interests of individual scientists are often sacrificed to projects favoured by the government. A 2005 article in *Nature* reported that 'if a project looks likely to earn foreign currency or meet the government's social objectives, it is backed to the hilt.'[54] This concentrated effort, though restricting scientific freedom, results in considerable success in applied research. Furthermore, Cuban scientists can bring a drug to clinical trials more readily than scientists can in other countries because, also rather ironically, they do not face equivalent bureaucratic hurdles. The Cuban biomedical scientific community is closely intertwined into the health-care system, allowing unfettered testing of promising pharmaceuticals.[55]

In 1990 biotechnology was designated one of the government's priority sectors, giving it the status of agriculture and tourism and thus ensuring that investment in the sector would continue despite drastic cutbacks in other areas of the Cuban economy and society. Even during the 'special period' of severe economic crisis in the early 1990s, the Cuban government continued to allocate 1.5 per cent of its GNP for scientific research and development.[56] However, this crisis took its toll on science in Cuba. At that time, according to José de la Fuente, a Cuban scientist now living in the United States, Cuba's scientific community suffered greatly. Unable to support continued research in some areas, the Cuban government sent some of its scientists to Europe so they could continue to conduct research.[57] Basic research especially suffered as money was directed first to applied research.[58] The government became increasingly involved in micromanaging the dwindling resources. The secretary of the Consejo de Estado (State Council), José M. Miyar Barrueco, reviewed the most minor decisions of the various research centres, including deciding whether individual scientists could attend conferences. This created disaffection within the scientific community and a thorough culling of many of the leading scientists in the country. Many were fired from their posts or left Cuba to continue their research elsewhere.[59]

However, Cuban biotechnology appears to have rebounded from its low point. Although priority is still given to applied research, Cuban scientists have made significant breakthroughs and they and their work receive considerable recognition from the international scientific community. For example, Michael Levin, a British medical researcher who is collaborating with Havana's Finlay Institute, explained that Cuba has 'excellent laboratories, and their doctors and scientists have maintained world-class standards.'[60] A Harvard professor of medical anthropology, Paul Farmer, had praise for Cuba's Instituto de Medicina Tropical 'Pedro Kouri' IPK: 'With a comparatively tiny budget – less than that, say, of a single large research hospital at Harvard – IPK has conducted important basic science research, helped to develop novel vaccines, trained thousands of researchers from Cuba and from around the world.'[61] In the mid-1990s, Smith-Kline Beecham PLC, now GlaxoSmithKline PLC, signed an agreement with the Finlay Institute to market the world's only vaccine for meningitis B.[62] Cuban researchers have been granted over 100 patents. A 2004 article in *Nature Biotechnology* reported: 'Cuba's outstanding achievements in health biotechnology are a source of inspiration for the developing world.'[63] Analysts expect Cuba's record of achievement to continue. James Larrick, a U.S. biotechnology entrepreneur, explains: 'Their pipeline is very, very deep now … It's gone into an adolescence and it's looking pretty good.'[64]

Cuba, Terrorism, and the Dual-Use Dilemma:
The American Perception

> *The dual-use dilemma arises in the context of research in the biological and other sciences as a consequence of the fact that one and the same piece of scientific research sometimes has the potential to be used for harmful as well as good purposes. Discoveries that may lead to important advances in science and medicine might therefore also facilitate development of biological weapons of mass destruction.*
>
> – Seumas Miller and Michael J. Selgelid, *Ethical and Philosophical Consideration of the Dual-Use Dilemma in the Biological Sciences*

In the biological sciences, the very technology that can be used to save human lives can also be used to create biological weapons. Capability to make one is easily translated to the other. Cuba's obvious success in this field has been fodder for speculation in the United States.

American accusations in 2002 about Cuba and bioterrorism were partially attributed to historical rumblings about the state's involvement in terrorist activities, a concern forcefully expressed by Under-Secretary John Bolton when he asserted that 'Havana has long provided safehaven for terrorists' and referred to Cuba's inclusion on the State Department's list of terrorist-sponsoring states. Cuba was included on this list in 1982 because the Cuban government had supported insurgent groups in Latin America including the FMLN (Farabundo Martí National Liberation) guerrillas in El Salvador and the M-19 in Colombia.[65] In April 1999 Michael Sheehan, the acting coordinator for the Office for Counterterrorism, stated: 'Cuba, quite bluntly, continues to provide safe haven for terrorists, period. They will remain on the list while they continue to provide safe haven for a number of terrorist organizations.'[66] In 2001 the State Department again listed Cuba as one of the seven state sponsors of terrorism. At that time the other countries on the list were Iran, Iraq, Libya, North Korea, Sudan, and Syria. Washington also argues that Cuba was on the list because Havana had 'permitted up to 20 Basque Fatherland and Liberty members to reside in Cuba and provided some degree of safe-haven and support to members of the Colombian Revolutionary Armed Forces (FARC) and National Liberation Army (ELN) groups.'[67] Cuba has also been accused of harbouring U.S. fugitives. The Cuban state denies these charges and points out that it has signed the twelve UN resolutions against terrorism.

. The events of 11 September 2001 changed perceptions of threat in the United States. From this point on, terrorism has topped the list of threats to the American way of life. To accuse Cuba of supporting terrorism in this environment has enormous consequences for the bilateral relationship and certainly adds to Cuba's insecurity.

After the attacks on the World Trade Center and the Pentagon, speculation about Cuba's role in international terrorism took centre stage in many Washington discussions about the island nation, the most provocative charge being Under-Secretary Bolton's claim in the spring of 2002 that Cuba was developing biological weapons[68] and currently had 'at least a limited, offensive biological warfare research-and-development effort.'[69] That same year, speculation was further fuelled by Cuba's decision to license biotechnology techniques to countries considered enemies of the United States. For example, according the State Department, Iran had given Cuba a 20-million Euro line of credit for biotechnology investment. Furthermore, the deputy assistant secretary of state for western hemisphere affairs accused the Castro government of supplying false information to the U.S. investigation into international terrorism, effectively sending

American officials on 'wild goose chases' and thus 'impeding our efforts to defeat the threat of terrorism.'[70]

These accusations and Cuba's inclusion on the list of sponsors of terrorism are challenged by many, who call into question the underlying security rationale. After all, Cuba had offered to assist the United States immediately following the 9/11 attacks. Shortly afterwards, the Cuban government announced: 'The government of our country rejects and condemns with full force the attacks against the mentioned installations and expresses its sincerest condolences to the American people for the painful and unjustifiable loss of human life.' Another message said: 'The Cuban government heard news of the attacks with pain and sadness ... At this bitter time, our people express solidarity with the U.S. people and express total willingness to cooperate, as far as our modest possibilities allow.'[71] Cuba's foreign minister, Felipe Perez Roque, stated: 'We deeply regret the loss of human life, and our position is of total rejection of this sort of terrorist attack.'[72] Cuba offered its airports to flights bound for the United States that were unable to enter American airspace. It also offered medical aid. Since 2001 Cuba has offered to sign agreements with the United States that would facilitate cooperation between the two countries in combating terrorism.

According to most estimates, Cuba does not pose a terrorist threat and, when pressed for specifics, even the American government sources that issued the various accusations are hard-pressed to come up with significant or recent evidence of such a danger. Many government documents that address terrorism omit any mention of the Cuban threat even though Cuba's place on the list of terror-sponsoring suggests it is one of the most serious offenders. In fact, in 1998, the Defense Department concluded that Cuba did not present a military threat to the United States. Paul Pillar, the former deputy chief of the CIA Counterterrorist Center, wrote the following about Cuba's inclusion on the list: 'Cuba's remaining links with terrorism consist of providing a home for a handful of members of the Basque Fatherland and Liberty group (ETA) and other fugitives, and providing some accommodations to the Revolutionary Armed Forces of Colombia and National Liberation Army ... The Castro government's post-cold war retrenchment has been so extensive that it is doing nothing either in terrorism or other military or external activities that would appear to qualify it for its pariah status.'[73] When pressed, Michael Sheehan also admitted that Cuba's inclusion on the list was questionable. He stated: 'It is true, in fact, that Cuba and several other states on that list could take what we would consider not difficult steps to move them off the list of state-sponsorship.'[74] Thus, the inclusion of Cuba on the list has little to do with the seriousness of the terrorist threat emanating from the island. Instead, the prevalence of a certain way of thinking about Cuba and the identities that underlie that thinking have influenced the popular and often official depiction of revolutionary Cuba as a terrorist state.

The horrific attacks on the World Trade Center and the Pentagon were immediately understood by Americans as a deliberate attack on American values – in particular, democracy and freedom. It was believed that the terrorists attacked the United States because the country represents these values. On 20 September 2001 President George W. Bush told a Joint Session of Congress and the American people: 'Americans are asking, why do they hate us? They hate what we see right here in this chamber – a democratically elected government. Their leaders are self-appointed. They hate our freedoms – our freedom of religion, our freedom of speech, our freedom to vote and assemble and disagree with each other.'[75]

The Cuban state, seen as a long-term enemy of these values, was naturally perceived to be on the side of the terrorists. American officials had often compared Fidel Castro to Saddam Hussein and other leaders considered pariahs, even going so far, to quote President Eisenhower, as calling him a 'little Hitler.'[76] In the aftermath of 9/11, the image was updated to reflect the 'villains' of the twenty-first century. Dana Rohrabacher (R-Calif.) told Congress that Castro was 'demonstrably stronger than (Iraqi President) Saddam Hussein in his ability to hurt the U.S.'[77] Dennis Hays, the former head of the State Department's Cuba section and then the executive vice-president of CANF, argued that 'enlisting Castro in the fight against terrorism is like deputizing John Gotti in the fight against organized crime.'[78]

To assume that a state led by Castro would be engaged in the production of chemical or biological weapons, regardless of Cuba's declared support for international norms or agreements against their production, is a natural evolution of that line of thought. The narrative of 'Cuba has the capacity to make these weapons' becomes 'Cuba is engaged in biological weapons production.' And so, though most official reports do not unequivocally state that Cuba has these weapons, they do intimate that *because* the Cuban state has the means to do so, it is more than likely that biological weapons are being produced on the island. For example, Secretary of State Colin Powell said that the United States was concerned about Cuba's 'capacity and capability to conduct such [biological] research.'[79]

However, a few members of the Bush administration took this narrative to the next step. Under-Secretary of State Bolton asserted:

> For four decades, Cuba has maintained a well-developed and sophisticated biomedical industry, supported until 1990 by the Soviet Union. This industry is one of the most advanced in Latin America and leads in the production of pharmaceuticals and vaccines that are sold worldwide. Analysts and Cuban defectors have long cast suspicion on the activities conducted in these biomedical facilities ... The United States believes that Cuba has at least a limited offensive biological warfare research and development effort. Cuba has provided dual-use biotechnology to other rogue states.[80]

Shortly after Bolton made this speech to the Heritage Foundation, both Colin Powell and Defense Secretary Donald Rumsfeld were careful to distance themselves from his remarks, stressing that the United States could not go further than to state that Cuba has the capacity to produce these weapons.[81] Yet the 2006 State Department report on state sponsors of terrorism reiterated Bolton's concerns. It noted:

> Cuba invests heavily in biotechnology, and there is some dispute about the existence and extent of Cuba's offensive biological weapons program. The Cuban Government maintains friendly ties with Iran and North Korea. Cuban Foreign Minister Perez Roque visited Iran on November 13. Earlier in the year, Iran offered Cuba a 20 million euro line of credit, ostensibly for investment in biotechnology. The Cuba-Iran Joint Commission met in Havana in January. Cuba and North Korea held military talks at the general staff level in May in Pyongyang. The North Korean trade minister visited Havana in November and signed a protocol for cooperation in the areas of science and trade.[82]

Most states with pharmaceutical-research capabilities have the same wherewithal to produce these weapons as Cuba and many also have scientific ties with states considered to be unfriendly to the United States. The crucial difference is the perception of Cuba in the United States.[83]

Furthermore, Cuba's location within the American sphere of influence heightens both the strategic and value-based rationales for these concerns. The island's location 'only ninety miles from U.S. shores' is stressed in discussions about the Cuban government's alleged terrorist activities. Dennis Hays stated: 'We need to know if a nation 90 miles from our shores is experimenting with deadly biological agents.'[84] Similarly, John Bolton asserted: 'In addition to Libya and Syria, there is a threat coming from another BWC signatory, and one that lies just 90 miles from the U.S. mainland – namely, Cuba.'[85] This fact is emphasized for both strategic and normative reasons. If Cuba does have biological weapons, its proximity to the United States would make an attack on the country easier. However, the location is stressed for another implicit reason – because Cuba is so intimately a part of the American sphere of influence, its interests cannot be separated from those of the United States. The argument, then, justifies American involvement in Cuban affairs.

Lincoln Diaz-Balart (R-Fl.) repeatedly stressed the connection between the western hemisphere and policy towards Cuba in an attempt to convince other members of Congress to vote down a 2002 amendment that would have made public financing available for sales to the Cuban government. 'Cuba is in this hemisphere,' he declared. 'It is the only country oppressed by tyranny in this hemisphere ... Cuba remains in this hemisphere, despite what some would like on the other side of this debate. It remains in this hemisphere, and the Cuban people deserve our continued solidarity, and not financing for the terrorist government.'[86] Diaz-Balart clearly believes that Cuba's location within the hemisphere is an important consideration in the determination of American policy towards the island. It is also obvious that he thinks this fact is important to the other members of Congress because he used it in an attempt to convince them to oppose the 2002 amendment. The image of the Cuban government as a pariah and the location of Cuba within the American sphere of influence have contributed to the American designation of Cuba as a terrorist-sponsoring state and influenced the more recent accusations about the government's involvement in biological-weapons production.

The View from North of the Border:
Canadian-Cuban Biotech Collaboration

In contrast, these perceptions are not prevalent in Canadian discussions about the island even though terrorism is considered one of the top threats to Canadian security. Canadians do not perceive Cuba as a country with a long history of ties to terrorism. A 1999 report of the Canadian Security Intelligence Service (CSIS) entitled 'Trends in Terrorism' lists forty-two categories of terrorist threats including threats from Latin America. Colombia and Peru are singled out as potential sources of danger but there is no mention of any threat from Cuba.[87] On the contrary, Cuba is seen as a partner in the fight against terrorism. Point 9 of the 1997 Joint Declaration between Canada and Cuba states that the two will work together to facilitate 'conversations on international terrorism and its prevention.'[88] In 2008 the Department of Foreign Affairs and International Trade stated on its website that Canadian and Cuban officials have had 'discussions on international efforts to combat terrorism.'[89]

Though Fidel Castro is no longer considered the honourable freedom fighter he once was, he is not considered a pariah either, and during the late 1990s and early 2000s Canadians were highly dubious of claims that his government was engaged in terrorist-friendly activities. Just as Americans are inclined to believe the worst about the Castro brothers, Canadians are predisposed to downplay reports that they are involved in terrorist activities. A *Globe and Mail* article about U.S.-Cuba relations captures the Canadian response to the charge that Cuba has biological weapons: 'John Bolton publicly widened the Bush "axis of evil" to include Cuba, which Mr. Bolton claimed is developing biological weapons. Conceivably – just – that might be true. As with Iraq there is no way to tell. But more likely it is not.'[90] Canadians remain highly sceptical of the American characterization of Castro as a terrorist or that he is engaged in bioweapons production.

In Ottawa, the issue of Cuba's links to terrorism is conspicuous by its absence. When the possibility of a Cuban biological weapons effort was being discussed in the United States, the issue was not once mentioned in the Canadian Parliament.[91] The only reference to the controversy ignored the subject of biological weapons and simply emphasized the similarity between Canadian perceptions of Cuba and former president Jimmy Carter's. A Canadian MP stated: 'Mr. Carter's visit to Cuba would indicate that he is probably a fellow traveler in what we are trying to do here.'[92]

In fact, the Canadian government has actively supported connections between Canadian and Cuban scientists.[93] The Canadian International Development Agency funds programs to aid Cuba's biotechnology sector. For example, CIDA funded a project between the

Universidad Central de Las Villas 'Marta Abreu' (UCLV), Santa Clara, Cuba, and the Institute of Biomedical Engineering at the University of New Brunswick (UNB). The stated objective of the project was 'to establish a Biomedical Engineering Education Infrastructure in Cuba.'[94] CIDA later funded another project between the Institute of Biomedical Engineering at UNB and three Cuban universities – UCLV in Santa Clara, Instituto Superior Politecnico José A. Echeverra (ISPJAE) in Havana, and Universidad de Oriente (UO) in Santiago de Cuba. This six-year project also involves the Hospital for Sick Children in Toronto. UNB's Ed Biden, the project's principal investigator, said that it will 'transfer the skills and knowledge of Canadian experts in biomedical and clinical engineering' to their Cuban counterparts.[95] Also according to a UNB press release, 'the project will equip advanced laboratories in each of the three partner universities in Cuba.'[96]

These types of associations have led to collaborative research. The University of Ottawa and the University of Havana collaborated on a human vaccine for flu and meningitis. Jointly patented by the universities in 1999, this vaccine was the first human vaccine made with a synthetic antigen and prevents one of the causes of childhood meningitis and pneumonia.[97] The opportunity for Canadian and Cuban scientists to meet relatively freely paved the way for this successful collaboration. Professor René Roy of the University of Ottawa met Dr Vicente Verez Bencomo of the University of Havana at a scientific conference in Ottawa in 1994 and the two began to work together after further discussion at a 1995 conference in Havana.[98]

There are also connections between Canadian NGOs and Cuba in the biomedical field. In 1995 former prime minister Pierre Trudeau grew concerned about the lack of basic medicines available to Cubans as a result of the embargo and the economic collapse following the end of the Soviet Union. On Trudeau's initiative and with the cooperation of the Canadian government, Health Partners International of Canada, a humanitarian NGO, implemented a medical-aid program designed to deliver medicines in short supply in Cuba to the island. The NGO arranged for Aventis Pasteur to donate $4.5-million worth of flu vaccine to Cubans through the program.[99] Between 1995 and 2005, almost $40 million in medical aid was sent to Cuba via this program.[100]

The Canadian business community has developed ties, albeit limited ones, to Cuba's biotechnology sector. In 1995 an Ontario company, YM Biosciences, collaborated with the Centro de Immunología Molecular (CIM) in Havana to commercialize cancer vaccines being developed by CIM. However, pressure from the United States does pose additional difficulties for Canadian companies like YM Biosciences. The chief executive of YM Biosciences, David Allen, explained: 'Developing a product that originates in Cuba is definitely a greater challenge than developing a product that originates elsewhere.'[101] Complications include having to raise equity in Europe and eventually needing to obtain approval from the American Food and Drug Administration (FDA) to market the drug in the United States.[102] That said, many Canadian scientists believe that the Cuban research community has the potential to become a scientific partner and are not concerned about the bioweapons charges levelled by Washington. David Allen declared: 'We don't care where science comes from if it is good science ... The fact it happens to be from the University of Havana, well, we are seeking good science where we can find it.'[103]

The Canadian tendency to disregard or minimize the possibility that the Cuban state supports terrorism reflects the identities Canadians perform on the international stage. Discussions of terrorism in general in Canadian government circles emphasize the values Canadians want to see reflected in their foreign policy. In March 2002 Bill Graham, then Canada's minister of foreign affairs, told an audience that 'our challenge in responding to terrorism is to not lose sight of the values and norms we cherish. Respect for the rule of law underpins Canadian society and is fundamental to Canadian values and identity. Canadians believe in the rule of law and in legal institutions to remedy injustice. Throughout our history, the rule of law has been our strength and the foundation upon which we have built this country. It is a fundamental part of our democratic tradition and is a principle that Canada promotes internationally.'[104] It is for this reason that Cuba's signature on the twelve UN resolutions against terrorism is seen as significant in Canadian circles.

Furthermore, Canadians have a great deal invested in their policy towards Cuba, since that policy represents independence from the United States. The very fact that reports of the existence of Cuban bioweapons emanate from Washington make Canadians more sceptical of them. During a CBC interview about the 9/11 attacks, Prime

Minister Chrétien mentioned Cuba but only in the context of Canadian policy towards the island, suggesting how American foreign policy could be improved to deter terrorism. He said that the United States and the Western world needed to shoulder some of the blame for the attacks because the West is 'looked upon as being arrogant, self-satisfied, greedy and with no limits.'[105] He used American policy towards Cuba as an example of misguided policy. He explained that, because the United States is so powerful, it should be 'nicer.'[106]

Canadians also have a history of identifying with Cuba. Though some Canadians occasionally draw tenuous comparisons (such as the one-party-state comparison discussed in Chapter 3) and others are upset about the level of closeness between the two countries, most empathize with Cuba and thus would be prone to question the American accusations of Cuba as a terrorist state. Furthermore, the 'Cuba as a terrorist' theme runs counter to the deeply held perception of Fidel Castro as essentially a well-meaning though sometimes misguided leader. To acknowledge a terrorist connection, Canadians would have to question seriously their whole picture of the Cuban government and their relationship with Cuba. It is much easier to chalk it up to another example of the 'American bully' in action.

Thus, the United States and Canada, in many ways so much alike, believe very different things about Cuba. Americans place the Cuban government on their list of sponsors of terrorism and insinuate that the Cubans are developing biological weapons and misleading the global effort to combat terrorism. Canadians are highly sceptical of all of these charges. The values, identities, and past perceptions at work in both countries have influenced these different characterizations of Fidel Castro and his connections to terrorism. Since it would be difficult to underestimate the effect of the designation of a state as terrorist-friendly in a post-9/11 world, this perception is exceedingly relevant to policy formulation.

Conclusion

Canada and the United States have long had distinct policies towards Cuba. Clearly, we cannot discount the effect of the Cuban American community on the U.S. response to the downing of the Brothers to the Rescue planes and the absence of a similar factor in determining the Canadian response. Also, the Cuban American community has a role in the identification of Fidel Castro as a terrorist in the United States and the absence of such a clearly anti-Castro group in Canada has likely had an impact on the Canadian perspective on this issue. Yet, as the examples in this chapter have demonstrated, neither policy can be reduced to a simple political or economic variable since they also reflect a complex interplay of identities and perceptions. By comparing the Canadian and American responses to the same issues, this chapter has further demonstrated the relevance of these variables. Both the shoot-down of the Brothers to the Rescue planes and the possibility that Cuba is engaged in bioterrorism research were understood differently in Canada and the United States largely because of the unique combination of identities and perceptions at work in both countries.

In the United States, the shoot-down was seen as an act of evil that demanded an immediate response. This interpretation reflected the long-standing perception of Fidel Castro and Cuba's place within the American 'family.' Helms-Burton, more than any other document of the post-Cold War era, explicitly reveals the degree to which the Americans place Cuba within their 'sphere of influence' and the latitude they believe that gives them to determine the future of the island country. In contrast, Canadians, generally sympathetic to sovereignty issues vis-à-vis the United States, saw the downing of the planes more as an unfortunate overreaction to repeated incursions on Cuban sovereignty. In typical Canadian fashion, they tried to defuse the tension between the United States and Cuba by talking to both sides. However, Canadians were most concerned with the enactment of the Helms-Burton bill because they saw it as another attempt by Americans to dictate Canadian policy.

Similarly, both countries reacted very differently to suggestions that the Cuban state has ties to terrorism. Based on long-standing views of Fidel Castro, Americans were inclined to believe the worst about him and so were receptive to charges that he was trying to scuttle the American efforts to combat terrorism and was involved in the production of biological weapons. Canadians, inclined to have a fairly positive view of Castro (and to question the American version of events when Cuba is involved), are highly sceptical of the American charges.

However, as the next chapter will reveal, both Canadian and American policies towards Cuba are changing as a result of new perceptions of the island nation that began to emerge in the late 1990s. Ironically, in some ways, the two strategies are becoming more similar as both sets of perceptions about the island and the rule of Fidel and now Raúl Castro evolve. A number of incidents have played a critical role in this evolution: in the United States, the visit to Cuba of Pope John Paul II and the Elían Gonzalez affair; and in Canada, the failure of Prime Minister Chrétien to secure the release of the dissidents during his visit to the island and Fidel Castro's criticisms of Canada following the 1999 Pan-American Games in Winnipeg.

5 Conclusion

The previous chapters have told a story of two complex, and very dissimilar, foreign policies that are based on perceptions rooted in different identities. Does this mean that these policies are destined to remain as they are today? Will the United States continue its policy of isolation until Cuba becomes a model of Western-style liberal democracy? Will Canada continue to engage with the island state under any and all circumstances?

The two policies are dynamic, like the underlying identities and perceptions; they are constantly ebbing and flowing. They are socially constructed and thus open to change. Indeed, in the last decade, the two policies have shown a potential for considerable change. This chapter will describe the recent alterations in both approaches, highlighting how these changes are connected to ideational factors.

Changing Perceptions and Evolving Policies

Chapter 1 argued that people are cognitive misers who interpret new information based on prior related experiences and ideas. They attempt to place the new information in context in ways that do not disrupt previously accepted ideas, beliefs, and concepts. Research has shown that individuals will even ignore or distort information that does not fit with previously held ideas.

That said, perceptions are not fixed but are socially constructed and thus flexible. They can evolve. Admittedly, established perceptions are not easily changed, especially when they are tied to relatively stable identities. Yet, though perceptions are rooted in identity factors, it is possible for perceptions to evolve independent of any change in identity, particularly when the newer perceptions remain consistent with established identity.

Newer perceptions of the U.S.-Cuba relationship remain consistent with the idea of American exceptionalism. Most of the arguments for normalization of relations do not dispute the legitimacy of American views of Cuba during the Cold War or of American superiority in the western hemisphere. They instead make the case that circumstances have now changed and that U.S. policy should evolve based on the updated circumstances. Some advocates of normalization argue that American policy should be altered because Cuba is changing. More argue that isolation is no longer in line with U.S. values and goals in Cuba. Though the U.S. identity is still seen as embodying the ideas of exceptionalism, those pressing for normalization argue that the isolationist approach towards Cuba no longer reflects this U.S. identity. They are attempting to interrupt the pathway between U.S. exceptionalism and U.S. policy via changing perceptions. This task is not easily accomplished.

The perceptions driving Canadian policy are equally socially constructed but they have not undergone a similar evolution. Canadian perceptions of Cuba shift and at times these shifts have caused Ottawa to narrow relations with Havana. The 1990s was one such period, and this example demonstrates just how closely identity and perceptions are linked since Canadian perceptions and thus policy shifted most dramatically when the Canadian identity was contested. Since our self-images become internalized, obvious challenges to those self-images can be important catalysts for change. States do not respond well when their identities are challenged. Cuba, as it has been governed since the early 1960s, has posed a direct challenge to the American self-image. As a matter of course, Cuba's actions do not contest the Canadian identity, but, when they begin to do so, relations sour considerably. The rest of this chapter will delve into the relationship between changing perceptions, identity, and policy by exploring recent developments in the two relationships.

Recent Developments in U.S. Cuban Policy

The norms, identities, and images that underlie the construction of U.S. policy towards Cuba are not easily altered. They have, to different degrees, become internalized or institutionalized. However, relatively recent international and domestic events have caused some

perceptions to shift. The perceptions reflected in this discourse continue to be constructed in a way that is consistent with the American
self-image. Though this restricts the degree and range of change possible, change can happen more easily when perceptions fit within
prevalent identities.

Slowly, American perceptions of Cuba are evolving. Having won the
Cold War, Americans are less likely to fear communism and consequently the Cuban state. Surveys indicate that most Americans still
perceive that Cuba is an enemy but that the numbers believing this
have declined since the Cold War ended.[1] Over half of the Americans
polled in 2000 thought that Cuba did not represent a serious threat to
the United States. Only 15 per cent thought the island was a 'very
serious threat.'[2]

Yet the changing perception of threat, while remaining important, is
only one of the variables that have caused some Americans to re-
examine their policy towards Cuba. Another is the media frenzy surrounding the custody battle over Elían Gonzalez. This six-year-old
Cuban boy, who was part of a group that fled the island in November
1999, lost his mother when their boat sank off the coast of Florida. After
he was rescued, the Immigration and Naturalization Service turned him
over to his relatives in Miami. The custody battle that ensued between
those relatives and Elían's father in Cuba made headlines for months.

The publicity altered many people's perceptions of Cuba, Cubans,
and Cuban Americans. First, it served to humanize Cubans. Americans
identified with Elían's father, Juan Miguel Gonzalez, and his family in
Cuba. People remarked that they 'seemed like just like us' and
reported that they felt empathy for Juan Miguel. Additionally, many
people questioned their perception of life in Cuba after Elían's father
refused an offer to remain in the United States. Lastly, during the
custody fight, the Cuban American community often appeared overly
emotional and sometimes irrational, thereby encouraging a growing
scepticism of its capacity for objectivity. A former senior government
official who remains very influential in policy towards Cuba told the
author that a *New Republic* article correctly analysed the impact of this
crisis on the community. This article claimed that the community's
reputation was tarnished during the custody battle. Many of its
members' insistence that Elían had been saved by angels in the form of
dolphins – as well as their passionate outbursts on national television
and the impression they gave that they thought themselves above the
law – hurt their credibility.[3]

Opinion polls taken at the time confirm these perceptions. Americans were asked if they approved or disapproved of the way the parties involved handled the Elían Gonzalez case. 'The boy's father' achieved the highest approval rating; 67 per cent said they approved of his actions. In contrast, only 34 per cent of those polled approved of the way 'the boy's relatives in Miami' handled the case. The publicity also influenced the public's view of the wider Cuban American community. Only 27 per cent of those polled approved of the way the community handled the case.[4] A NBC/Wall Street Journal poll reported that even fewer respondents thought that the Cuban American relatives (23 per cent) and the wider community (20 per cent) acted responsibly. In contrast, 71 per cent of those polled said they believed that Elían's father acted responsibly.[5] These events have caused a re-examination of some of the most prevalent images, norms, and ideas of Cuba and the Cuban American community. The custody battle called into question some long-held perceptions – specifically, that the Cuban American community's view of Cuba is correct and that life in Cuba is as bad as Washington reports.

Many arguments that favour ending the embargo have been framed in ways that draw on the moral issues and values embedded within the tradition of American exceptionalism. For instance, these arguments often refer to the 1998 visit of Pope John Paul II to Cuba.[6] Many Americans, believing in their country's exceptional character and thinking that the United States is taking the most morally correct position in relation to Cuba, were surprised by the pope's message. Since the Vatican and the Catholic Church have considerable moral authority, the pope's opinion of the embargo as 'deplorable' made many people question whether their government was pursuing the best policy.[7] Though his visit did not cause a major policy change, his remarks about the U.S. embargo and the plight of the Cuban people did have an impact in Washington and beyond. A senior U.S. official said that the pope swayed the American public, the Clinton administration, and even some hard-line Cuban Americans.[8] Democratic Representative Lee Hamilton said that the pope's visit 'got an awful lot of people thinking. The Pope's approach is the exact opposite of the American Government's. The Pope is trying to engage the Cuban people. The U.S. policy is to isolate the Cuban people. The contrast is apparent.'[9] After visiting Cuba for the pope's visit, the archbishop of Boston, Bernard Cardinal Law, argued for a change to the U.S. approach towards the island. He stated that he was accompanied by 'heads of social service agencies and representatives of foundations, there were lawyers and judges, congressmen, presidents of colleges, a law school dean and a university professor, and the editor of a national magazine. We were a wondrously diverse group, but we found unity in our conviction that the time is now for a change.'[10] President Bill Clinton stated after he introduced a number of changes to Cuba policy that 'the measures I have announced today are designed to build on [the pope's] visit.'[11]

The pope's visit was still having an impact on U.S. policy years later. In 2002 the House of Representatives' Cuba Working Group stated that it 'heartily' embraced the pope's message in Cuba.[12] The pope's remarks prompted a re-examination of the assumption that U.S. policy towards the Cuban government was morally correct. By interrupting the logical pathway between the American identity as an exceptional country (a moral leader) and the isolation of Cuba, his statements caused some Americans to question their policy towards the island.

Former president Jimmy Carter's visit to Cuba in 2002 also had an impact on people's perceptions of Cuba and of the U.S. policy. This was the first visit by an American of this stature since Fidel Castro had assumed power. Carter is one of the most popular former presidents; indeed, he is more popular now than he was during his presidency.[13] His work in human rights and other humanitarian issues is well respected. Thus, when Carter spoke out in favour of engagement during this trip, he prompted even greater discussion about the appropriateness of the U.S. policy towards the island.

Perceptions within the Cuban American community are also changing. Surveys conducted in the 1970 and 1980s indicated that a large majority of Cuban Americans favoured isolation or removing Castro from power by force. Dialogue was opposed by as many as 80 per cent of the community.[14] In those days, Cuban Americans who advocated dialogue were harassed by fellow expatriates. One was even killed in 1975.[15]

Over the last few years, the community has become much less united behind a single solution, reflecting growing divisions among Cuban immigrants. A majority of Cubans in the Miami area are recent immigrants. These 'economic refugees,' who arrived from the 1980s on, are known to favour dialogue much more than their predecessors.[16] Surveys taken in 2003 indicate that more than half of all Cuban immigrants believe that the U.S. approach towards Cuba has failed to improve the lives of people in Cuba. A majority also believe that exiles should be talking to the Cuban government and approved of a meeting between the two groups held in April 2003.[17] The Miami *Herald* reports that polls taken of Cuban Americans in Florida during 2003 show 'a major shift towards moderation by Cuban exiles.'[18] The New York *Times* observes that 'the change in attitudes reflects an ideological split between the original Cuban exiles and their children and grandchildren, a recent influx of immigrants who fled for economic rather than political reasons, and a concerted effort by some exile groups to improve the image of Cuban Americans after a nationally televised struggle over the young shipwreck survivor Elian Gonzalez.'[19] The change within the community has continued to progress. A 2009 poll of Cuban Americans revealed that '67 percent of the community now supports the removal of all restrictions for travel to Cuba.'[20]

To a certain degree, the Cuban American National Foundation has also changed its views, rhetoric, and policies. The organization is now willing to meet with members of the current Cuban government to discuss democracy issues. This would have been virtually unthinkable in the 1990s. It is telling that CANF did not come out in opposition to Carter's visit. It asked only that Carter raise the issue of human rights while he was in Cuba.[21] CANF's new stance is not accepted by everyone. The change in the main Cuban American lobby group caused divisions among its members. As we have seen, those members who have been upset with the changes in the organization's hard-line views have banded together in the new Cuban Liberty Council.[22] However, given the evolving views of the community, this group is unlikely to achieve the monolithic status achieved by CANF in 1980s Miami. Though the CLC's major influence comes from its ideational agreement with Washington's consensus about Cuba, without a solid base of support in Miami the organization is unlikely to achieve the level of influence enjoyed by CANF in its heyday.

The pope's visit to the island, the reporting of the Elían Gonzalez saga, the end of the Cold War, and divisions with the community changed perceptions and influenced the norms directing U.S. policy. Significant elements of the American public began to question isolation during this period. Americans also started voicing their opinions by defying their government over Cuba. Approximately 50,000 Americans illegally visited Cuba in 2001.[23] Business leaders and lawmakers also travelled to the island in record numbers in the early 2000s. Over 700 American business people, representing almost 300 companies, participated in the 2002 Havana Trade Show.[24] Although the number of Americans attending the Havana Trade Show and vacationing in Cuba declined under the final years of the Bush administration when the United States tightened travel restrictions, the interest in establishing relations with Cuba remains strong. In fact, when asked in 2007 'Do you think the United States should continue the trade embargo with Cuba or should the United States end the trade embargo and permit normal trade with Cuba?' 40 per cent of Americans polled said that they favoured an end to the embargo.[25]

In the last decade there has also been a movement in Washington to lift the embargo. The Cuba Policy Foundation, founded in 2001 by some key powerbrokers, made a concerted attempt in the first few years of the twenty-first century to press for engagement. Similarly, both the House of Representatives and the Senate formed Cuba working groups for the explicit purpose of critically examining American policy towards Cuba. The Senate group, formed in March 2003, announced in its first public statement that it would look at the right of Americans to travel to Cuba and the capacity of the island nation to serve as a market for American products.

The working groups listed numerous reasons for lifting the embargo. There was some sense that a new approach was warranted because Cuba was changing in ways that were consistent with U.S. values and goals. The groups argued that 'bereft of Soviet bloc aid and trade for a decade, Cuba is experimenting with elements of markets and capitalism, such as small enterprise, free-market sales of farm produce, foreign investment, and state enterprise reform, to generate jobs and growth.'[26]

Rather than focusing solely on changes within Cuba, many of the arguments also try to adjust the logic that connects the exceptionalist self-image with a policy based on isolation. In its 'Review of U.S. Policy toward Cuba,' the U.S. House of Representatives' Working Group began by referring to the pope's message. It then argued that policy towards Cuba is 'at odds with the values and long-term strategies that the President and Secretary of State passionately advocate when they promote engagement around the world.' Appealing to the U.S. role in the hemisphere, the group stated: 'Because Cuba is a neighbor and our nations share deep historical ties and current interests, Cuba should be at the center of our engagement policy.' The embargo, it concluded, is contrary to the U.S. vision of a democratic Cuba. 'Current U.S. policy seeks to assist the Cuban people and to promote a "rapid and peaceful" transition to democracy, yet many of its elements work in the opposite direction.' The travel ban should be repealed because 'freedom to travel is a basic right of Americans.' The United States should also remove restrictions on agricultural trade because 'far from focusing attention on Cuba's failed domestic policies, U.S. restrictions send the signal that America wants to use economic deprivation as a tool for political change.'[27] In a nutshell, the group argued that, in the post-Cold War environment, a policy based on engagement is more consistent with American values and the U.S. role in the world than a policy based on isolation.

These arguments do not contest the American self-image or abandon the link between identity and foreign policy. Instead, they try to change how people connect the two concepts, a strategy that is feasible because these concepts and the policies they give rise to are socially constructed. Thus, the working groups are attempting to change policy by appealing to the values, ideas, and norms within the exceptionalist identity. In so doing, they are attempting to change the pathway between the American identity and policy towards Cuba.

Though the embargo remains in place, policy is beginning to reflect these changing perceptions and norms. Americans were given permission to sell agriculture products to Cuba on a cash-sale basis in 2000. Between 2001 and 2007, Cuba purchased almost $2 billion in U.S. agricultural products.[28] The pressure to ease the embargo continues. In 2007–8 a series of bills were introduced into Congress to change policy towards Cuba. One would have allowed American oil and gas companies to engage in joint ventures with the Cuban state to develop the Cuban offshore oil fields. Another pushed for ending all travel restrictions and another would have dispensed with the requirement that the Cuban state pay cash in advance for agriculture imports from the United States.[29] Though these bills were not passed, there clearly has been an unmistakable movement in many quarters to normalize U.S. relations with Cuba. The new policies being proposed reflect changing perceptions and norms about the island, its people, the Cuban American community, and the relationship between the American identity and foreign policy.

However, there has also been an increase in countervailing pressures in support of isolation. Emphasizing the long-established images of Cuba, the Bush administration made a case for taking a harder approach towards the island. The events of 9/11 and the subsequent war on terrorism were used to further negative perceptions of Cuba since the 'rogue regime' was on the State Department's list of terror-sponsoring states. As Chapter 4 showed, the inclusion of Cuba on this list and charges that Cuba supports bioterrorism are serious barriers to normalization.

President Bush took a harder line with Cuba than did his predecessor. In 2001 he said that his administration 'will oppose any attempt to weaken sanctions against Cuba's government.'[30] Further, President Bush filled openings in his administration with representatives of the hard-line elements of the community. In 2004 the Bush administration imposed additional restrictions on family visits to the island, limiting visits to once every three years. Cash remittances from expatriates were also tightened.

At the same time, Bush increased support for human-rights activists in Cuba. He adopted a more confrontational approach and, according to some, actively goaded the Cuban government.[31] Much of the new tension in the relationship has taken place between the American diplomats in Havana and the Cuban government. According to the Associated Press, the principal officer in Havana during Bush's first two years in office, Vicki Huddleston, 'walked a rocky road that turned sharply to the right when President Bush took office in 2001.' They report that, in contrast, 'during the Clinton administration, Huddleston kept a relatively low profile, meeting quietly with dissidents.'[32] Under Bush, Huddleston distributed to Cuban activists both books and short-wave radios programmed to receive Radio Martí. She also increased her criticisms of the Cuban government and her support of dissidents.[33]

Huddleston's replacement, James Cason, further increased the tension between the U.S. Interests Section and the Cuban state by intensifying the contact between the dissidents and U.S. diplomats. Dissidents were frequently invited to Cason's home and also to the U.S. mission. Cason spoke at opposition meetings.[34] The Cuban leadership reacted by severely limiting the movement of U.S. personnel in Cuba.

Havana claims that the effort to harass and jail dissidents that occurred in the spring of 2003 was a reaction to the 'American offensive.' A representative of the Cuban government in Washington, Juan Hernadez Acen, claimed: 'These people have not been arrested for what they think ... They were arrested because they are directly linked to the active conspiracy and subversion being done by James Cason.'[35] Though firmly stating that Castro alone was responsible for the 2003 crackdown, Washington insiders admit that Cason's activities gave the Cuban leadership the excuse it needed to engage in repressive behaviour.[36] In any case, this series of arrests and trials has been described as the most serious repression in years. Some dissidents were given jail sentences as long as twenty-seven years.

Michael E. Parmly replaced Cason in 2005 and for a time appeared to be taking the rhetoric down a notch. However, in 2006, tensions escalated again. In January of that year, the United States put up a scrolling electronic billboard that displayed messages critical of the Cuban government. The Cuban government responded by erecting a monument across the street from the embassy in 'Anti-Imperialism Park.' The tall, black, imposing flags on the monument obscured the billboard. Parmly said that Castro's Cuba 'makes Ceausescu's Romania look like real amateurs,' after accusing the Cuban government of deliberately turning off the electricity to the mission for a couple of days. Castro responded by calling Parmly a 'little gangster.'[37] Parmly was replaced in 2008 by Jonathan D. Farrar, a former senior official at the State Department's Bureau of Democracy, Human Rights and Labor. Farrar has said that the transfer of power to Raúl Castro has not led to any changes in the human-rights situation on the island. The Cuban state simply changed one Castro 'for the other.'[38]

Lastly, the American attack on Iraq in 2003 made many Cubans nervous. The American government's new pre-emptive approach to rogue regimes spurred speculation that Washington might take unilateral action against Cuba. This conjecture was fuelled by the jingoism of the Bush administration. On 10 April 2003 the U.S. ambassador to the Dominican Republic warned that Iraq was a 'very good example for Cuba.'[39]

However, when the Americans elected Barack Obama in 2008 on a platform based on change, many Cuba watchers believed that the new president would overturn the embargo early on in his administration. Certainly, as a presidential candidate and even before, Obama had come out on the side of loosening restrictions. His early public remarks indicated that he would work towards normalization; in 2004 he declared that 'it is time for us to end the embargo.'[40] Later, in the election campaign, he stated that he would not end the embargo but that his administration would instead 'grant Cuban-Americans unrestricted rights to visit family and send remittances to the island.'[41] Yet, even in making those statements, he echoed the discourse of previous administrations. Reflecting ideas about the U.S. role in promoting democracy and human rights in the hemisphere and drawing on negative and opposing images of Cuba, Obama stated: 'It is a tragedy that, just 90 miles from our shores, there exists a society where such freedom and opportunity are kept out of reach by a government that clings to discredited ideology and authoritarian control. A democratic opening in Cuba is, and should be, the foremost objective of our policy.' He continued: 'I will use aggressive and principled diplomacy to send an important message: If a post-Fidel government begins opening Cuba to democratic change, the United States (the president working with Congress) is prepared to take steps to normalize relations and ease the embargo that has governed relations between our countries for the last five decades.'[42]

President Obama followed through on his campaign promise to ease restrictions on travel by Cuban Americans and allow greater levels of remittances. Just before heading off to the Summit of the Americas meeting in Trinidad and Tobago in the spring of 2009, he announced that Americans with relatives in Cuba could visit Cuba without any restrictions and could also send as much money as they like to family on the island. In July 2009 he removed the electronic billboard that had displayed messages from the Interests Section critical of the Cuban government and reopened migration talks with the Cuban government that had been suspended in 2003.[43] Yet Obama has also said that the next major move is up to the Cubans. His administration reiterates the traditional calls for change within Cuba. Secretary of State Hillary Clinton has explained: 'We're continuing to explore ways to further democracy in Cuba and provide the Cuban people with more opportunities.'[44] When Obama's changes were criticized as insufficient by Fidel Castro, Hillary Clinton responded: 'Well, we would welcome him releasing some political prisoners.'[45]

The American self-identification as an exceptional country and, as such, a moral and political leader is deeply internalized. Revolutionary Cuba continues to be seen as the antithesis of the U.S. identity, something that will not change in the foreseeable future. Likewise, the belief that Cuba is within the U.S. sphere of influence is unlikely to change and tension between Washington and Havana over the direction of Cuba's future is likely to continue too. However, perceptions that are related to certain images about daily life in Cuba, Cubans, and Cuban Americans are more easily changed. Those perceptions have been evolving along with mounting questions about the appropriateness of the isolationist solution and have thus facilitated the movement towards normalization.

That said, the future of the movement in Congress and among the American public to end the embargo will not be completely divorced from what happens in Cuba. If it appears there might be a new round of repression, few members of Congress will feel confident arguing for a relaxation. This became apparent in 2003 when the move towards relaxation that was gaining steam hit an abrupt halt in response to events in Cuba. As the Cuba Policy Foundation put it: 'If the move to end the embargo was like a political campaign, we had a great candidate ... This dissident roundup is the candidate being caught with the intern. The fear is people will be less inclined to listen to a positive message. Because of the fear, distrust and justifiable outrage, the message of engaging Cuba will be lost.'[46] If repression is seen as easing, the pressure to change U.S. policy is likely to continue in tandem with evolving perceptions, and it is very possible that specific elements within the wider policy will be altered (perhaps the further easing of travel restrictions and allowing the sale of other products in addition to food and medicine). Such piecemeal changes will eventually nullify 'isolation.' However, if the repression is seen to intensify under Raúl Castro, perceptions of Cuba and of the isolationist policy will be harder to change. At that point, any piecemeal changes will come to a halt. Furthermore, unless there is substantial change in Cuba (along the lines indicated in Helms-Burton), the ingrained ideational factors will continue to work against the full normalization of U.S.-Cuba relations. Thus, though there is the possibility for significant policy change because of evolving perceptions, the identity at the root of the policy remains relatively stable. Furthermore, the logical pathway between the American self-image and isolationist policy, though much less entrenched than the exceptionalist identity itself, remains dominant.

Recent Developments in Canada's Cuba Policy

Canada's policy towards Cuba is equally influenced by ideational variables, though in its case these factors promote engagement with the island. While the relationship has ebbed and flowed since 1959, events occasionally challenge the Canadian identity in relation to Cuba policy and thereby erode some support for Canada's approach. This happened in the late 1990s.

During the mid-1990s, Canadian-Cuban relations seemed to be flourishing. At this point, high-level ministerial visits and other signs of good will characterized the relationship. In 1997 Ottawa and Havana signed the much celebrated Joint Declaration, which established cooperation between the two governments in a number of areas including human rights and good governance.[47] However, by the end of the 1990s, the amicable relationship between the two governments had waned. The initial fallout arose from the 1998 visit by Prime Minister Chrétien to Cuba.[48] This was the first visit at this level in three decades and was played up in the Canadian press. During that visit, Chrétien made a point of raising with Castro the case of four dissidents who were scheduled to be tried in Cuba. He pressed for an open trial and felt fairly confident that President Castro would follow through. His optimism proved unwarranted: the four were summarily tried and convicted in a closed trial.[49] This greatly embarrassed the prime minister and contributed to Canadians' sense of disillusionment with their efforts on the island. Castro's action was a direct challenge to the Canadian identity since Canada was not able to achieve the desired release even though the dialogue had occurred at the very highest levels. Canada immediately cooled relations. Ministerial visits were suspended.

Relations worsened during the subsequent 1999 Pan-American Games held in Winnipeg. Fidel Castro was angry about a number of issues surrounding the games. 'Never before had we seen such abusive and trickery actions in a Pan American sport competition,' he said. 'The whole purpose was to harass Cuba, to displace Cuba from the second position in order to benefit the host country and to discredit our sport.'[50] As noted earlier, he charged that Canada allowed sports scouts to promote the defection of Cuban athletes, withdrew medals from Cuban winners under false charges, and tried to disadvantage Cuban teams. Castro concluded his speech with the declaration that 'it is in that spirit that our athletes have been competing in the face of hostility, seduction and traps, on a field that has been turned into enemy ground. So, be it. The same has happened in other places where authorities from the North have been present. But, there are two in that North now; the one that was already there and another one further North.'[51] Lumping Canada and the United States together was not only the most serious insult that Fidel Castro could muster but was also a challenge to the Canadian identity. Relations had reached a new low.

At the same time, Canadian development programs were encountering difficulty in Cuba. A number of Cuban students attending Canadian universities defected while in Canada, creating tension between the two countries. Furthermore, the CIDA program to modernize the Cuban taxation system backfired as the Cuban government used it to hinder the establishment of private enterprise.[52] In 2000 Fidel Castro visited Canada for Pierre Trudeau's funeral but did not meet with the prime minister.

Canadian investors also began to shy away from Cuba. The *Wall Street Journal* reported as early as 1999 that 'for many Canadian companies as well as for the government, it's the morning after their love affair with the island nation.'[53] Archibald Ritter, a well-known expert on Canadian-Cuban relations at Carleton University, Ottawa, confirmed the *Journal* report in 2001 when he told an audience at the City University of New York that Canadian businesses were becoming more disillusioned with Cuba at that time.[54] Furthermore, when Cuba accepted the offer of cash-sale agricultural exports from the United States in 2001, Canadian agricultural sales to Cuba fell quite drastically, prompting concern about the future of Canadian trade with the island.

Cuba's exclusion from the 2001 Summit of the Americas meeting in Quebec City caused even more tension in the bilateral relationship. John Manley, the minister of foreign affairs, told the author at a meeting of the Canadian Society in New York in April 2001 that Cuba would not be invited to the Summit of the Americas because it was not a democracy. Manley's remarks at that meeting were published in Canadian newspapers. Fidel Castro was infuriated. He responded by encouraging the protesters at the Summit as well as criticizing Canada's treatment of the protesters. Challenging Canada's image of itself as a just and peaceful society, he stated: 'We have just seen the images of the brutal way in which Canadian authorities repressed the peaceful demonstrations ... They cannot sustain this unjust order imposed on humanity. We send you our total solidarity. Cuba supports you.'[55]

However, when the last member of the 'Group of Four' was released in August 2002, relations warmed. These four dissidents were the same four that Prime Minister Chrétien had spoken to Fidel Castro about on his visit to the island. DFAIT explains: 'In March 1999, Canada had suspended ministerial visits as a signal of our dissatisfaction with Cuba's response to our demarches on various human rights issues (including the sentencing of four prominent political dissidents, the "July Four"). In May 2002, the last of the four dissidents, Vladimiro Roca, was released.'[56] Thus, the release of the four was an important step in the relationship.

Public evidence of a friendlier attitude came in September 2002 during a CBC interview with the prime minister. During that interview, Chrétien emphasized that Canada had a 'normal' relationship with Cuba and criticized the American approach towards the island.[57] High-level visits were resumed. In November 2002 Denis Paradis, secretary of state for Latin America, Africa, and la Francophonie, went to Cuba to attend the Havana International Trade Fair. During that visit the secretary also inaugurated an exhibit honouring Pierre Trudeau.[58] The Department of Foreign Affairs and International Trade asserted, 'Denis Paradis visited Cuba in November 2002, the first ministerial visit in almost four years. Secretary of State Paradis' visit signals Canada's willingness to reinvigorate political dialogue with Cuban officials and to support Canadian interests in Cuba.'[59] In Cuba, Paradis explained: 'We should be encouraging as wide a dialogue as possible, comparing perspectives and values. The large numbers of Canadians that visit Cuba every year are testament to the affection between our two peoples and the importance of understanding each other better.'[60]

In addition, in March 2003, the Canadian embassy in Cuba held a photographic exposition entitled 'Canada-Cuba: A View over One Hundred Years.' The Department of Foreign Affairs and International Trade proclaimed that 'the images will cover the wide diversity of contacts between the two countries including political visits, commercial projects, development programs, cultural, scientific and educational exchanges and sporting activities.'[61] Canada was once again celebrating its friendship with Cuba.

Nevertheless, this warming trend came to a temporary halt in the spring of 2003 when the Cuban state initiated a repression of the dissident movement. According to the *Globe and Mail*: 'Foreign Affairs Minister Bill Graham summoned Cuba's ambassador to Canada to his office last night to express "extreme concern" over a dramatic crackdown on peaceful dissent by Fidel Castro's regime. The highly unusual move came after the sentencing of dozens of dissidents to prison terms of 12 to 27 years. Their trials had been brief and closed, some on charges of cooperating with the United States to oppose the Communist government.'[62] Ottawa could not let such a severe and public crackdown go unnoticed. Yet it was not enough to convince Canadians that isolation was the answer. Unlike the Europeans, the

Canadians did not impose sanctions against Cuba at this time, and after a short period relations returned to their 'normal' state.

Many expected relations between Canada and Cuba to encounter problems under the leadership of Stephen Harper. In 2006 there was speculation that 'Canada's historically friendly relationship with Cuba could see signs of stress as the Conservative government continues its pro-democracy foreign policy and the Communist country fosters closer links to countries like Iran and Venezuela.'[63] Under Harper, there certainly has been an increase in the rhetorical emphasis on human rights and democracy vis-à-vis Cuba. Maxime Bernier, Canada's minister of foreign affairs, gave a nod towards the Bush policy on Cuba in May 2008 when he 'congratulated' Cuba on their 'independence day.' The 20th of May is a date that Cubans do not recognize as their independence day but it is the one that Cuban exiles celebrate as such (the Bush administration called it 'Cuban Solidarity Day'). In his press release, Bernier stressed the strong ties between Canada and Cuba but also said that 'Canada continues to monitor developments in Cuba closely, and we are concerned about the plight of political prisoners, especially those suffering from poor health. It is our hope that recent shifts will open the way for the Cuban people to pursue a process of political and economic reform.'[64] The following year, Minister of State for the Americas Peter Kent ratcheted up the rhetoric, referring to Cuba as a 'dictatorship, any way you package it.'[65] In advance of his planned May 2009 visit to Havana, he announced that he would 'reinforce the message that the prime minister delivered to the Summit of the Americas, to encourage productive, constructive responses to the U.S. gesture.' He also publicly stated that he would 'stress again our encouragement of the release of political prisoners and the opening of institutions to democratic practices.'[66] This rhetoric, more characteristic of statements emanating from Washington than Ottawa, was met with a chilly silence in Havana. The Cuban state then abruptly 'postponed' Kent's visit to the island and Ottawa delayed issuing a visa for Cuba's minister of trade and investment.

Yet, despite this rhetoric, relations continue to remain on solid footing. Peter Kent's visit was quietly rescheduled and successfully conducted in November 2009. According to Peter McKenna and John Kirk, the 'apparent pause or drift in the Canada-Cuba diplomatic policy game [under Harper] should not be misconstrued as any significant rupture or downturn in official relations.'[67] Indeed, some people are disappointed that Prime Minister Harper has not criticized Cuba more directly. Ana Faya, a specialist at the Canadian Foundation for the Amercias (FOCAL), has written: 'Actually, during the Conservative Party's rule in Canada, I have seen an increase of Canadian business investments in Cuba. Ask Toronto-based mining and energy company Sherritt International.' She continued: 'And I haven't heard one single word coming from Ottawa about violations of human rights in the island, which are happening daily, or about the more than 200 political prisoners that somehow survive in Cuban jails, or about the recent break up by Havana's police and an organized mob of a peaceful demonstration by the Ladies in White near Revolution Square.'[68]

In fact, Harper has drawn on the same elements of the Canadian self-image stressed by Canadian governments for decades in describing his approach towards the region. For example, when signalling that his government was going to make relations with Latin America a priority, he made a point of distinguishing Canadian and American involvement in the hemisphere. In a speech given in Chile, Harper said: 'Canada's political structures differ substantially from those in the United States. Our cultural values and social models have also been shaped by unique forces and we've made our own policy choices to meet our own needs. We want our role in the hemisphere to reflect these differences while emphasizing the economic and political fundamentals necessary for progress. In other words, we want a role that reflects our commitment to open markets and free trade, to democratic values and accountable institutions, but also to our national identity, and our traditions of order and community values.'[69] Commenting on Canada's relationship with Cuba in May 2008, Cuba's first deputy foreign minister, Bruno Rodriguez Parrilla, said: 'If Canada could build their pattern of relations with the Latin American and Caribbean countries in the same styles, experiences, benchmarks as Canada does it with Cuba, in my view, would be excellent. Because relations between Canada and Cuba could be an excellent model.'[70] Thus, though Ottawa's policy towards Havana has evolved over time and become closer to the American approach, Ottawa has not responded to Cuban challenges to the Canadian self-image by adopting an isolationist posture – even in cases when other countries, such as those of the European Union, have imposed sanctions.

How much would changes in Cuba itself, independent of its relations with Canada or the United States, influence the relationships it has with these two North American states? The next section explores this question by addressing one of the most significant changes to take place within Cuba since 1959.

Changes in Cuba: From Fidel to Raúl Castro

In July 2006 Fidel Castro, about to undergo gastric surgery, temporarily gave up his governing authority to his brother, Raúl. The younger Castro continued to govern Cuba 'temporarily' until February 2008 when Fidel formally retired. Raúl Castro then became president of Cuba.

Since he assumed power, Raúl Castro has made a number of changes that have been viewed positively by the West. Cuba signed two UN human-rights covenants shortly after he became president of Cuba. Domestically, the younger Castro brother began with a significant reform of the Cuban agricultural sector, reducing the number of state-controlled farms, allotting land for private farms, and allowing farmers to sell directly to consumers. He has also allowed Cubans to stay in hotels that were earlier restricted to tourists and removed the ban on the private ownership of cellphones and computers. Much more significantly, in June 2008, he said that the Cuban state plans to abolish salary equality. Raúl Castro has modified the well-known Marxist slogan 'From each according to his ability, to each according to his need' to 'From each according to his ability, to each according to his work.'[71] However, in July 2008 he told Cubans that these reforms could be stalled because of the rising cost of food and oil around the globe.

Given that Washington has declared that the U.S. approach towards Cuba will not be altered until Havana initiates reforms, some might expect a significant shift in the American policy under these circumstances. In fact, the changes that took place in Cuba following the leadership transfer, though seemingly important, have not yet altered the U.S.-Cuba relationship. After the transfer of power in Cuba, George W. Bush claimed that 'all Cuba has done is replace one dictator with another.' When Raúl Castro initiated changes to the cellphone policy, Bush complained: 'If Raúl is serious about his so-called reforms, he will allow these phones to reach the Cuban people.' He then said: 'If the Cuban people can be trusted with mobile phones, they should be trusted to speak freely in public.'[72] Although President Obama has not made similar statements, his administration has not made much of the modifications within Cuba and indicates that further change is necessary for improved relations. Likewise, these changes have not led to any shift in Canadian policy either.

Foreign-Policy Impotence and Cuba

Cuba remains an island in many senses of the word. For five decades, the Cuban state has kept tight control over the country regardless of international events. Under Fidel Castro, Cuba survived as the only Warsaw Pact country in the western hemisphere, and Castro himself survived countless assassination attempts during that period; he survived the end of the Cold War and the death of the Soviet Union; he survived Helms-Burton; and he survived chaotic relations with various friends and enemies, including Canada and the United States, only to finally release his hold on power because of health issues. Furthermore, even though he is no longer Cuba's leader, Castro's vision of Cuba lives on.

It seems as though Cuba is relatively unaffected by international events and other countries' foreign policies. Just as Canadian-Cuban relations were warming, just as the embargo was under the most serious congressional attack in its history, just as Cuban Americans were becoming more moderate, Havana initiated the most serious crackdown on activists and journalists in years. The Cuban leadership blames the 2003 crackdown on the Bush team in Havana and Washington but this argument ignores the serious warming trend that was then under way in Miami and on Capitol Hill.

The repression elicited the expected reactions. Countries all over the globe expressed their opposition to the 2003 crackdown and cooled relations with Havana as a result. Yet it is clear that the Cuban government is much less concerned with other countries' policies towards Cuba than everyone else thinks. Fidel Castro came to power denouncing foreign intervention and he has apparently succeeded in making Cuba one of the most independent states on the globe. Neither the Canadian nor the American policy has been successful in altering the political landscape in Cuba. Thus, this study predicts that neither isolation nor engagement nor something in between will fundamentally change things in Cuba. Even the improbable use of force, similar to the U.S. invasion of Iraq, is unlikely to produce the desired transition to stable democracy. If Western style-democracy is in Cuba's future, it will have to come from within.

Summary and Theoretical Implications

This study began with the question why Canada and the United States have adopted such dramatically different approaches towards revolutionary Cuba. The contrasting policies are especially apparent in the post-Cold War environment as both countries claim to have the same end in mind – greater respect for democracy and human rights on the island – yet continue to employ different means. American policy contends that the best way to ensure change in Cuba is to isolate the current government. Canadians have taken the opposite approach, that engagement is the most effective means to promote democracy and human rights.

The most widely accepted explanations for both policies ignore ideational variables. The Cuban American community's influence over elections is presumed to explain, fully and simply, the U.S. approach. This explanation assumes that the community favours a hard-line, isolationist policy towards the Cuban homeland. It then contends that, because the Cuban American population is concentrated in Miami-Dade County in Florida (and to a lesser extent also in Jersey City, New Jersey), it has a disproportionate influence over elections, thus ensuring that its policy preferences are followed in Washington. Although the Canadian policy of engagement is not to the same degree attributed to a single monolithic cause, economic interests are seen as having considerable sway over this policy. This argument maintains that, because many American businesses are prevented from investing in or selling to the Cuban people, Canadian companies have an advantage and are keen to trade with Cuba. Thus, the Canadian government, wanting to support Canadian-Cuban trade, follows a policy of engagement.

This study has adopted a constructivist approach to this question, challenging both of the conventional explanations and examining the role of ideational factors such as identity, norms, and perceptions in the two policies. In doing so, it has demonstrated that the widely accepted explanations for the two policies are inadequate. Though each offers some insight into the respective bilateral relationships, they are incomplete. For example, the Cuban American electoral thesis cannot explain how the community first began to wield power when, at that time, they represented a very small, unorganized electoral base. The constructivist analysis shows that the community was given this power by Washington because its perceptions and policy preferences were directly in line with the views prevalent in Washington during that period. Furthermore, the fact that George W. Bush's policy towards Cuba became more hard line than that of the previous two administrations while the Cuban American community itself was growing more divided also reveals the incongruity between Cuba policy and the wishes of the community. As this chapter has shown, an isolationist platform is attracting less and less support among members of the Cuban American community. In sum, contrary to popular opinion, policy towards Cuba is not directed from Miami offices of the Cuban American National Foundation or the Cuban Liberty Council.

Similarly, the Canadian policy towards Cuba is not a sole reflection of economic interests and has far more to do with identity and perception than most scholars maintain. Canadian trade with the United States is far more important than any trade with Cuba. Canadians trade more in one day with the United States than they do in a whole year with Cuba. If trade was the main reason for Canada's policy towards Cuba, Ottawa would have adopted an isolationist policy decades ago.

This study has not just pointed out the weaknesses of the accepted explanations but has shown that ideational factors have significant independent explanatory power. Americans' belief in the natural superiority of the United States and their emphasis on the values of democracy and freedom, which they see as entailing greater rights as well as a commitment to corresponding duties in the hemisphere, have had a major influence on the way American policy makers conceptualize Cuba and the U.S.-Cuba relationship. This study argues that Americans, believing in their natural superiority in political and economic matters, and stressing the value of democracy and freedom, are affronted by what they perceive to be the total absence of democracy and freedom in Cuba. The United States believes it must take action in Cuba because it has a duty to promote democracy and freedom globally, and especially in the western hemisphere. Furthermore, Cuba has always been seen as 'special' because of its geographical and historical ties to the United States. U.S. policy suggests that the Cubans need American guidance even if they do not realize it. Thus, the United States feels a responsibility to ensure that democracy and freedom are in Cuba's future. In addition, since the Castro brothers are understood to be the root of the 'Cuba problem,' American policy has long reflected a determination to remove them from power. The very idea of working with the Cuban leadership is abhorrent to many people in Washington. The policy of isolation reflects this visceral reaction.

This does not mean that policy change becomes impossible. In fact, this chapter has shown that change, especially when it is facilitated by new perceptions that remain logically consistent with established identities, is entirely possible. This begs the following question: How are perceptions at all relevant if many different perceptions can reflect the same identity? Though identity itself is socially constructed and thus open to change, this book maintains that identities that have persisted over time become entrenched and thus are not easily or quickly changed. Still, since we construct our perceptions, we are capable of reconstructing them, and, though our perceptions reflect the way we see the world and our role in it, a particular identity can have many perceptions that are consistent with it. To be sure, while identity does not dictate a particular perception, it does put a limit on the range of perceptions likely to be adopted. In addition, once a perception about a particular topic is accepted, future perceptions tend to be consistent with it. The way we see the world ultimately dictates what we do. As a result, perceptions become key to policy formation. Though there is not a hard-and-fast line of causality between identity, a single perception, and a certain policy outcome, patterns of perceptions reinforce certain policy choices over others.

This pattern becomes the default and to break from it requires either a fundamental event that cannot be ignored or easily dismissed or a slow evolution of perceptions. This can help explain why the United States has continued to isolate Cuba long after many people outside the United States (and a significant number within it as well) think it is clear that the policy is the relic of an earlier era. Washington is unlikely to adopt fully the Canadian perception of Cuba or of Fidel Castro and Ottawa is unlikely to adopt the American view of the island since to do so would contest many elements within the two countries' self-images. Notions of what it means to be 'American' or 'Canadian' limit the range of perceptions that are likely to be widely adopted in each country. Yet gradual change is possible, especially when the evolving perceptions remain consistent with the prevalent identities.

The Canadian approach towards Cuba is as much rooted in identities and perceptions as the American one. This study argues that the

Canadian identity as a good international citizen and as distinct from the United States contributes to the Canadian policy of engagement. Canada's self-image includes an emphasis on international law, communication, dialogue, social justice, mediation, and maintaining a few key foreign policy legacies that speak to the country's independence in world affairs.

All these elements of the Canadian identity coalesce to reinforce perceptions and produce the Canadian policy towards Cuba. Ottawa's emphasis on communication and mediation help to construct a policy based on engagement. The importance given to international law and independence from the United States contributes to the Canadian opposition to Helms-Burton. The emphasis on sovereignty and social justice encourages empathy with Cuba, and the desire to be distinct from the United States also predisposes Ottawa to choose engagement over isolation. Lastly, Canadians see isolation as an inherently hostile policy, likely to lead to instability and international disorder. They believe that engagement in the Cuba case is compatible with peace and order.

This approach also helps us understand that we should expect tension when one state, either directly or indirectly, challenges another state's self-image. Although Canadian-Cuban relations have been traditionally friendly, the Cuban challenge to the Canadian identity in the late 1990s intensified the downturn in the relationship. By charging Canada with being just another 'United States' and refusing to heed the concerns about the Group of Four voiced directly by the prime minister, Cuba set up a challenge to the Canadian idea of itself both as distinct from the United States and as an international good citizen.

In short, the examination of identity and its related perceptions and norms offers an alternative way of making sense of U.S.-Cuba and Canada-Cuba relations. These two case studies reveal how ideational variables influence foreign policy and enable us to better understand international relations.

Theoretical Applications

Policy towards Cuba is only one example of the influence of ideational variables on foreign policy. For instance, the American exceptionalist identity, with its belief in the natural superiority of the United States and the political and economic inferiority of others, influences the idea that the United States has rights and duties above and beyond those of other states. This produces a missionary norm that the United States must 'assist' other states, particularly where democracy and freedom are concerned. Consequently, the American self-identity has wide implications for foreign policy. The ideas, values, perceptions, and norms associated with the exceptionalist identity that has portrayed Cuba as the absolute opposite of the United States, demonized Castro, and predisposed empathy with the hard-line Cuban American narrative of life in Cuba are probably influencing how the American foreign-policy establishment characterizes other leaders and states. Similar case studies of U.S. policy towards other 'rogue' states would prove illuminating. Nor is this true of the United States alone. A constructivist analysis of the Canadian preoccupation with establishing an international prohibition on anti-personnel landmines would be fruitful. Why did Canada take the lead on this issue? Initial research indicates that ideational variables can offer considerable insight into this question.

Further, the constructivist approach to the study of international relations is not limited to the Canadian and American contexts but can offer insight into any country's foreign policies. Indeed, given that Canadians and Americans can differ fundamentally both in their perceptions and in their policies even though they are mistaken for each other abroad, the constructivist approach may hold even greater promise for understanding foreign-policy differences among states that have less in common than these two North American neighbours. It would be interesting to investigate other incidents when one state's actions either directly or indirectly challenge another state's idea of itself.

This book has contended that we must look to the domestic and international environments to find the sources of identity. Most mainstream constructivist theorizing downplays or even dismisses the role of domestic sources of identity. I suggest that a broader analysis, which does not focus on one source of identity, will illuminate issues that would be otherwise obscured. We need to expand the ways we study international relations by borrowing from the research interests of comparative politics and foreign-policy analysis.

A more self-consciously constructivist approach to the study of foreign policy and comparative politics would also benefit these subfields. Though there has been a resurgence in the study of ideational variables in comparative politics, the dependent variables continue to be domestic politics or economic variables, most often political culture. This study has shown that the comparative politics' study of political culture is a rich literature. However, an accusation that haunted the national-characteristic studies in the 1940s and 1950s – that some of the research resorted to stereotypes – is often still levelled at today's cultural studies. By seeing ideational factors as not static, constructivism works against these types of characterizations.

Although they are accustomed to addressing domestic-level variables, including ideational factors, most foreign-policy studies that address these topics reflect their dialogue with comparative politics and thus focus primarily on political culture and public opinion. Adding constructivist analyses would not only broaden their research but would also open up the study of foreign policy to the influence of international ideational factors. Foreign-policy analysis, with its focus on the domestic determinants of foreign policy and the state, has tended to ignore the influence of international norms, values, and perceptions. The field would benefit, for example, from research on epistemic communities or studies of how international norms influence state behaviour in conjunction with its own studies of domestic- or state-level factors.

Lastly, opening up constructivist theorizing to the methods, concepts, and questions prevalent in comparative politics and foreign-policy studies will help answer some constructivist critics. For example, Jeffrey Checkel criticizes constructivism for not considering cases 'when "the dog doesn't bark," that is, where state identity/interests, in the presence of a norm, do not change.'[73] Comparative-politics studies that examine domestic-level attributes and foreign-policy analyses that take these variables and apply them to foreign policy can help constructivists point out why the 'dog doesn't always bark.' Also, a focus on domestic-level ideational variables addresses another, related, common criticism of constructivism – why 'social construction ... varies cross nationally.'[74] Domestic factors are most likely at the heart of much cross-national variation. Further, it is important to understand how international norms initially develop and that often requires an examination of domestic variables.

This study has only touched the surface of what borrowing from studies in comparative politics, international relations, and foreign policy can offer to our understanding of international interactions. Furthermore, many other disciplines such as psychology, anthropology, sociology, and economics are treasure troves of information regarding ideational variables. Research that borrows from these fields will further our comprehension of the role of ideational factors in foreign policy.

Notes

1. Introduction

1 PBS Online Newshour, 'Lloyd Axworthy,' 23 January 1997, http://www
   .pbs.org/newshour/bb/latin_america/january97/canada_1-23.html
   (accessed 24 June 2008). Although the Godfrey-Milliken Bill was not
   passed, its more serious counterpart, Bill C-54, did pass in an effort to
   neutralize the impact of the Helms-Burton Act.
2 It is important to remember that, especially in the post-Cold War era,
   policy makers in Ottawa and Washington often claim to have the same
   ends in mind – the transformation of Cuba into a more democratic state
   respectful of human rights. Yet the two have chosen opposite routes to
   that same goal, and, despite movements in both countries to adopt policies that resemble their neighbour's approach – in Canada some feel that
   the foreign-policy establishment has been naive and want a harsher line
   taken with Castro; in the United States there is a sustained movement to
   persuade the government to try engagement – the powers that be continue to be relatively confident that their policy is the best.
3 Minister of Public Works and Government Services Canada, *Canada-United
   States Accord on Our Shared Border – Update 2000* (Ottawa: Minister of Public
   Works and Government Services Canada 2000), http://www .dsp-psd
   .pwgsc.gc.ca/Collection/Ci51-95-2000E.pdf (accessed 30 July 2008).
4 Gordon Giffen, 'The Road to the Future: The U.S.-Canada Relationship,'
   in Gareth S. Seltzer and Edward P. Badovinac, eds., *The Empire Club of
   Canada Speeches 1997–1998* (Toronto: Empire Club Foundation 1998),
   415–29.
5 See the table and figure in Chapter 3 for more information on Canadian
   trade and investment in Cuba.
6 However, it is necessary to note that European scholars of international

relations did not abandon these factors. The rise of realism and behav-
ioural methods in the study of IR was never as popular in Europe. Thus,
when we speak of the 'return' of the study of culture and identity, we are
referring primarily to a change in North American scholarship.

7 See Richard Ned Lebow and Thomas Risse-Kappen, eds., *International
Relations Theory and the End of the Cold War* (New York: Columbia University Press 1996), for an excellent analysis of this topic.

8 In *World of Our Making: Rules and Rule in Social Theory and International
Relations* (Columbia: University of South Carolina Press 1989), Onuf was
building on the recent work of other scholars such as Friedrich Kratochwil and John Ruggie, who in 1986 stressed the necessity of 'opening
up the positivist epistemology to more interpretive strains.' See Friedrich
Kratochwil and John Ruggie, 'International Organization: A State of the
Art and an Art of the State,' *International Organization* 40, no. 4 (1986):
753–5. The work of Alexander Wendt, who brought attention to the
agent-structure question in 1987, and John Ruggie, who in 1989 criticized
IR for its inability to account for historical transformations, was an
important precursor to constructivism in international relations. See John
Ruggie, 'International Structure and International Transformation,' in
James N. Rosenau and Ernst-Otto Czempiel, eds., *Global Changes and
Theoretical Challenges* (Lexington, Ky.: Lexington Books 1989); Alexander
Wendt, 'The Agent-Structure Problem in International Relations Theory,'
International Organization 41, no. 3 (1987): 335–70; and Friedrich Kratochwil, *Rules, Norms, Decisions* (Cambridge: Cambridge University Press
1989). Similarly, in 1988, Robert Keohane argued for the creation of a
'reflective' research program in IR. These, and many other, works in
international relations in the mid- to late 1980s formed the basis of what
would soon become widely understood as constructivist thought. See
Robert Keohane's presidential address to the International Studies Association, published as *International Institutions and State Power* (Boulder,
Colo.: Westview Press 1989).

9 This quote is from Onuf's later summary of the argument he made in
World of Our Making. Nicholas Onuf, 'Constructivism: A User's Manual,'
in Vendulka Kubalkova, Nicholas Onuf, and Paul Kowert, eds., *International Relations in a Constructed World* (Armonk, N.Y.: ME Sharpe 1998), 59.

10 Alexander Wendt, 'Anarchy Is What States Make of It: The Social Construction of Power Politics,' *International Organization* 46 (spring 1992):
391–425.

11 Ibid., 396.

12 Ibid., 397.

13 Ibid., 398.

14 Ibid.

15 Ibid., 406.

16 Ibid., 158.

17 Ibid., 141.

18 Most of this literature also ignores why some international norms take hold in certain countries and not in others. Jeffery T. Checkel, A. Florini, and Andrew Moravcski have criticized constructivist scholarship on this point. See Andrew Moravcsik, 'Taking Preferences Seriously: A Liberal Theory of International Politics,' *International Organization* 51, no. 4 (1997): 513–53; Jeffery T. Checkel, 'Norms, Institutions, and National Identity in Contemporary Europe,' *International Studies Quarterly* 43 (1999): 83–114; and Ann Florini, 'The Evolution of International Norms,' *International Studies Quarterly* 40, no. 3 (1996): 363–90.

19 See Robert Hermanin, 'Identity, Norms, and National Security: The Soviet Foreign Policy Revolution and the End of the Cold War,' and Thomas U. Berger, 'Norms, Identity, and National Security in Germany and Japan,' in Peter J. Katzenstein, ed., *The Culture of National Security* (New York: Columbia University Press 1996). See also Peter Katzenstein, *Cultural Norms and National Security: Police and Military in Postwar Japan* (Ithaca, N.Y.: Cornell University Press 1996).

20 See Susan Fiske and Shelley E. Taylor, *Social Cognition* (Reading, Mass.: Addison-Wesley 1984), for a good review of the early literature on this topic.

21 Robert Jervis, *Perception and Misperception in International Politics* (Princeton, N.J.: Princeton University Press 1976).

22 Yaacov Y.I. Vertzberger, *The World in Their Minds: Information Processing, Cognition, and Perception in Foreign Policy Decisionmaking* (Stanford, Calif.: Stanford University Press 1990); and Glen Chafetz et al., 'Introduction: Tracing the Influence of Identity on Foreign Policy,' *Security Studies* 8, nos. 2 and 3 (1998–9): 7–22.

23 See, for example, Hazel Markus, Jeanne Smith, and Richard L. Moreland, 'Role of the Self-Concept in the Perception of Others,' *Journal of Personality and Social Psychology* 49, no. 6 (1985): 1494–512.

24 A.W. Combs and D. Snygg, *Individual Behavior: A Perceptual Approach to Behavior* (New York: Harper 1959). Quoted in Markus, Smith, and Moreland, 'The Role of the Self-Concept in the Perception of Others.'

25 Chafetz et al., 'Introduction: Tracing the Influence,' viii.

26 Vertzberger, *The World in Their Minds*, 348.

27 Chafetz et al., 'Introduction: Tracing the Influence,' viii.

28 Christopher Gelpi, 'Crime and Punishment: The Role of Norms in Crisis Bargaining,' *American Political Science Review* 91, no. 2 (1997): 339–60.

29 Alexander Wendt, *Social Theory of International Politics* (Cambridge: Cambridge University Press 1999), 186.

30 Philip Dur and Christopher Gilcrease, 'US Diplomacy and the Downfall of a Cuban Dictator: Machado in 1933,' *Journal of Latin American Studies* 34, no. 2 (2002): 259.

31 Quoted in Morris H. Morley, *Imperial State and Revolution: The United States and Cuba, 1952–1986* (Cambridge: Cambridge University Press 1987), 47.

32 John Scanlan and Gilburt Loescher, 'U.S. Foreign Policy, 1959–80: Impact on Refugee Flow from Cuba,' *Annals of the American Academy of Political and Social Science* 467, no. 1 (1983): 124.

33 See Wayne Smith, *The Closest of Enemies* (New York: W.W. Norton 1987), Chapter 8, for an interesting and informative discussion of the Mariel exodus.

34 'U.S. Policy: Balancing Strategic and Humanitarian Concerns,' *Congressional Digest* (March 1999): 73.

35 Hugh Thomas, *Cuba: The Pursuit of Freedom* (New York: Harper and Row 1971), 275, 537.

36 John Kirk, Peter McKenna, and Julia Sagebien, *Back in Business: Canada-Cuba Relations after 50 Years* (Ottawa: FOCAL [Canadian Foundation for the Americas] 1995), 7.

37 James Rochlin, *Discovering the Americas: The Evolution of Canadian Foreign Policy towards Latin America* (Vancouver: UBC Press 1994), 238. For more information on the early history of the Canada-Cuba relationship, see also Hal Klepak, 'Canada, Cuba, and Latin America: A Paradoxical Relationship,' in Robert Wright and Lana Wylie, eds., *Our Place in the Sun: Canada and Cuba in the Castro Era* (Toronto: University of Toronto Press 2009).

38 For more detail on Canada's relations with Batista and early opinions about Fidel Castro's rebel movement, see Don Munton and David Vogt, 'Inside Castro's Cuba: The Revolution and Canada's Embassy in Havana,' in Wright and Wylie, eds., *Our Place in the Sun.*

39 Not wanting to cause any undue tension with Cuba, Castro was eventually invited to visit Ottawa after the conclusion of his trip to the United States. In the end, Castro did come to Canada but he restricted his visit to Montreal, his representatives claiming that problems in Cuba forced him to cut his trip short. See Robert Wright, *Three Nights in Havana: Pierre Trudeau, Fidel Castro and the Cold War World* (Toronto: HarperCollins 2007), 25.

40 Documents on Canadian External Relations, Volume #26–466, Chapter X,

Latin America Part 2, Cuba Section, A Fidel Castro et le Gouvernement Révoltionnaire, 466, DEA/10224–40, Secretary of State for External Affairs to Ambassador in Cuba, Despatch D-214, Ottawa, 25 September 1959, http://www.international.gc.ca/department/history-histoire/dcer/details-en.asp?intRefid=11284 (accessed 13 July 2009).

41 Knowlton Nash, *Kennedy and Diefenbaker: Fear and Loathing across the Undefended Border* (Toronto: McClelland and Stewart 1990).

42 Kirk, McKenna, and Sagebien, *Back in Business*, 66.

43 James Guy, 'The Growing Relationship of Canada and the Americas,' *International Perspectives* (July–August 1977): 6.

44 U.S. Trade and Economic Council, 'Foreign Investment and Cuba,' http://www.cubatrade.org (accessed 5 January 2003). See also Chapter 3 in this volume.

45 Canada, Department of Foreign Affairs and International Trade, 'Canada-Cuba Relations,' http://www.dfait-maeci.gc.ca/latinamerica/cubarela-tions-en.asp (accessed 23 January 2002).

2. The Exceptionalist and the Cuban Other

1 Seymour Martin Lipset, *American Exceptionalism: A Double-Edged Sword* (New York: W.W. Norton 1996).

2 John L. O'Sullivan, 'On Manifest Destiny,' in J. and H.G., Publishers, 'The Great Nation of Futurity,' *United States Democratic Review* 6, no. 23 (1839): 426–30, http://www.mtholyoke.edu/acad/intrel/osulliva.htm (accessed 7 March 2003).

3 State Department's Office of the Historian, 'National Security Affairs; Foreign Economic Policy,' *U.S. Department of State* 1 (1950).

4 Madeleine K. Albright, Secretary of State, 'Sustaining Democracy in the Twenty-First Century' (Speech delivered at Johns Hopkins University, Washington, D.C., 18 January 2000), http://www.secretary.state.gov /www/statements/2000/000118.html (accessed 30 April 2003).

5 President George W. Bush, 'State of the Union' (Speech delivered at the U.S Capitol, Washington, D.C., 28 January 2003), http://www.white-house.gov/news/releases/2003/01/20030128-19.html (accessed 16 March 2003).

6 See Howard J. Wiarda, *American Foreign Policy: Actors and Processes* (New York: HarperCollins College Publishers 1999), for a discussion of the myriad number of different government agencies involved in the construction of foreign policy.

7 See, for example, Christopher A. Vaughan, 'Cartoon Cuba: Race, Gender

and Political Opinion Leadership in *Judge*, 1898,' *African Journalism Studies* 24, no. 2 (2003): 195–217.

8 William McKinley, quoted in Michael H. Hunt, *Ideology and US Foreign Policy* (New Haven, Conn.: Yale University Press 1987), 38.

9 U.S. Congress, *In Support of an American Empire*, 56th Cong., 1st sess., 9 January 1900, 704, quoted in Stephen W. Twing, *Myths, Models, and U.S. Foreign Policy: The Cultural Shaping of Three Cold Warriors* (Boulder, Colo.: Lynne Rienner Publishers 1998), 22.

10 Woodrow Wilson, 'The Ideals of America' (1902), quoted in David Hollinger and Charles Capper, eds., *The Liberal Intellectual Tradition* (New York: Oxford University Press 2001).

11 Condoleezza Rice, Secretary of State, Chair, 'Report of the Commission for Assistance to a Free Cuba,' 10 July 2006, http://www.cafc.gov/rpt/ (accessed 22 July 2008).

12 Polling the Nations (1986 through 2001), *Portrait of America* (Matthews, N.C.: Rasmussen Research 2000).

13 U.S. Department of State, 'Toward a Democratic Cuba' (Speech by President George W. Bush, Washington, D.C., 13 July 2001), http://www.usinfo.state.gov/regional/ar/us-cuba/ (accessed 20 August 2001).

14 How Cubans perceive the United States is also important. However, that is beyond the scope of this work.

15 U.S. House of Representatives, 'Cuban Liberty and Democratic Solidarity (*Libertad*) Act of 1996,' PL 104–14, http://www.usinfo.state.gov /regional/ar/us-cuba/libertad.htm (accessed 26 August 2001).

16 Foreign and Commonwealth Office, 'Creating Stronger and Better Relations with Cuba, April 2, 2003,' United Kingdom Parliament, Publications and Records, http://www.fco.gov.uk/en/newsroom/latest-news/? view=News&id=1559096 (accessed 31 July 2008).

17 Ibid.

18 Dante Fascell, Human Rights in Cuba: Hearings before the Subcommittees on Human Rights and International Organizations and on Western Hemisphere Affairs of the Committee on Foreign Affairs, House of Representatives, 98th Cong., 2nd sess., 27 June 1984, 2.

19 Rice, 'Report of the Commission for Assistance to a Free Cuba.'

20 U.S. Interests Section, Havana, 'Basic Policy: To Support Peaceful Change from within, January 1998,' Embassy of the United States of America, http://www.usembassy.state.gov/havana/wwwh0012.html (accessed 24 March 2003).

21 U.S. Senate, 'America's Free Trade Act, January 22, 2001,' Library of Con-

gress, http://www.thomas.loc.gov/cgi-bin/query/D?c107:11:./temp
/~c107usOUxu (accessed 22 March 2001).

22 U.S. House of Representatives, 'Cuban Liberty and Democratic Solidarity
(*Libertad*) Act of 1996.' The Helms-Burton Act tightened the embargo.
Among other things, it expanded the categories of parties that were
· targets of sanctions, including foreign individuals and companies; set out
the conditions that Cuba must meet before the United States can re-
engage with Cuba, including the ouster of Fidel and Raúl Castro; and, by
codifying regulations, removed the president's power to alter U.S.-Cuba
policy significantly.

23 Ibid.

24 Daniel W. Fisk, 'Cuba in US Policy: An American Congressional Perspective,' quoted in Heather N. Nicol, ed., *Canada, the US and Cuba: Helms-
Burton and Its Aftermath* (Kingston, Ont.: Centre for International Relations, Queen's University, 1999), 46.

25 Theodore Roosevelt, 'The Roosevelt Corollary to the Monroe Doctrine'
(Annual Message to Congress, 6 December 1904), http://www.uiowa.edu
/~c030162/Common/Handouts/POTUS/TRoos.html (accessed 21
March 2001).

26 Ibid.

27 Jorge Dominguez makes the argument that U.S.-Cuba policy is a continu-
ation of a pattern going back to the Monroe Doctrine. See 'US-Cuban
Relations: From the Cold War to the Colder War,' *Journal of Interamerican
Studies and World Affairs* 39, no. 3 (1997): 49–73.

28 Confidential interview with senior U.S. government official, 2000.

29 Louis A. Perez, Jr, *Cuba: Between Reform and Revolution* (Oxford: Oxford
University Press 1988), 109.

30 Leland Jenks, *Our Cuban Colony: A Study in Sugar* (New York: Arno Press
1970), 13.

31 United States Department of State, *Foreign Relations of the United States,
Statement of 11 April 1898* (Washington, D.C.: Government Printing Office
1899), 757.

32 Juan Del Aguila, 'Development, Revolution, and Decay in Cuba,' in
Howard Wiarda and Harvey Kline, eds., *Latin American Politics and Development* (Boulder, Colo.: Westview Press 1996), 378.

33 Luis E. Agular, 'Cuba c. 1860–1930,' in Leslie Bethell, ed., *Cuba: A Short
History* (Cambridge: Cambridge University Press 1993), 43.

34 Thomas G. Paterson, *Contesting Castro: The United States and the Triumph
of the Cuban Revolution* (New York: Oxford University Press 1994),
5.

35 Ibid., 14.

36 Ibid.

37 Elihu Root, quoted in ibid., 5.

38 José Martí, 'Congreso Internacional en Washington (II),' *La Nación (Buenos Aires 6)* (Havana: Editorial Ciencias Sociales 1975), 56–62, quoted in Rafael Hernández, 'Cuba and the United States: Political Values and Interests in a Changing International System,' in Jorge Dominguez and Rafael Hernández, eds., *U.S.-Cuban Relations in the 1990s* (Boulder, Colo.: Westview Press 1989), 34.

39 David Dent, *The Legacy of the Monroe Doctrine* (Westport, Conn.: Greenwood Press 1999), 125.

40 U.S. Department of State, Bureau of Public Affairs 6 (1962), quoted in Jutta Weldes, 'The Cultural Production of Crisis: U.S. Identity and Missiles in Cuba,' in *Cultures of Insecurity: States, Communities, and the Production of Danger* (Minneapolis: University of Minnesota Press 1999), 43.

41 Fisk, 'Cuba in US Policy,' 46.

42 U.S. House of Representatives, Cuban Liberty and Democratic Solidarity (*Libertad*) Act of 1996, Report 104–68, sec. 201, 1 March 1996.

43 Ibid., sec. 206.

44 Office of the Press Secretary, 'Fact Sheet: Commission for the Assistance of a Free Cuba,' White House, http://www.whitehouse.gov/news /releases/2003/12/20031208-8.html (accessed 31 August 2008).

45 Colin L. Powell, 'Foreword,' Report on the Commission for Assistance for a Free Cuba, http://www.cafc.gov/rpt/ (accessed 22 July 2008).

46 Rice, 'Report of the Commission for Assistance to a Free Cuba.'

47 Jim Lobe, 'Learn from Cuba, Says World Bank,' Inter Press Service (IPS), 1 May 2001, http://www.hartford-hwp.com/archives/43b/185.html (accessed 2 May 2007).

48 Neta C. Crawford, 'The Passion of World Politics: Propositions on Emotion and Emotional Relationships,' *International Security* 24, no. 4 (2000): 116–56.

49 Fidel Castro, 'Appearance of Castro before the Press' (Interview conducted in Cuba, 19 February 1959), http://www.lanic.utexas.edu/project /castro/db/1959/19590219.html (accessed 22 July 2008).

50 Fidel Castro, 'Castro Denounces Imperialism and Colonials at the United Nations' (Speech delivered at UN General Assembly, Washington D.C., 26 August 1960), http://www.lanic.utexas.edu/project/castro/db/1960 /19600926.html (accessed 22 July 2008).

51 Jeffrey Davidow, 'The U.S. Vision: Cuba and Hemisphere Policy' (Remarks to the American Enterprise Institute and Friedrich Hayek Uni-

versity, Cuba Vision Series, in Washington D.C., 28 July 1997),
http://www.state.gov/www/regions/wha/970728-davidow.html
(accessed 19 April 1999).

52 Dwight D. Eisenhower, *July 6, 1960, The Eisenhower Diaries*, Robert H.
Ferrell, ed. (New York: W.W. Norton 1981).

53 Howard W. Odum, 'Survey Collection: Harris/ 1643, IRSS Study
Number: S1643,' Institute for Research in Social Science, University of
North Carolina at Chapel Hill, http://www.veblen.irss.unc.edu
(accessed 17 July 2001).

54 Gallup Poll, 'Favorability: People in the News,' Gallup, Inc., http://www
.galluppoll.com/content/?ci=1618&pg=1, and Gallup Poll, 'Cuba,'
Gallup, Inc., http://www.galluppoll.com/content/?ci=1630&pg=1
(accessed 21 June 2007).

55 Susan Eckstein, 'The Clash between Cuban Immigrant Cohorts,' in
Mauricio A. Font, ed., *Cuba Today: Continuity and Change since the 'Periodo
Especial'* (New York: Bildner Center for Western Hemisphere Studies, City
University of New York, 2004), http://www.web.gc.cuny.edu/dept
/bildn/publications/cubatodaybook.pdf (accessed 21 May 2008).

56 International-relations theorists have explored the importance of
'common-sense' notions for the conduct of international relations. Many
of these borrow from Clifford Geertz's writings on culture. Geertz,
describing culture as 'stories we tell about ourselves,' argues that these
stories could be both conscious and unconscious. What we take as
'common sense' are unconscious, taken-for-granted assumptions. Yet what
is understood as common sense, Geertz and others point out, differs significantly between cultures. See Clifford Geertz, *Local Knowledge: Further
Essays in Interpretive Anthropology* (New York: Basic Books 1983).

57 María de los Angeles Torres, *In the Land of Mirrors: Cuban Exile Politics
in the United States* (Ann Arbor: University of Michigan Press 2001),
113.

58 Ibid., 182.

59 Jorge Dominguez, 'Cooperating with the Enemy? U.S. Immigration Policies toward Cuba,' in Christopher Mitchell, ed., *Western Hemisphere Immigration and United States Foreign Policy* (University Park: Pennsylvania
State University Press 1992), 31–88.

60 Peter Schwab, *Cuba: Confronting the U.S. Embargo* (New York: St Martin's
Press 1999), 137.

61 Patrick J. Haney and Walt Vanderbush, 'The Role of Ethnic Interest
Groups in U.S. Foreign Policy: The Case of the Cuban American National
Foundation,' *International Studies Quarterly* 43, no. 2 (1999): 348.

62 Cuban Information Archives, DOCUMENT 0146a, 'Broadcasting to Cuba Radio Martí & C.A.N.F. 1960-1990 part 1,' http://www.cuban-exile.com/doc_126-150/doc0146a.html (accessed 23 July 2009).

63 Jay Nordlinger, 'Meet the Diaz-Balarts: A Couple of Castro's "Nephews" – in Congress (Lincoln and Mario Diaz-Balart),' *National Review*, 10 March 2003.

64 Walt Vanderbush, 'Exiles and the Marketing of U.S. Policy,' *Foreign Policy Analysis* 5 (2009): 287–306.

65 Emanuel Adler and Peter Haas, 'Conclusion: Epistemic Communities, World Order, and the Creation of a Reflective Research Program,' *International Organization* 46, no. 1 (1992): 379.

66 Cuban American National Foundation, 'About the Cuban American National Foundation,' http://www.canfnet.org/About/aboutmain.htm (accessed 17 August 2001).

67 See information about Jorge Mas Canosa at Cuban American National Foundation, 'Who Founded CANF?' http://www.canf.org/ingles/about-CANF/jorge-mas-canosa.htm (accessed 17 August 2001).

68 Ernesto Betancourt, quoted in Carla Anne Robbins, 'Dateline Washington: Cuban-American Clout,' *Foreign Policy* 88 (1992): 165.

69 Confidential interviews with senior U.S. government officials, 1999, 2000.

70 Francisco 'Pepe' Hernandez, 'Send U.S. Funds Directly to Cuba's Democratic Opposition,' Cuban American National Foundation, 15 May 2008, http://www.canf1.org/cgi-bin/artman/search.cgi?action=search&page=1&perpage=5&template=articleLists/categor yIndex.html&categoryNum=33 (accessed 15 May 2008).

71 Angeles Torres, *In the Land of Mirrors*, 147.

72 Haney and Vanderbush, 'The Role of Ethnic Interest Groups,' 348.

73 Ibid., 347.

74 Angeles Torres, *In the Land of Mirrors*, 59.

75 Confidential interview with senior government official, 2000.

76 Confidential interview with senior government official, 1999.

77 For more information on Elían Gonzalez, see discussion in Chapter 5.

78 Confidential interview with senior U.S. government official, 2000.

79 Stanley Meisler, 'U.N. Rebuffs U.S. on Cuba Embargo-Trade: Allies Desert Washington in 59–3 General Assembly Vote That Urges Lifting of Latest Restrictions. American Interference in Foreign Subsidiaries Is Alleged,' Los Angeles *Times*, 25 November 1992.

80 Neil MacFarquhar, 'U.S. Embargo on Cuba Again Finds Scant Support at U.N.,' New York *Times*, 29 October 2009.

81 United Nations, Press Release GA/9814, 'For Ninth Successive Year, General Assembly Calls for End of United States Embargo against Cuba,' http://www.un.org/News/Press/docs/2000/20001109.ga9814.doc.html (accessed 31 August 2008).

82 Confidential interview with senior U.S. government official, 2000.

83 Paul Koring, 'Axworthy, Helms Aide Slug It out on Cuba,' *Globe and Mail*, 7 March 1998.

84 These measures included the resumption of direct charter flights between the United States and Cuba, allowing Cuban Americans to send up to $300 four times a year to their families in Cuba, and the facilitation of the sale of medicines to Cuba. See President William Clinton's 'Statement on Cuba,' *Administration of William J. Clinton, 1998* (20 March 1998), 475.

3. The Independent International Citizen and the Other Cuba

1 See Robert Wright, *Three Nights in Havana: Pierre Trudeau, Fidel Castro and the Cold War World* (Toronto: HarperCollins 2007), for an engaging account of Prime Minister Pierre Trudeau's historic three-day visit to Havana in 1976.

2 Documents on Canadian External Relations, Volume 27 #639, Chapter IX, Latin America, Part 1, Cuba 639, J.G.D./VI/848/C962, Minister of Citizenship and Immigration to Prime Minister, Ottawa, 10 November 1960, http://www.international.gc.ca/department/history-histoire/dcer/details-en.asp?intRefid=13193 (accessed 13 July 2009).

3 Canada, Department of Foreign Affairs and International Trade (DFAIT), 'Canada-Cuba Relations,' http://www.dfait-maeci.gov.ca/latinamerica/cubarelations-e.asp (accessed 23 January 2002).

4 DFAIT, 'Canada's Relations with Cuba,' http//www.dfait.maeci.gc.ca/latin/cuba/81600-e.htm (accessed 13 June 2008).

5 DFAIT, 'Canada-Cuba Joint Declaration Implementation Checklist.' Provided to the author by David Kilgour, secretary of state (Latin America and Africa), Ottawa (October 1999).

6 'Cuban Trial Step Backward, Axworthy Says,' *Globe and Mail*, 3 March 1999.

7 PBS, 'Castro: 1999 on PanAm Games' ('Excerpts from speech delivered by Dr. Fidel Castro, President of the Republic of Cuba, in Cienfuegos, Cuba, July 26, 1999'), http://www.pbs.org/stealinghome/sport/castro99b.html (accessed 31 January 2002).

8 Archibald Ritter, 'Cuba Project' (Speech delivered to the City University of New York's Queens College and Graduate School, 2001).

9 Confidential interview with senior Canadian government official, 2000.

10 Lloyd Axworthy, quoted in Joe Jockel and Joel Sokolsky, 'Lloyd Axworthy's Legacy,' *International Journal* 56, no. 1 (2000–1): 2.

11 Ibid., 2.

12 Canadian-American Committee, 'Canada's Trade with Cuba and Canadian-American Relations' (6 February 1961), 6. The Canadian-American Committee was a joint committee of the Private Planning Association of Canada and the National Planning Association, USA, which included leaders of big business in both countries.

13 See, for example, a letter from the Canadian ambassador in Havana: Documents on Canadian External Relations, Volume 27 #643, Chapter IX, Latin America Part 1, Cuba 643, DEA/288–40, Ambassador in Cuba to Secretary of State for External Affairs, Despatch no. D-937, Havana, 13 December 1960, Canadian Position in Cuba, http://www.international .gc.ca/department/history-histoire/dcer/details-en.asp?intRefid=13197 (accessed 13 July 2009).

14 Ibid., 7.

15 Confidential interviews with senior Canadian government officials, 1999.

16 Luke Fisher et al., 'Canada Protests Controversial Bill,' *Maclean's*, 18 March 1996.

17 *Globe and Mail*, 2 May 1998.

18 Gillian McGillivray, 'Trading with the "Enemy": Canadian-Cuban Relations in the 1990s,' *Cuba Briefing Paper Series*, no. 15 (December 1997): 1.

19 John Kirk and Peter McKenna, *Canada-Cuba Relations: The Other Good Neighbor Policy* (Gainesville, Fla.: University of Florida Press 1997), 173.

20 Oficina Nacional de Estadísticas República de Cuba, 'Intercambio comercial de mercancías de países seleccionados agrupados por áreas geográficas, Sector Externo,' http://www.one.cu/aec2006/anuariopdf2006/capitulo7/VII.4.pdf (accessed 1 July 2008).

21 Canadian International Development Agency, 'Programming Framework Canadian Cooperation Program in Cuba,' http://www.acdi-cida.gc.ca /CIDAWEB/acdicida.nsf/En/NIC-223122217-NDJ (accessed 28 June 2008).

22 Statistics Canada, 'Latin America and the Caribbean: Exports and Imports: December 1996' (Statistics Canada, Merchandise Trade Statistics, May 1997). Figures in Canadian dollars.

23 Archibald R.M. Ritter, 'Canadian-Cuban Economic Relations: Past, Present, and Prospective,' in Robert Wright and Lana Wylie, eds., *Our*

   Place in the Sun: Canada and Cuba in the Castro Era (Toronto: University of
   Toronto Press 2009).
24 DFAIT, *Cuba: A Guide for Canadian Business* (Ottawa: Minister of Supply
   and Services, July 1997), 5.
25 Industry Canada, 'Canadian Trade by Industry,' Trade Data Online,
   http://www.ic.gc.ca/sc_mrkti/tdst/tdo/tdo.php?lang=30&product-
   Type=NAICS (accessed 28 June 2008).
26 DFAIT, 'Canada-United States: Trade and the Economy,'
   http://www.dfait-maeci.gc.ca/can-am/menu-en.asp?mid=1&cat=1029
   (accessed 4 April 2003).
27 Industry Canada, 'Canadian Trade by Industry.' Figures in Canadian
   dollars.
28 David Campbell, *Writing Security: The United States Foreign Policy and the
   Politics of Identity* (Minneapolis: University of Minnesota Press 1998).
29 See, for example, Gad Horowitz, 'Tories, Socialists, and the Demise of
   Canada,' *Canadian Dimension* 2, no. 4 (1965): 12–15; William Christian and
   Colin Campbell, *Political Parties and Ideologies in Canada*, 3rd ed. (Toronto:
   McGraw-Hill Ryerson 1990); and Denis Stairs, 'The Political Culture of
   Canadian Foreign Policy,' *Canadian Journal of Political Science* 15 (December 1982): 667–90.
30 See Horowitz, 'Tories, Socialists, and the Demise of Canada,' and 'Conservatism, Liberalism, and Socialism in Canada: An Interpretation,' *Canadian Journal of Economics and Political Science* 32, no. 2 (1966): 143–71. See
   also Louis Hartz, ed., *The Founding of New Societies* (New York: Harcourt,
   Brace and World 1964).
31 Cranford Pratt, 'Canada's Development Assistance: Some Lessons from
   the Last Review,' *International Journal* 49, no. 1 (1993–4): 121. This quote is
   also used to make a similar point in Paul Gecelovsky and Tom Keating,
   'Liberal Internationalism for Conservatives: The Good Governance Initiative,' in Nelson Michaud and Kim Richard Nossal, eds., *Diplomatic Departures: The Conservative Era in Canadian Foreign Policy, 1984–93* (Vancouver:
   UBC Press 2001), 194.
32 DFAIT, 'Canada's Foreign Policy: Principles and Priorities for the Future,'
   Report of the Special Joint Committee Reviewing Canadian Foreign Policy
   (November 1994), 1.
33 'Canada's World Poll,' 9–22 January 2008, Environics Research,
   http://www.canadasworld.ca/quizzesa/pollresu (accessed 13 July 2009).
34 The Pearson Peacekeeping Centre sponsors many of these type of educational events. See Pearson Peacekeeping Centre, 'Think about Peace,'
   http://www.thinkaboutpeace.ca/en/winners_en.html, and 'Welcome,'

http://www.peaceoperations.org/ (accessed 21 July 2008). I would like to thank Lynn Rider for describing the Ontario high school curriculum.

35 DFAIT, 'Backgrounder: Canada and Peacekeeping,' http://www.dfait-maeci.gc.ca/peacekeeping/back-e.asp1/23/02 (accessed 23 January 2002).

36 David Kilgour, 'Canada's Peacekeeping Role: Then and Now,' Remarks by David Kilgour, MP for Edmonton Southeast, 'Picking up the Peaces' (Speech Delivered at the Shell Canada Lecture Theatre, Edmonton, University of Alberta International Week 2004, 26 January 2004), http://www.david-kilgour.com/mp/Peacekeeping%20U%20of%20A .htm (accessed 20 January 2008).

37 DFAIT, 'A Dialogue on Foreign Policy: A Better Canada, A Better World,' http://www.foreign-policy-dialogue.ca/en/discusspaper/index.html (accessed 4 April 2003).

38 Ibid.

39 DFAIT, 'Canada's Relations with Cuba.' Emphasis added.

40 Paul Knox, 'PM Uses Cuban TV to Push Trade Links,' *Globe and Mail*, 27 April 1998.

41 PBS Online, 'Lloyd Axworthy,' NewsHour, 23 January 1997, http://www .pbs.org/newshour/bb/latin_america/january97/canada_1-23.html (accessed 3 April 2003).

42 Ibid.

43 Paul Koring, 'Axworthy, Helms Aide Slug It out on Cuba,' *Globe and Mail*, 7 March 1998.

44 Lloyd Axworthy, quoted in Peter M. Boehm, ambassador and permanent representative of Canada to the Organization of American States, 'Notes for a Speech to the Annual Meeting of the Cuban Committee for Democracy,' Miami, 12 September 1998, http://www.dfait-maeci.gc.ca/oas /oas04d-e.htm (accessed 23 January 2002).

45 DFAIT, 'Notes for an Address by the Honourable Christine Stewart, Secretary of State (Latin America and Africa)' (Speech delivered to the 26th General Assembly of the Organization of American States, Panama City, Panama, 3 June 1996), http://www.w01.international.gc.ca/minpub /PublicationContentOnly.asp?publication_id= 376997&Language= E&MODE=CONTENTONLY&Local=False (accessed 16 August 2007).

46 Joe Clarke, quoted in Kirk and McKenna, *Canada-Cuba Relations*, 134.

47 This approach has its risks, at times angering both the Cubans and the Americans.

48 U.S. Department of State, 'Secretary of State Madeleine K. Albright and Canadian Foreign Minister Axworthy: Remarks in Press Briefing' (speech

delivered in Ottawa, 10 March 1998), http://www.secretary.state.gov
/www/statements/1998/980310a.html (accessed 22 February 2002).

49 Michelle Collins, 'Canadian Companies Hit A Snag in Cuba,' *Embassy*, 10
December 2008.

50 Anglican Church of Canada, 'Resolution A280: Cuba,' http://www.angli-
can.ca/gs2001/rr/resolutions/resolution.php?res+a280 (accessed 22 February 2002).

51 In a television commercial for Molson's now known as 'the Rant,' Joe
Canada proudly shouts: 'I have a Prime Minister, not a President. I speak
English and French, NOT American … I believe in peace keeping, NOT
policing. DIVERSITY, NOT assimilation … CANADA IS THE SECOND LARGEST
LANDMASS! THE FIRST NATION OF HOCKEY! AND THE BEST PART OF NORTH
AMERICA! MY NAME IS JOE! AND I AM CANADIAN!' View the commercial online
at Molson Canada, 'I Am Canadian,' YouTube, http://www.youtube.com
/watch?v=BRI-A3vakVg (accessed 26 January 2008).

52 Master Corporal Frank Misztal, 'I am Canadian,' Canadian Peacekeeper's
Home Page, http://www.peacekeeper.ca/stories3.html#17 (accessed 11
July 2007).

53 Documents on Canadian External Relations, Volume 27 # 638, Chapter IX,
Latin America Part 1, Cuba 638.DEA/2444–40, Ambassador in Argentina
to Secretary of State for External Affairs, Despatch no. 53, Buenos Aires,
10 November 1960, http://www.international.gc.ca/department/history-
histoire/dcer/details-en.asp?intRefid=13192 (accessed 14 July 2009).

54 Though Cuba was not mentioned in this memo, it convinced Diefenbaker
not to follow the American lead on many issues. Cuba soon became a
sore point in the bilateral relationship and eventually developed into a
symbol of Canadian independence.

55 Evidence that Diefenbaker linked the Rostow memo with U.S. pressure
over Cuba appears in H. Basil Robinson's notes in *Diefenbaker's World*. He
recounts an incident in January 1962 when Kennedy adviser Arthur
Schlesinger complained about Canadian policy towards Cuba. Robinson
writes that this 'reminded him [Diefenbaker] of Rostow's "pushing" at
time of Kennedy visit to Ottawa.' Two days later, Robinson writes that 'I
think Schlesinger's indiscretion a few days ago solidified PM's views
against moving any closer to the US on Cuba policy.' See *Diefenbaker's
World: A Populist in Foreign Affairs* (Toronto: University of Toronto Press
1989), 246.

56 Denis Molinaro, 'Calculated Diplomacy: John Diefenbaker and the
Origins of Canada's Cuba Policy,' in Wright and Wylie, eds., *Our Place in
the Sun*.

57 See Knowlton Nash, *Kennedy and Diefenbaker: Fear and Loathing across the Undefended Border* (Toronto: McClelland and Stewart 1990), for a detailed discussion of the relationship between the two leaders.

58 Charles Ritchie, *Storm Signals: More Undiplomatic Memories, 1962–1971* (Toronto: Macmillan 1983), 16–17, quoted in Kirk and McKenna, *Canada-Cuba Relations*, 41.

59 J.L Granatstein and Robert Bothwell, *Pirouette: Pierre Trudeau and Canadian Foreign Policy* (Toronto: University of Toronto Press 1990), 195.

60 James Guy, 'The Growing Relationship of Canada and the Americas,' *International Perspectives* (July–August, 1977): 6. See also Wright, *Three Nights in Havana*, for an excellent discussion of Trudeau's approach towards Cuba and his relationship with Fidel Castro. For a summary of the cooling of the relationship caused by Cuba's involvement in Angola, see Greg Donaghy and Mary Halloran, 'Viva el pueblo cubano: Pierre Trudeau's Distant Cuba, 1968–78,' in Wright and Wylie, eds., *Our Place in the Sun*.

61 Confidential interview with former Canadian embassy official, Ottawa, October 1999.

62 André Ouellet, 'Canadian Foreign Policy,' House of Commons *Debates*, 35th Parliament, 1st sess., 15 March 1994, 2259.

63 Confidential interview with senior Canadian government official, 1999.

64 DFAIT, 'Cuba: Trade and Economic Overview,' http://www.dfait.maeci.gc.ca/cubatrade.htm (accessed January 2002).

65 R. Gary Edwards and Jon Hughes, 'Status Quo Favoured in Business Relationship with Cuba,' *Gallup Poll*, 56, no. 25 (1996): 2.

66 Koring, 'Axworthy, Helms.'

67 Author interview with a former senior Canadian official with the United Nations, New York, September 1999.

68 Nash, *Kennedy and Diefenbaker*, 190.

69 Mark Entwistle, 'Canada-Cuba Relations: A Multiple-Personality Foreign Policy,' in Wright and Wylie, eds., *Our Place in the Sun*.

70 David Sheinin, 'Cuba's Long Shadow: The Progressive Church Movement and Canadian-Latin American Relations, 1970–87,' in Wright and Wylie, eds., *Our Place in the Sun*.

71 Ibid.

72 Ibid.

73 Wright, *Three Nights in Havana*, 25.

74 Bruce Wallace, 'Jean and Fidel,' *Maclean's* 3, no. 19 (1998): 30.

75 Wright, *Three Nights in Havana*, 23, 28.

76 Ibid., 28.

77 Ivan Head, quoted in Granatstein and Bothwell, *Pirouette*, 274.

78 Pew Global Attitudes Project, 'Global Opinion Trends 2002–2007,' 24 July 2007, http://www.pewglobal.org/reports/pdf/257.pdf (accessed 3 February 2008).

79 Cynthia Wright, 'Between Nation and Empire: The Fair Play for Cuba Committees and the Making of Canada-Cuba Solidarity in the Early 1960s,' in Wright and Wylie, eds., *Our Place in the Sun*.

80 Canadian Network on Cuba, 'Cuba Friendship groups in ONTARIO,' http://www.canadiannetworkoncuba.ca/ON/index.shtml (accessed 20 July 2009).

81 Canadian-Cuban Friendship Association, 'Who We Are,' http://www.ccfatoronto.ca/index.php?option=com_content&view=article&id=44&Itemid=53 (accessed 20 July 2009).

82 Hamilton Friendship Association with Cuba, 'About Us,' http://cubacanada.org/about (accessed 20 July 2009).

83 The Nova Scotia-Cuba Association, 'About Us,' http://www.nscuba.org/About_Us.html (accessed 20 July 2009).

84 Confidential interviews with Canadian officials, 1999 and 2000.

85 DFAIT, 'Relations with Cuba.'

86 Wallace, 'Jean and Fidel,' 30. Emphasis added.

87 Marcus Gee, 'Recognize Castro for What He Is,' *Globe and Mail*, 10 March 1999.

88 Canadians and Americans express equivalent preferences for democratic political systems. In 1999–2000, 90 per cent of Americans and 89 per cent of Canadians responded either very good or fairly good to this World Values Survey question: 'I'm going to describe various types of political systems and ask what you think about each as a way of governing this country. For each one, would you say it is a very good, fairly good, fairly bad or very bad way of governing this country? Having a democratic political system.' See '1999–2001 World Values Survey,' Institute for Social Research, University of Michigan, http://www.worldvaluessurvey.org/ (accessed 2 February 2008).

89 This does not represent the official Canadian position vis-à-vis Cuba, but it does demonstrate a much greater diversity of acceptable views on the subject within the Canadian foreign-policy establishment.

90 'MPs Irate over Cuba Comments: House Speaker's Remarks Assailed,' Miami *Herald*, 11 March 1998.

91 'Canada's Cuban Confusion,' *Globe and Mail*, 11 March 1998.

92 This perception was also evident during interviews with senior Canadian officials.

93   'Cuba Si! Discussion with Deputy Chief of Cuban Embassy,' *Marxist-Leninist Daily*, 26 January 2005, http://www.cpcml.ca/Tmld2005/D35003.htm (accessed 15 May 2008).

94   Confidential interviews with American and Canadian officials, 2000.

95   The Nova Scotia-Cuba Association, 'FAQ: Common Questions about Cuba,' http://www.nscuba.org/FAQ.html (accessed 21 July 2009).

96   DFAIT, 'Notes of an Address by the Honourable Christine Stewart, Secretary of State (Latin America and Africa)' (Speech Delivered to the Symposium on Helms-Burton and International Business Sponsored by the Canadian Foundation for the Americas and the Centre for International Policy, Ottawa, 16 May 1996), http://www.dfait-maeci.gc.ca/english/news/statements/96_state/96_023e.htm (accessed 22 February 2002).

97   Bruce Wallace, 'I Think He Is Changing,' *Macleans* 111, no. 19 (1998).

98   'Secretary of State Madeleine K. Albright and Canadian Foreign Minister Axworthy: Remarks in Press Briefing, Ottawa, Canada, March 10, 1998,' http://www.secretary.state.gov/www/statements/1998/980310a.html (accessed 22 February 2002).

99   Jeff Sallot, 'Cuba Policy Gives Ottawa Leverage for Change, PM Says,' *Globe and Mail*, 17 March 1999.

100   DFAIT, 'Canada-Cuba Relations.'

101   Ibid.

4. Exploring Cuba Policy in Tandem

1   Basil Robinson, *Diefenbaker's World: A Populist in Foreign Affairs* (Toronto: University of Toronto Press, 1989), 146.

2   John Kirk and Peter McKenna, *Canada-Cuba Relations: The Other Good Neighbor Policy* (Gainesville, Fla.: University of Florida Press 1997), 49–50.

3   Interestingly, the United States was seen as the country that stood out as a negative force for the greatest number of Canadians (52 per cent). See results at 'Canada's World Poll,' 9– 22 January 2008, Environics Research, http://www.canadasworld.ca/quizzesa/pollresu (accessed 13 July 2009).

4   Lydia Saad, 'Americans' Most and Least Favored Nations,' Gallup http://www.gallup.com/poll/104734/Americans-Most-Least-Favored-Nations.aspx, and 2008 video report 'Americans Rate Canada Best, Iran Worst,' http://www.gallup.com/video/104710/Americans-Rate-Canada-Best-Iran-Worst.aspx, 13 July 2009. Interestingly, Canada ranked as the most favoured country, with 92 per cent of Americans having a favourable opinion of Canada (accessed 14 July 2009).

5 Department of Foreign Affairs and International Trade (DFAIT), 'Cuba Fact Sheet,' http://www.infoexport.gc.ca (accessed 14 February 2002).

6 U.S. Department of State, 'Background Note: Cuba (09/01),' http://www.state.gov/r/pa/bgn/2886.htm (accessed 15 February 2002).

7 CNN, 'U.N. "Strongly Deplores" Cuban Action,' CNN Interactive, http://www.cnn.com/US/9602/cuba_shootdown/27/8am/index.html (21 July 2002).

8 U.S. Government Printing Office, 'Remarks Announcing Sanctions against Cuba following the Downing of Brothers to the Rescue Airplanes,' *Weekly Compilation of Presidential Documents*, 26 February 1996, http://frwebgate4.access.gpo.gov (accessed 15 April 2002).

9 U.S. Department of State, 'Cuban Liberty and Democratic Solidarity [Libertad] Act of 1996 – Conference Report (Senate – March 05, 1996),' http://www.senate.gov/~dood/press/Speeches/104_96/0303.htm (accessed 28 January 2002).

10 Richard Nuccio, 'Cuba: A U.S. Perspective,' in Richard N. Haass, ed., *Trans-Atlantic Tensions* (Washington, D.C.: Brookings Institution Press 1999), 7–28. See also Jorge Domínguez, 'U.S.-Cuban Relations: From the Cold War to the Colder War,' *Journal of Interamerican Studies and World Affairs* 39, no. 3 (1997): 62.

11 U.S. Department of State, 'Cuban Liberty and Democratic Solidarity [Libertad] Act of 1996 – PL104–114,' http://www.usinfo.state.gov/regional /ar/us-cuba/libertad.htm (accessed 26 August 2001).

12 Stuart Eizenstat, quoted in Heather N. Nicol, 'The Geopolitical Discourse of Helms-Burton,' in Heather N. Nicol, ed., *Canada, the US and Cuba: Helms Burton and Its Aftermath* (Kingston, Ont.: Centre for International Relations, Queen's University, 1999), 96.

13 U.S. Department of State, 'Cuban Liberty and Democratic Solidarity [Libertad] Act of 1996.'

14 Ibid.

15 The idea of spheres of influence is completely accepted by the U.S. foreign-policy establishment. The academic and foreign-policy communities in other countries do not as readily accept theories that place the United States at the centre of international relations. For example, see Robert M.A. Crawford and Darryl S.L. Jarvis, eds., *International Relations – Still an American Social Science?* (Albany: University of New York Press 2001).

16 U.S. Department of State, 'Cuban Liberty and Democratic Solidarity [Libertad] Act of 1996.'

17 U.S. Department of State, 'Cuba: U.S. Policy Now and in the Future –

Remarks by Michael Rannaberger, Coordinator for Cuban Affairs, before the Governor's Cuba Advisory Group,' Miami, 28 February 1997, http://www.state.gov/www/regions/wha/970228_ranneberger.html (accessed 9 September 2002).

18 U.S. House of Representatives, *Cuban Liberty and Democratic Solidarity Act of 1996*, Report 104–168, sec. 201, 1 March 1996.

19 Ibid., sec. 206.

20 Domínguez, 'U.S. Cuban Relations,' 58.

21 U.S. House of Representatives, 'Shoot-Down of the Brothers to the Rescue Planes, Hearing before the Subcommittee on Crime of the Committee on the Judiciary,' 106th Cong., 1st sess., 19 July 1999, http://www.commdocs.house.gov/committees/judiciary/hju63608.000/ lju63608_0.htm (accessed 21 August 2002).

22 Ibid.

23 Keith Martin, 'America's Cuban Debacle,' *TV Times*, Ottawa, 15 March 1996, http://www.keithmartin.org/policy/foreign/foreign_cuba.shtml (accessed 17 July 2002). Martin was elected as a Reform Party MP in 1993; in 2004 he joined the Liberal Party.

24 Ibid.

25 Confidential interview with senior Canadian government official, 1999.

26 Canada, Parliament, 'Foreign Affairs, Issue 11, Evidence Proceedings of the Standing Senate Committee on Foreign Affairs, Ottawa, November 5, 1996,' http://www.parl.gc.ca/search/qfullhit-E.htw?CiWebHitsFile= /35/2/parlbus/commbus/senate/com (accessed 16 April 2002). Emphasis added.

27 Canada, Parliament, 'Government Orders (071) 4507 Government Orders – Foreign Extraterritorial Measures Act, Ottawa, September 20, 1996,' http://www.parl.gc.ca (accessed 16 April 2002).

28 James J. Blanchard, *Behind the Embassy Door: Canada, Clinton and Quebec* (Toronto: McClelland and Stewart 1998), 147.

29 Canada, Parliament, 'Routine Proceedings – Statements by Members [English]: 130 Cuba, February 29, 1996,' http://www.parl.gc.ca/35/2 /parlbus/chambus/house/debates/003_96-02-29/003SM1E.html (accessed 16 April 2002).

30 Canada, Parliament, 'Proceedings of the Standing Senate Committee on Foreign Affairs Issue 2 – Evidence, Ottawa, May 28, 1996,' http:// www.parl.gc.ca/35/2/parlbus/commbus/senate/com-e/FORE-E/02EV-E.htm (accessed 16 April 2002).

31 Ibid.

32 Confidential interview, October 1999.

33 Canada, Parliament, 'Routine Proceedings – Statements by Members
    [Translation]: 707 Cuba, March 14, 1996,' http://www.parl.gc.ca/35/2
    /parlbus/chambus/jouse/debates/013_96-03-14/013SM1E.html
    (accessed 16 April 2002).

34 Canada, Parliament, 'Routine Proceedings – Government Orders
    [English]: 4508 Foreign Extraterritorial Measures Act, Ottawa, September
    20, 1996,' http://www2.parl.gc.ca/HousePublications/Publication
    .aspx?DocId=2332610&Language =E&Mode=1&Parl=35&Ses=2#4507
    (accessed 28 July 2008).

35 Ibid.

36 Canada, Parliament, 'Foreign Affairs, Issue 11, Evidence Proceedings of
    the Standing Senate Committee on Foreign Affairs, Ottawa, November 5,
    1996,' http://www.parl.gc.ca/search/qfullhit-E.htw?CiWebHits-
    File=/35/2/parlbus/commbus/senate/com (accessed 16 April 2002).

37 Canada, Parliament, 'Routine Proceedings – Government Orders
    [English]: 4508 Foreign Extraterritorial Measures Act.'

38 Peter Schwab, *Cuba: Confronting the US Embargo* (New York: St Martin's
    Press 1999), 56.

39 María G. Guzmán, 'Deciphering Dengue: The Cuban Experience,' *Global
    Voices of Science* 309, no. 5740 (2005): 1495.

40 Ibid.

41 Julie Margot Feinsilver, *Healing the Masses* (Berkeley: University of Cali-
    fornia Press 1993), 129.

42 World Health Organization, 'Cuba: Mortality and Burden of Disease,'
    World Health Organization Country Profiles, http://www.who.int/coun-
    tries/cub/en/ (accessed 12 December 2005).

43 Michael Kranish, 'Incubating Biotech: US Charges Highlight Castro's
    Efforts to Build Industry,' Boston *Globe*, 15 May 2002.

44 Jose de la Fuente, 'Wine into Vinegar – The Fall of Cuba's Biotechnology,'
    Nature Biotechnology 19, no. 10 (2001): 906.

45 José Ferández Alvarez, quoted in Feinsilver, *Healing the Masses*, 123.

46 Fuente, 'Wine into Vinegar,' 905–7.

47 Ibid.

48 Jon Beckwith, 'Cuba Report: Science and Society Are Inseparable,' *Science
    for the People* 17, no. 5 (1985): 20–4. Quoted in Feinsilver, *Healing the
    Masses*, 131.

49 Fuente, 'Wine into Vinegar,' 905–7.

50 See Ernesto Lopez et al., 'Development of Cuban Biotechnology,' *Journal
    of Commercial Biotechnology* 9, no. 2 (2003): 147–52; Schwab, *Cuba: Con-
    fronting the US Embargo*, 1999.

51 Halla Thorsteinsdóttir et al., 'Cuba – Innovation through Synergy,' *Nature Biotechnology* 22 (2004): DC23.
52 Miguel A. Galindo, 'Immunization and Vaccine Research in Cuba: Cuba's National Immunization Program,' *Medical Education Cooperation with Cuba (MEDICC) Review*, http://www.medicc.org/medicc_review/1004/pages/spotlight.html (accessed 12 December 2005).
53 Jocelyn Kaiser, 'Synthetic Vaccine Is a Sweet Victory for Cuban Science,' *Science* 305, no. 5683 (2004): 460.
54 Editorial, 'Socialism in One Country,' *Nature* 43, no. 7049 (2005): 303.
55 Feinsilver, *Healing the Masses*, 125. Feinsilver also notes that the absence of an FDA equivalent in Cuba does not mean that Cuban clinical research is unethical. In fact, she explains that the Cubans refuse to conduct placebo trials because it would mean withholding treatment from people who need it.
56 Chen may Yee, 'Cutting-edge Biotech in Old-world Cuba,' *Christian Science Monitor*, 17 April 2000, http://www.csmonitor.com/2003/0417/p14s03-stct.html (accessed 28 July 2008).
57 Ibid.
58 Jim Giles, 'Cuban Science: ¿Vive la revolución?' *Nature* 436, no. 7049 (2005): 322–4.
59 Fuente, 'Wine into Vinegar,' 905–7.
60 Tom Fawthrop, 'Cuba Ailing? Not Its Biomedical Industry,' *Straits Times*, 26 January 2004, reprinted in *YaleGlobal Online*, http://www.yaleglobal.yale.edu (accessed 8 December 2005).
61 Ibid.
62 Yee, 'Cutting-edge Biotech in Old-world Cuba.'
63 Thorsteinsdóttir et al., 'Cuba – Innovation through Synergy,' DC19.
64 Kaiser, 'Synthetic Vacine,' 460.
65 By 1991, the FMLN had gained recognition as a political party in El Salvador.
66 U.S. Department of State, 'Patterns of Global Terrorism 1998,' Press Briefing, Washington, D.C., 30 April 1999.
67 U.S. Department of State, 'Patterns of Global Terrorism – 2002 Overview of State-Sponsored Terrorism,' Office of the Coordinator for Counterterrorism, Washington, D.C., 30 April 2003, http://www.state.gov/s/ct/rls/crt/2002/html/19988.htm (accessed 15 March 2008).
68 Christopher Marquis and Eric Schmitt, 'Bush Faces Pressure from Congress to Alter Cuba Policy,' New York *Times*, 19 May 2002.

69 John R. Bolton, Under-Secretary for Arms Control and International Security, 'The U.S. Position on the Biological Weapons Convention: Combating the BW Threat' (speech delivered at Tokyo America Center, Tokyo, Japan, 26 August 2002), http://www.state.gov/t/us/rm/13090.htm (accessed 18 September 2002).

70 Christopher Marquis, 'U.S. Accuses Cuba of Trying to Disrupt Antiterrorism Effort,' New York *Times*, 18 September 2002.

71 David Mozer, 'Cuba and the September 11, 2001 Attacks,' 'Cuba, U.S. Policy, Travel and Resources,' http://www.ibike.org/cuba/911.htm (accessed 29 July 2008).

72 Ibid.

73 Paul R. Pillar, *Terrorism and U.S. Foreign Policy* (Washington D.C.: Brookings Institution Press 2001), 161.

74 U.S. Department of State, 'Patterns of Global Terrorism 1998.'

75 President George W. Bush, 'Address to a Joint Session of Congress and the American People' (Speech delivered at the U.S. Capitol, Washington, D.C., 20 September 2001), http://www.whitehouse.gov/news/releases/2001/09/20010920-8.html (accessed 26 September 2002).

76 Dwight D. Eisenhower, 'July 6, 1960,' *The Eisenhower Diaries*, ed. Robert H. Ferrell (New York: W.W. Norton 1981), 379. Quoted in Dennis Molinaro, '"Calculated Diplomacy": John Diefenbaker and the Origins of Canada's Cuba Policy,' in Robert Wright and Lana Wylie, eds. *Our Place in the Sun: Canada and Cuba in the Castro Era* (Toronto: University of Toronto Press 2009).

77 Dan Morgan, 'Federal Pay Raise Near House Passage: End to Cuba Travel Curbs Also Backed,' Washington *Post*, 24 July 2002.

78 Latino News Network, 'CANF Deplores Interpol Chief's Acceptance of Cuba Terrorism Ties,' 22 January 2002, http://www.latnn.com (accessed 21 July 2002).

79 Comcast Interactive Media, 'Powell Backs down on Cuba Weapons Claims,' Comcast News, http://www.comcast.net/smedia/abcnews.com (accessed 14 May 2002).

80 John R. Bolton, 'Beyond the Axis of Evil: Additional Threats from Weapons of Mass Destruction,' Heritage Foundation Heritage Lecture #743, 6 May 2002, http://www.heritage.org/Research/MissileDefense/HL743.cfm (accessed 26 September 2002).

81 Marquis and Schmitt, 'Bush Faces Pressure.'

82 U.S. Department of State, 'Country Reports on Terrorism – State Sponsors of Terror Overview,' Office of the Coordinator for Counterterrorism,

Washington, D.C., 28 April 2006, http://www.state.gov/s/ct/rls/crt
/2005/64337.htm (accessed 29 May 2008).

83 Interpol (the international police organization) investigated Cuba's ties to
terrorism and was satisfied that Cuba was committed to the fight against
terrorism. See Latino News Network, 'CANF Deplores Interpol Chief's
Acceptance of Cuba Terrorism Ties.'

84 Dennis Hays, 'Inspect Cuba for Production of Biological Weapons,'
Miami *Herald*, 29 July 2002.

85 Bolton, 'Beyond the Axis of Evil.'

86 Hon. Lincoln Diaz-Balart of Florida, U.S. House of Representatives,
'Motion to Instruct Conferees on H.R. 2646, Farm Security Act of 2001'
(House of Representatives/Extension of Remarks – 18 April 2002) [Page:
H1453]), http://www.house.gov/apps/list/speech/fl21_diaz-
balart/st020418.html (accessed 20 September 2002).

87 Canadian Security and Intelligence Service, 'Report #2000/01 Trends in
Terrorism,' *Perspectives: A Canadian Security Intelligence Service Publication*
(18 December 1999), http://www.csis-scrs.gc.ca/eng/miscdocs/200001
_e.html (accessed 5 April 2002).

88 DFAIT, 'Canada-Cuba Joint Declaration Implementation Checklist.' Provided to the author by David Kilgour, secretary of state (Latin America
and Africa), Ottawa (October 1999).

89 DFAIT, 'Canada's Relations with Cuba,' 'Doing Business Abroad,'
http://www.infoexport.gc.ca/ie-en/DisplayDocument.jsp?did=992
(accessed 13 June 2008).

90 'The Old Foe in Havana,' *Globe and Mail*, 16 May 2002, sec. A18.

91 Lana Wylie, 'Perceptions and Foreign Policy: A Comparative Study of
Canadian and American Policy toward Cuba,' *Canadian Foreign Policy* 11,
no. 3 (2004): 39–62.

92 John Bryden, Canadian Liberal MP, 'The Sub-Committee of the Standing
Committee on Public Accounts on Combating Corruption,' 37th Parliament, 1st sess., 22 May 2002, http://www.parl.gc.ca.libaccess.lib.mcmas-
ter.ca (accessed 1 September 2004).

93 Lana Wylie, 'Ambassador MD: The Role of Health and Biotechnology in
Cuban Foreign Policy,' in Wright and Wylie, eds., *Our Place in the Sun*.

94 See information at Institute of Biomedical Engineering, 'Research,' University of New Brunswick, http://www.unb.ca/biomed/ (accessed 29
July 2008).

95 Sandra Howland, 'UNB Know-How Boosts Cuba's Biomedical Capability,' UNB Fredericton News Release: C891 (30 January 2004),
http://www.unb.ca/news/view.cgi?id=442. (accessed 29 July 2008).

96 Ibid.
97 Thorsteinsdóttir, et al., 'Cuba – Innovation through Synergy,' DC20.
98 Susan Hurlich, 'The World's First Synthetic Vaccine for Children,' CubaNow.net, http://www.cubanow.cult.cu/global/loader.php ?secc=10&cont=culture/num10/8.htm (accessed 7 January 2006).
99 Canada NewsWire, 'Trudeau Legacy Produces $23 Million Medical Lifeline to Cuba,' http://www.newswire.ca/en/, 8 March 2002.
100 Canada NewsWire, 'HPIC Marks 10th Anniversary of Medical Aid Program for Cubans – Trudeau's Legacy Includes Medical Aid for Cuba,' http://www.newswire.ca/en/, 24 March 2005. For more information, see: www.hpicanada.ca.
101 Leonard Zehr, 'Biotech Builds on Cuban Innovation,' Cubanet, 2 May 2001, http://www.cubanet.org/CNews?y01/may01?02e8.hm (accessed 8 December 2005).
102 Ibid.
103 Kranish, 'Incubating Biotech.'
104 Hon. Bill Graham, Minister of Foreign Affairs, 'Notes for an Address to the Terrorism, Law and Democracy Conference Organized by the Canadian Institute for the Administration of Justice' (speech delivered in Montreal, 26 March 2002), http://www.webapps.dfaitmaeci.gc.ca /minipub/Publication.asp?FileSpec+/Min_Pub/1050 49.htm (accessed 5 April 2002).
105 Jean Chrétien, 'Chrétien Interview on Sept. 11,' Canadian Broadcasting Corporation (interview conducted by the CBC News on 16 September 2002), http://www.cbc.ca/news/features/chretien_interview.html (accessed 18 September 2002).
106 Ibid.

5. Conclusion

1 See, for example, Darren Carlson, 'Poll Analyses: 40 Years after Bay of Pigs, Most Americans Have Unfavorable Opinion of Cuba, April 17, 2001,' Gallup Poll Organization, http://www.gallup.com/poll/releases /pr010417.asp (accessed 13 August 2001).
2 'Polling the Nations (1986 through 2001),' Cuba (Matthews, N.C.: Rasmussen Research 2000).
3 Charles Lane, 'And a Child Shall Lead Them: Miami's Passionate, Self-defeating Fight for Elian Gonzalez,' New Republic, 24 January 2000, http://www.thenewrepublic.com (accessed 19 August 2001).
4 ABC News Poll, 'Elian Gonzalez, April 24, 2000,' PolllingReport.com,

http://www.pollingreport.com/oldnews.htm (accessed 17 August 2001).

5 NBC/Wall Street Journal Poll, 'Elian Gonzalez, April 29–May 1, 2000,' PollingReport.com, http://www.pollingreport.com/oldnews.htm (accessed 17 August 2001).

6 See Max Azicri, *Cuba Today and Tomorrow: Reinventing Socialism* (Gainesville: University Press of Florida 2004), especially 251–74, for background and information on the pope's visit to Cuba.

7 Donna Cassata, 'Foreign Policy: Papal Visit Highlights Divisions over Cuban Embargo,' *Congressional Quarterly* (24 January 1998): 195.

8 Confidential interview with senior U.S. government official, 2000.

9 Lee Hamilton, quoted in Tim Weiner, 'Pope vs. Embargo: Still a Sharp Divide in U.S.,' New York *Times*, 21 January 1998.

10 Quoted by Senator Chris Dodd, 'His Eminence Bernard Cardinal Law, Archbishop of Boston, Reflecting on Cuba, Senate, March 19, 1998,' http://www.senate.gov/~dood/pres/speeches/105_98/0319.htm (accessed 28 January 2000).

11 President Bill Clinton, 'Statement on Cuba, March 20, 1998,' American Presidency Project Online, University of California at Santa Barbara, http://www.presidency.ucsb.edu/ws/print.php?pid=55654 (accessed 26 August 2008).

12 Cuba Working Group, 'A Review of US Policy toward Cuba, May 15, 2002,' U.S. House of Representatives, http://www.cubafoundation.org/CWG-Review.htm (accessed 13 April 2003).

13 Daniel Merkle, 'Carter Improves with Age,' ABCNews.com, 1 October 1999, http://www.abcnews.go.com/sections/politics/DailyNews/poll990929.html (accessed 14 April 2003).

14 Andrea Elliot and Elaine De Valle, 'Cuban Exiles Shifting Hard-line Position,' Miami *Herald*, 12 February 2003, http//www.miami.com/mld/miamiherald/news/world/cuba/5160039.htm (accessed 13 April 2003).

15 Ibid.

16 Christopher Marquis and Eric Schmitt, 'Bush Faces Pressure from Congress to Alter Cuba Policy,' New York *Times*, 19 May 2002.

17 Dana Canedy, 'Cuban Exiles Finding Spirit of Reconciliation,' New York *Times*, 23 March 2003.

18 Elliot and De Valle, 'Cuban Exiles Shifting Hard-line Position.'

19 Canedy, 'Cuban Exiles Finding Spirit of Reconciliation.'

20 Damien Cave, 'U.S. Overtures Find Support among Cuban-Americans,' New York *Times*, 20 April 2009.

21 David Gonzalez, 'Carter's Trip to Cuba Raises Many Hopes from All Sides,' New York *Times*, 11 May 2002.

22 Canedy, 'Cuban Exiles Finding Spirit of Reconciliation.'
23 'Former President Carter on Landmark Visit to Cuba,' *Globe and Mail*, 12 May 2002, http://www.theglobeandmail.com (accessed 13 May 2002).
24 Cuba Policy Foundation, 'At Least 104 U.S. Congressional Districts, 66 Senate Seats Represented at Havana Trade Expo,' Press Release, 10 October 2002.
25 USA Today/Gallup Poll, 'Cuba, Feb. 21–24, 2008,' http://www.pollingreport.com/cuba.htm (accessed 4 August 2008).
26 Cuba Working Group, 'A Review of U.S. Policy toward Cuba.'
27 Ibid.
28 See Mark Sullivan, *CRS Report for Congress: Cuba: Issues for the 110th Congress* (Congressional Research Service, 21 August 2007), and Cuba Policy Foundation, 'Embargo Update, March 28, 2003,' http://www.cubafoundation.org/Embargo_Update-0303.28w.htm (accessed 13 April 2003). These sales are restricted to cash-in-advance terms.
29 U.S. Library of Congress, 'Cuba' (search term used to obtain list of bills introduced in 110th Congress), http://www.thomas.loc.gov/cgi-bin/thomas (accessed 28 July 2008).
30 President George W. Bush, quoted in Cuba Policy Foundation, 'History of U.S. Policy,' http://www.cubapolicyfoundation.org/policy.html (accessed 1 April 2002).
31 Paul Knox, 'Why Did Washington Goad Cuba?' *Globe and Mail*, 9 April 2003.
32 Anita Snow, 'U.S. Diplomat in Cuba Walks an Often Rocky Road as Chief of Mission on Communist Island, June 7, 2002,' Cuban American National Foundation, http://www.canfnet.org/News/archived/020607newsa.htm (accessed 14 April 2003).
33 Andrew Cawthorne, 'Cuba Protests "Subversive" U.S. Radio Handouts, April 5, 2002,' Cuban American National Foundation, http://www.canf.org (accessed 12 April 2003).
34 Knox, 'Why Did Washington Goad Cuba?'
35 David Gonzalez, 'Cuba Arrests More Dissidents amid Outcry,' New York *Times*, 22 March 2003.
36 Knox, 'Why Did Washington Goad Cuba?'
37 Juan O. Tamayo, 'Jonathan Farrar to Replace Michael Parmly as "Ambassador" to Cuba,' Miami *Herald*, 16 May 2008.
38 Will Weissert, 'Cuban Activists Briefed on Human Rights, March 7, 2007,' Cubanet, http://www.cubanet.org/CNews/y07/mar07/16e7.htm (accessed 28 July 2008).
39 Ann Louise Bardach, 'A Purge with a Purpose,' New York *Times*, 13 April

2003, and 'Fidel's Reply to Statement by U.S. Ambassador in the Dominican Republic,' *Granma*, 11 April 2003, http://www.granma.cu/ingles/abril03/vier11/15respuest.html (accessed 14 April 2003).

40 President Barack Obama, 'Barack Obama on the Cuban Embargo, January 20, 2004,' http://www.youtube.com/watch?v=cZ3SVok9g34 (accessed 14 July 2009).

41 Barack Obama, 'Editorial,' Miami *Herald*, 22 August 2007.

42 Ibid.

43 Lesley Clark, 'U.S., Cuba to Reopen Talks on Migration,' Miami *Herald*, 13 July 2009.

44 Jacqueline Charles, 'Hillary Clinton: Haiti, Cuba Policies Are under Review,' Miami *Herald*, 15 April 2009.

45 Ibid.

46 David Gonzalez, 'Cuban Crackdown on Critics Stalls a Drive to Ease U.S. Embargo,' New York *Times*, 13 April 2003.

47 See Department of Foreign Affairs and International Trade (DFAIT), 'Canada's Relations with Cuba,' http://www.dfait.maeci.gc.ca/latin/cuba/81600-e.htm (accessed 13 June 2008). In recent years the success of the Joint Declaration has been called into question since there appears to be little progress on these issues in Cuba. Canadian government officials respond that they did not expect rapid change in Cuba and that constructive engagement is a long-term policy. Based on confidential interviews with senior Canadian government officials, Ottawa and Havana, 1999 and 2000.

48 For further information on Chrétien's Cuba policy, see Robert Wright, 'Northern Ice: Jean Chrétien and the Failure of Constructive Engagement in Cuba,' in Robert Wright and Lana Wylie, eds., *Our Place in the Sun: Canada and Cuba in the Castro Era* (Toronto: University of Toronto Press 2009).

49 'Cuban Trial Step Backward, Axworthy Says,' *Globe and Mail*, 3 March 1999.

50 Fidel Castro, 'Castro: 1999 on PanAm Games in Winnipeg' (speech delivered in Cienfuegos, Cuba, 26 July 1999), http://www.pbs.org/stealing-home/sport/castro99b.html (accessed 31 January 2002).

51 Ibid.

52 Archibald Ritter, 'Cuba Project' (speech delivered at the City University of New York's Queens College and Graduate School, 2001).

53 Jose de Cordoba and Carlta Vitzthum, 'Canadian Woes with Cuba,' *Wall Street Journal*, 28 June 1999, http//www.fiu.edu/~fcf/cawo.html (accessed 31 January 2002).

54 Ritter, 'Cuba Project.'

55 'Fidel Castro Sends Message of Solidarity to Protesters in Quebec,' 21 April 2001, http://www.radiohc.org (accessed 31 January 2002).

56 DFAIT, 'Canada-Cuba Relations,' http://www.dfait-maeci.gc.ca/latinamerica/cubarelations-en.asp0 (accessed 23 January 2002).

57 CBC News, 'Chrétien Interview on Sept. 11,' http://www.cbc.ca (accessed 19 September 2002).

58 DFAIT, 'Secretary of State Paradis to Visit Cuba,' News Release, 1 November 2002, http://www.webapps.dfait-maeci.gc.ca/minpub/Publication.asp?FileSpec=/Min_Pub_Docs/105614.htm&bPrint=Fal se&Year=&Language=E (accessed 13 April 2003).

59 DFAIT, 'Canada-Cuban Relations.'

60 DFAIT, 'Paradis Promotes Trade, Investment and Canadian Values in Cuba,' News Release, 8 November 2002, http://www.webapps.dfait-maeci.gc.ca/minpub/Publication.asp?FileSpec=/Min_Pub_Docs/105649.htm (accessed 14 April 2003).

61 DFAIT, 'Canada-Cuban Relations.'

62 Paul Knox, 'Graham Protests against Cuban Trials,' *Globe and Mail*, 8 April 2003, http://www.theglobeandmail.com/servlet/story/RTGAM.20030408.ucuba0408/BNStory/I nternational/?query=Cuba (accessed 14 April 2003).

63 Lee Berthiaume, 'Cuba Saga Shows Signs of Complication in Ottawa,' *Embassy*, 20 December 2006, http://www.embassymag.ca/html/index.php?display=story&full_path=/2006/december/2 0/cuba (accessed 30 July 2008).

64 Mike Blanchfield, 'Canada Supports Cuban Reforms despite U.S. Jabs,' Edmonton *Journal*, 23 May 2008.

65 Mike Blanchfield, 'New Minister Sees a Future for Canada in Cuba,' *Financial Post*, 6 January 2009.

66 Mike Blanchfield, 'Minister to Make Rare High-level Visit to Cuba,' *National Post*, 26 April 2009.

67 Peter McKenna and John M. Kirk, 'Canadian-Cuban Relations: Muddling through the "Special Period,"' in Wright and Wylie, eds., *Our Place in the Sun*.

68 Ana Faya, 'Let's Be Honest about the Tories' Approach to Cuba,' *Embassy*, 28 May 2008, http://www.embassymag.ca/html/index.php?display=story&full_path=/2008/may/28/lette r3/ (accessed 30 July 2008).

69 Prime Minister Stephen Harper, 'Prime Minister Harper Signals Canada's Renewed Engagement in the Americas' (speech delivered in Santiago, Chile, 17 July 2007), http://www.pm.gc.ca/eng/media.asp?category=2&id=1759 (accessed 30 July 2008).

70 Lee Berthiaume, 'Cuba Warns Canada: Follow U.S. at Own Peril,' *Embassy*, 14 May 2008, http://www.embassymag.ca/html/index .php?display=story&full_path=/2008/may/14/cub a/ (accessed 30 July 2008).

71 Canadian Foundation for the Americas (FOCAL), 'Chronicle on Cuba – June 2008,' Cubasource, http://www.cubasource.org/publications /chronicles/coc200806ec_e.asp (accessed 29 July 2008).

72 Mike Blanchfield, 'Canada Talks Softly on Cuba, Bush Prefers Big Stick,' Ottawa *Citizen*, 22 May 2008.

73 Jeffrey T. Checkel, 'The Constructivist Turn in International Relations Theory,' *World Politics* 50 (January 1998): 339.

74 Ibid.

Bibliography

ABC News Poll. 'Elian Gonzalez, April 24, 2000.' PollingReport.com. http://www.pollingreport.com/oldnews.htm (accessed 17 August 2001).

Adler, Emanuel, and Peter Haas. 'Conclusion: Epistemic Communities, World Order, and the Creation of a Reflective Research Program.' *International Organization* 46, no. 1 (1992): 367–90.

Agular, Luis E. 'Cuba c. 1860–1930.' In Leslie Bethell, ed., *Cuba: A Short History*. Cambridge: Cambridge University Press 1993.

Albright, Madeleine K., Secretary of State. 'Sustaining Democracy in the Twenty-first Century.' Speech delivered at Johns Hopkins University, Washington, D.C., 18 January 2000. http://www.secretary.state.gov /www/statements/2000/000118.html (accessed 30 April 2003).

Angeles Torres, María de los. *In the Land of Mirrors: Cuban Exile Politics in the United States*. Ann Arbor: University of Michigan Press 2001.

Anglican Church of Canada. 'Resolution A280: Cuba.' http://www.anglican .ca/gs2001/rr/resolutions/resolution.php?res+a280 (accessed 22 February 2002).

Azicri, Max. *Cuba Today and Tomorrow: Reinventing Socialism*. Gainesville: University Press of Florida 2004.

Bardach, Ann Louise. 'A Purge with a Purpose.' New York *Times*, 13 April 2003.

Beckwith, Jon. 'Cuba Report: Science and Society Are Inseparable.' *Science for the People* 17, no. 5 (1985): 20–4.

Berger, Thomas U. 'Norms, Identity, and National Security in Germany and Japan.' In Peter J. Katzenstein, ed., *The Culture of National Security*. New York: Columbia University Press 1996.

Berthiaume, Lee. 'Cuba Saga Shows Signs of Complication in Ottawa.' *Embassy*, 20 December 2006. http://www.embassymag.ca/html

/index.php?display=story&full_path=/2006/dece mber/20/cuba
(accessed 30 July 2008).

– 'Cuba Warns Canada: Follow U.S. at Own Peril.' *Embassy,* 14 May 2008.
http://www.embassymag.ca/html/index.php?display=story&full_path=
/2008/may/14/cuba/ (accessed 30 July 2008).

Blanchard, James J. *Behind the Embassy Door: Canada, Clinton and Quebec.*
Toronto: McClelland and Stewart 1998.

Blanchfield, Mike. 'Canada Supports Cuban Reforms despite U.S. Jabs.'
Edmonton *Journal,* 23 May 2008.

– 'Canada Talks Softly on Cuba, Bush Prefers Big Stick.' Ottawa *Citizen,* 22
May 2008.

– 'Minister to Make Rare High-level Visit to Cuba.' *National Post,* 26 April
2009.

– 'New Minister Sees a Future for Canada in Cuba.' *Financial Post,* 6 January
2009.

Boehm, Peter M. Ambassador and Permanent Representative of Canada to
the Organization of American States. 'Notes for a Speech to the Annual
Meeting of the Cuban Committee for Democracy,' Miami, 12 September
1998. http://www.dfait-maeci.gc.ca/oas/oas04d-e.htm (accessed 23
January 2002).

Bolton, John R. Under-Secretary for Arms Control and International Security.
'Beyond the Axis of Evil: Additional Threats from Weapons of Mass
Destruction.' Heritage Foundation Heritage Lecture #743, 6 May 2002.
http://www.heritage.org/Research/MissileDefense/HL743.cfm (accessed
26 September 2002).

– 'The U.S. Position on the Biological Weapons Convention: Combating the
BW Threat.' Speech delivered at Tokyo America Center, Tokyo, Japan, 26
August 2002. http://www.state.gov/t/us/rm/13090.htm (accessed 18
September 2002).

Bryden, John [Canadian Liberal MP]. 'The Sub-Committee of the Standing
Committee on Public Accounts on Combating Corruption.' 37th Parliament, 1st sess., 22 May 2002. http://www.parl.gc.ca.libaccess.lib
.mcmaster.ca (accessed 1 September 2004).

Bush, George W., President. 'Address to a Joint Session of Congress and the
American People.' Speech delivered at the U.S. Capitol, Washington, D.C.,
20 September 2001). http://www.whitehouse.gov/news/releases/2001
/09/20010920-8.html (accessed 26 September 2002).

– 'State of the Union.' Speech delivered at the U.S Capitol, Washington, D.C.,
28 January 2003. http://www.whitehouse.gov/news/releases/2003/01
/20030128-19.html (accessed 16 March 2003).

Campbell, David. *Writing Security: The United States Foreign Policy and the Politics of Identity.* Minneapolis: University of Minnesota Press 1998.

Canada. Department of Foreign Affairs and International Trade. 'Backgrounder: Canada and Peacekeeping.' http://www.dfait-maeci.gc.ca /peacekeeping/back-e.asp1/23/02 (accessed 23 January 2002).
- 'Canada-Cuba Joint Declaration Implementation Checklist.' Provided to the author by David Kilgour, Secretary of State (Latin America and Africa), Ottawa (October 1999).
- 'Canada-Cuba Relations.' http://www.dfait-maeci.gov.ca/latinamerica /cubarelations-e.asp (accessed 23 January 2002).
- 'Canada's Foreign Policy: Principles and Priorities for the Future.' *Report of the Special Joint Committee Reviewing Canadian Foreign Policy* (November 1994).
- 'Canada's Relations with Cuba.' 'Doing Business Abroad.' http://www .infoexport.gc.ca/ie-/DisplayDocument.jsp?did=992 (accessed 13 June 2008).
- 'Canada-United States: Trade and the Economy.' http://www.dfait-maeci.gc.ca/can-am/menu-en.asp?mid=1&cat=1029 (accessed 4 April 2003).
- 'Cuba Fact Sheet.' http://www.infoexport.gc.ca (accessed 14 February 2002).
- *Cuba: A Guide for Canadian Business.* Ottawa: Minister of Supply and Services, July 1997.
- 'Cuba: Trade and Economic Overview.' http://www.dfait.maeci.gc.ca /cubatrade.htm (accessed January 2002).
- 'A Dialogue on Foreign Policy: A Better Canada, A Better World.' http://www.foreign-policy dialogue.ca/en/discusspaper/index.html (accessed 4 April 2003).
- Documents on Canadian External Relations, Volume 26 #466, Chapter X, 126 Latin America Part 2, Cuba Section, A Fidel Castro et le Gouverment Révoltionnaire, 466, DEA/10224–40, Secretary of State for External Affairs to Ambassador in Cuba, Despatch D-214, Ottawa, 25 September 1959, http://www.international.gc.ca/department/historyhistoire/dcer/details-en.asp?intRefid=11284 (accessed 13 July 2009).
- Documents on Canadian External Relations, Volume 27 #638, Chapter IX, Latin America Part 1, Cuba 638.DEA/2444–40, Ambassador in Argentina to Secretary of State for External Affairs, Despatch no. 53, Buenos Aires, 10 November 1960, http://www.international.gc.ca/department/history histoire/dcer/details-en.asp?intRefid=13192 (accessed 14 July 2009).
- Documents on Canadian External Relations, Volume 27 #639, Chapter IX, Latin America, Part 1, Cuba 639, J.G.D./VI/848/C962, Minister of Citizenship and Immigration to Prime Minister, Ottawa, 10 November 1960, http://www.international.gc.ca/department/historyhistoire/dcer/details-en.asp?intRefid=13193 (accessed 13 July 2009).

– A Letter from the Canadian Ambassador in Havana: Documents on Canadian External Relations, Volume 27 #643, Chapter IX, Latin America Part 1, Cuba 643, DEA/288–40, Ambassador in Cuba to Secretary of State for External Affairs, Despatch no. D-937, Havana, 13 December 1960, Canadian Position in Cuba, http://www.international.gc.ca/department /historyhistoire/dcer/details-en.asp?intRefid=13197 (accessed 13 July 2009).

– 'Notes for an Address by the Honourable Christine Stewart, Secretary of State (Latin America and Africa).' Speech delivered to the 26th General Assembly of the Organization of American States, Panama City, Panama, 3 June 1996. http://www.w01.international.gc.ca/minpub/Publication ContentOnly.asp?publicat ion_id=376997&Language=E&MODE= CONTENTONLY&Local–False (accessed 16 August 2007).

– 'Notes of an Address by the Honourable Christine Stewart, Secretary of State (Latin America and Africa).' Speech delivered to the Symposium on Helms-Burton and International Business Sponsored by the Canadian Foundation for the Americas and the Center for International Policy, Ottawa, 16 May 1996. http://www.dfaitmaeci.gc.ca/english/news /statements/96_state/96_023e.htm (accessed 22 February 2002).

– 'Paradis Promotes Trade, Investment and Canadian Values in Cuba.' News Release, 8 November 2002. http://www.webapps.dfait-maeci.gc.ca /minpub/Publication.asp?FileSpec=/Min_Pub_Docs/105649.htm (accessed 14 April 2003).

– 'Secretary of State Paradis to Visit Cuba.' News Release, 1 November 2002. http://www.webapps.dfait-maeci.gc.ca/minpub/Publication.asp ?FileSpec=/Min_Pub_Docs/105614.htm&bPr int=Fa se&Year=&Language=E (accessed 13 April 2003).

Canada. Parliament. 'Foreign Affairs, Issue 11, Evidence Proceedings of the Standing Senate Committee on Foreign Affairs, Ottawa, November 5, 1996.' http://www.parl.gc.ca/search/qfullhitE.htw?CiWebHitsFile=/35 /2/parlbus/commb us/senate/com (accessed 16 April 2002).

– 'Government Orders (071) 4507 Government Orders – Foreign Extraterritorial Measures Act, Ottawa, September 20, 1996.' http://www.parl.gc.ca (accessed 16 April 2002).

– 'Proceedings of the Standing Senate Committee on Foreign Affairs Issue 2 – Evidence, Ottawa, May 28, 1996.' http://www.parl.gc.ca/35/2/parlbus /commbus/senate/com-e/FORE-E/02EV-E.htm (accessed 16 April 2002).

– 'Routine Proceedings – Government Orders [English]: 4508 Foreign Extraterritorial Measures Act, Ottawa, September 20, 1996.' http://www2 .parl.gc.ca/HousePublications/Publication.aspx?DocId=2332610& LanguageE&Mode=1&Parl=35&Ses=2#4507 (accessed 28 July 2008).

– 'Routine Proceedings – Statements by Members [English]: 130 Cuba, Feb-
    ruary 29, 1996.' http://www.parl.gc.ca/35/2/parlbus/chambus/house
    /debates/003_9602-29/003SM1E.html (accessed 16 April·2002).
– 'Routine Proceedings – Statements by Members [Translation]: 707 Cuba,
    March 14, 1996.' http://www.parl.gc.ca/35/2/parlbus/chambus
    /house/debates/013_96-03 14/013SM1E.html (accessed 16 April
    2002).
Canada NewsWire. 'HPIC Marks 10th Anniversary of Medical Aid Program
    for Cubans – Trudeau's Legacy Includes Medical Aid for Cuba,'
    http://www.newswire.ca/en/, 24 March 2005.
– 'Trudeau Legacy Produces $23 Million Medical Lifeline to Cuba,'
    http://www.newswire.ca/en/, 8 March 2002.
Canadian-American Committee. 'Canada's Trade with Cuba and Canadian-
    American Relations.' 6 February 1961.
Canadian-Cuban Friendship Association. 'Who We Are,' http://www.ccfa
    toronto.ca/index.php?option=com_content&view=article&id=44
    &Itemid=53 (accessed 20 July 2009).
Canadian Foundation for the Americas (FOCAL). 'Chronicle on Cuba-June
    2008.'
Cubasource. http://www.cubasource.org/publications/chronicles
    /coc200806ec_e.asp (accessed 29 July 2008).
Canadian International Development Agency. 'Programming Framework
    Canadian Cooperation Program in Cuba.' http://www.acdi-cida.gc.ca
    /CIDAWEB/acdicida.nsf/En/NIC-223122217-NDJ (accessed 28 June 2008).
Canadian Security and Intelligence Service. 'Report #2000/01 Trends in Ter-
    rorism.' *Perspectives: A Canadian Security Intelligence Service Publication* (18
    December 1999). http://www.csis-scrs.gc.ca/eng/miscdocs/200001_e.html
    (accessed 5 April 2002).
Canedy, Dana. 'Cuban Exiles Finding Spirit of Reconciliation.' New York
    Times, 23 March 2003.
Carlson, Darren. 'Poll Analysis: 40 Years after Bay of Pigs, Most Americans
    Have Unfavorable Opinion of Cuba, April 17, 2001.' Gallup Poll Organiza-
    tion. http://www.gallup.com/poll/releases/pr010417.asp (accessed 13
    August 2001).
Cassata, Donna. 'Foreign Policy: Papal Visit Highlights Divisions over Cuban
    Embargo.' *Congressional Quarterly* (24 January 1998).
Castro, Fidel. 'Appearance of Castro before the Press.' Interview conducted
    in Cuba, 19 February 1959. http://lanic.utexas.edu/project/castro/db
    /1959/19590219.html (accessed 30 October 2009).
– 'Castro Denounces Imperialism and Colonials at the United Nations.
    Speech delivered at UN General Assembly, Washington, D.C., 26 August

1960.' http://lanic.utexas.edu/project/castro/db/1960/19600926.html (accessed 30 October 2009).

– 'Castro: 1999 on PanAm Games in Winnipeg.' Speech delivered in Cienfuegos, Cuba, 26 July 1999. http://www.pbs.org/stealinghome/sport /castro99b.html (accessed 31 January 2002).

Cave, Damien. 'U.S. Overtures Find Support among Cuban-Americans.' New York *Times*, 20 April 2009.

Cawthorne, Andrew. 'Cuba Protests "Subversive" U.S. Radio Handouts, April 5, 2002.' Cuban American National Foundation. http://www.canf .org (accessed 12 April 2003).

CBC News. 'Chrétien Interview on Sept. 11.' http://www.cbc.ca (accessed 19 September 2002).

Chafetz, Glen, et al. 'Introduction: Tracing the Influence of Identity on Foreign Policy.' *Security Studies* 8, nos. 2, 3 (1998–9): 7–22.

Charles, Jacqueline. 'Hillary Clinton: Haiti, Cuba Policies Are under Review.' Miami *Herald*, 15 April 2009.

Checkel, Jeffery T. 'The Constructivist Turn in International Relations Theory.' *World Politics* 50 (January 1998): 324–48.

– 'Norms, Institutions, and National Identity in Contemporary Europe.' *International Studies Quarterly* 43 (1999): 83–114.

Christian, William, and Colin Campbell. *Political Parties and Ideologies in Canada*, 3rd ed. Toronto: McGraw-Hill Ryerson 1990.

Clark, Lesley. 'U.S., Cuba to Reopen Talks on Migration.' Miami *Herald*, 13 July 2009.

Clinton, William. 'Statement on Cuba, March 20, 1998.' American Presidency Project Online, University of California at Santa Barbara. http://www .presidency.ucsb.edu/ws/print.php?pid=55654 (accessed 26 August 2008).

CNN. 'U.N. "Strongly Deplores" Cuban Action.' CNN Interactive. http://www.cnn.com/US/9602/cuba_shootdown/27/8am/index.html (accessed 21 July 2002).

Collins, Michelle. 'Canadian Companies Hit a Snag in Cuba.' *Embassy*, 10 December 2008.

Combs, A.W., and D. Snygg. *Individual Behavior: A Perceptual Approach to Behavior*. New York: Harper 1959.

Comcast Interactive Media. 'Powell Backs down on Cuba Weapons Claims.' Comcast News. http://www.comcast.net/smedia/abcnews.com (accessed 14 May 2002).

Cordoba, Jose de, and Carlta Vitzthum. 'Canadian Woes with Cuba.' *Wall Street Journal*, 28 June 1999. http://www.fiu.edu/~fcf/cawo.html (accessed 31 January 2002).

Crawford, Neta C. 'The Passion of World Politics: Propositions on Emotion and Emotional Relationships.' *International Security* 24, no. 4 (2000): 116–56.

Crawford, Robert M.A., and Darryl S.L. Jarvis, eds. *International Relations – Still an American Social Science?* Albany: University of New York Press 2001.

Cuba Policy Foundation. 'Embargo Update, March 28, 2003.' http://www.cubafoundation.org/Embargo_Update-0303.28w.htm (accessed 13 April 2003).

– 'History of U.S. Policy.' http://www.cubapolicyfoundation.org/policy.html (accessed 1 April 2002).

– 'At Least 104 U.S. Congressional Districts, 66 Senate Seats Represented at Havana Trade Expo.' Press Release. 10 October 2002.

Cuba Working Group. 'A Review of US Policy toward Cuba, May 15, 2002.' U.S. House of Representatives. http://www.cubafoundation.org/CWG-Review.htm (accessed 13 April 2003).

Cuban American National Foundation. 'About the Cuban American National Foundation.' http://www.canfnet.org/About/aboutmain.htm (accessed 17 August 2001).

– 'CANF Deplores Latest House Actions on Cuba; Expresses Confidence in President's Commitment to Maintain Policy.' http://www.canfnet.org/News/020725releasea.htm (accessed 20 September 2002).

– 'Who Founded CANF?' http://www.canf.org/ingles/about-CANF/jorge-mas-canosa.htm (accessed 20 May 2008).

Cuban Information Archives. DOCUMENT 0146a, 'Broadcasting to Cuba Radio Martí & C.A.N.F. 1960–1990 part 1,' http://www.cubanexile.com/doc_126-150/doc0146a.html (accessed 23 July 2009).

Davidow, Jeffrey. 'The U.S. Vision: Cuba and Hemisphere Policy.' Remarks to the American Enterprise Institute and Friedrich Hayek University, Cuba Vision Series, Washington, D.C., 28 July 1997. http://www.state.gov/www/regions/wha/970728-davidow.html (accessed 19 April 1999).

Del Aguila, Juan. 'Development, Revolution, and Decay in Cuba.' In Howard Wiarda and Harvey Kline, eds., *Latin American Politics and Development*. Boulder, Colo.: Westview Press 1996.

Dent, David. *The Legacy of the Monroe Doctrine*. Westport, Conn.: Greenwood Press 1999.

Diaz-Balart, Lincoln. U.S. House of Representatives. 'Motion to Instruct Conferees on H.R. 2646, Farm Security Act of 2001.' House of Representatives/Extension of Remarks – April 18, 2002 (Page: H1453).' http://www.house.gov/apps/list/speech/fl21_diaz-balart/st020418.html (accessed 20 September 2002).

Dodd, Chris, U.S. Senator. 'His Eminence Bernard Cardinal Law, Archbishop of Boston, Reflecting on Cuba, Senate, March 19, 1998.' http://www.senate .gov/~dood/pres/speeches/105_98/0319.htm (accessed 28 January 2000).

Dominguez, Jorge. 'Cooperating with the Enemy? U.S. Immigration Policies toward Cuba.' In Christopher Mitchell, ed., *Western Hemisphere Immigration and United States Foreign Policy*. University Park: Pennsylvania State University Press 1992.

– 'US-Cuban Relations: From the Cold War to the Colder War.' *Journal of Interamerican Studies and World Affairs* 39, no. 3 (1997): 49–73.

Donaghy, Greg, and Mary Halloran. 'Viva el pueblo cubano: Pierre Trudeau's Distant Cuba, 1968–78.' In Robert Wright and Lana Wylie, eds. *Our Place in the Sun: Canada and Cuba in the Castro Era*. Toronto: University of Toronto Press 2009.

Dur, Philip, and Christopher Gilcrease. 'US Diplomacy and the Downfall of a Cuban Dictator: Machado in 1933.' *Journal of Latin American Studies* 34, no. 2 (2002): 255–82.

Eckstein, Susan. 'The Clash between Cuban Immigrant Cohorts.' In Mauricio A. Font, ed., *Cuba Today: Continuity and Change since the 'Periodo Especial.'* New York: Bildner Center for Western Hemisphere Studies, City University of New York, 2004. http://www.web.gc.cuny.edu/dept/bildn /publications/cubatodaybook.pdf (accessed 21 May 2008). Online Publication.

Edwards, R. Gary, and Jon Hughes. 'Status Quo Favoured in Business Relationship with Cuba.' *Gallup Poll*, 56, no. 25 (1996): 1–2.

Eisenhower, Dwight D. '6 July 1960.' *The Eisenhower Diaries*. Robert H. Ferrell, ed. New York: W.W. Norton 1981. Quoted in Dennis Molinaro, '"Calculated Diplomacy": John Diefenbaker and the Origins of Canada's Cuba Policy.' In Robert Wright and Lana Wylie, eds. *Our Place in the Sun: Canada and Cuba in the Castro Era*. Toronto: University of Toronto Press 2009.

Elliot, Andrea, and Elaine De Valle. 'Cuban Exiles Shifting Hard-line Position.' Miami *Herald*, 12 February 2003. http://www.miami.com/mld /miamiherald/news/world/cuba/5160039.htm (accessed 13 April 2003).

Entwistle, Mark. 'Canada-Cuba Relations: A Multiple-Personality Foreign Policy.' In Robert Wright and Lana Wylie, eds., *Our Place in the Sun: Canada and Cuba in the Castro Era*. Toronto: University of Toronto Press 2009.

Environics Research. 'Canada's World Poll,' 9–22 January 2008. http://www.canadasworld.ca/quizzesa/pollresu (accessed 13 July 2009).

Fascell, Dante. Human Rights in Cuba: Hearings before the Subcommittees on Human Rights and International Organizations and on Western Hemisphere Affairs of the Committee on Foreign Affairs, House of Representatives, 98th Cong., 2nd sess., 27 June 1984.

Fawthrop, Tom. 'Cuba Ailing? Not Its Biomedical Industry.' *Straits Times*. 26 January 2004. Reprinted in *YaleGlobal Online*, http://yaleglobal.yale.edu (accessed 8 December 2005).

Faya, Ana. 'Let's Be Honest about the Tories' Approach to Cuba.' *Embassy*, 28 May 2008. http://embassymag.ca/html/index.php?display=story &full_path=/2008/may/28/let ter3/ (accessed 30 July 2008).

Feinsilver, Julie Margot. *Healing the Masses*. Berkeley: University of California Press 1993.

'Fidel Castro Sends Message of Solidarity to Protesters in Quebec.' 21 April 2001. http://www.radiohc.org (accessed 31 January 2002).

'Fidel's reply to statement by U.S. Ambassador in the Dominican Republic.' *Granma*, 11 April 2003. http://www.granma.cu/ingles/abril03 /vier11/15respuest.html (accessed 14 April 2003).

Fisher, Luke, et al. 'Canada Protests Controversial Bill.' *Maclean's*, 18 March 1996.

Fiske, Susan, and Shelley E. Taylor. *Social Cognition*. Reading, Mass.: Addison-Wesley 1984.

Florini, Ann. 'The Evolution of International Norms.' *International Studies Quarterly* 40, no. 3 (1996): 363–90.

Foreign and Commonwealth Office. 'Creating Stronger and Better Relations with Cuba, April 2, 2003.' United Kingdom Parliament, Publications and Records, http://www.fco.gov.uk/en/newsroom/latest-news/?view= News&id=1559096 (accessed 31 July 2008).

Fuente, Jose de la. 'Wine into Vinegar: The Fall of Cuba's Biotechnology.' *Nature Biotechnology* 19, no. 10 (2001): 905–7.

Galindo, Miguel A. 'Immunization and Vaccine Research in Cuba: Cuba's National Immunization Program.' *Medical Education Cooperation with Cuba (MEDICC) Review*. http://www.medicc.org/medicc_review/1004/pages /spotlight.html (accessed 12 December 2005).

Gallup Poll Inc.. 'Cuba.' http://www.galluppoll.com/content/?ci=1630 &pg=1 (accessed 21 June 2007).

– 'Favorability: People in the News.' http://www.galluppoll.com/content /?ci=1618&pg=1 (accessed 21 June 2007).

Gecelovsky, Paul, and Tom Keating. 'Liberal Internationalism for Conservatives: The Good Governance Initiative.' In Nelson Michaud and Kim Richard Nossal, eds., *Diplomatic Departures: The Conservative Era in Canadian Foreign Policy, 1984–93*. Vancouver: UBC Press 2001.

Gee, Marcus. 'Recognize Castro for What He Is.' *Globe and Mail*, 10 March 1999.

Geertz, Clifford. *Local Knowledge: Further Essays in Interpretive Anthropology*. New York: Basic Books 1983.

Gelpi, Christopher. 'Crime and Punishment: The Role of Norms in Crisis Bargaining.' *American Political Science Review* 91, no. 2 (1997): 339–60.

Giffen, Gordon. 'The Road to the Future: The U.S.-Canada Relationship.' In Gareth S. Seltzer and Edward P. Badovinac, eds., *The Empire Club of Canada Speeches 1997–1998.* Toronto: Empire Club Foundation 1998.

Giles, Jim. 'Cuban science: ¿Vive la revolución?' *Nature* 436, no. 7049 (2005): 322–4.

Globe and Mail. 'Canada's Cuban Confusion,' 11 March 1998.

– 'Cuban Trial Step Backward, Axworthy Says,' 3 March 1999.

– 'Former President Carter on Landmark Visit to Cuba,' 12 May 2002. http://www.theglobeandmail.com (accessed 13 May 2002).

– 'Letter to the Editor,' 2 May 1998.

– 'The Old Foe in Havana,' 16 May 2002.

Gonzalez, David. 'Carter's Trip to Cuba Raises Many Hopes from All Sides.' New York *Times,* 11 May 2002.

– 'Cuba Arrests More Dissidents amid Outcry.' New York *Times,* 22 March 2003.

– 'Cuban Crackdown on Critics Stalls a Drive to Ease U.S. Embargo.' New York *Times,* 13 April 2003.

Graham, Hon. Bill, Minister of Foreign Affairs. 'Notes for an Address to the Terrorism, Law and Democracy Conference Organized by the Canadian Institute for the Administration of Justice.' Speech delivered in Montreal, 26 March 2002. http://www.webapps.dfaitmaeci.gc.ca/minipub /Publication.asp?FileSpec+/Min_Pub/105049.hm (accessed 5 April 2002).

Granatstein, J.L., and Robert Bothwell. *Pirouette: Pierre Trudeau and Canadian Foreign Policy.* Toronto: University of Toronto Press 1990.

Guy, James. 'The Growing Relationship of Canada and the Americas.' *International Perspectives* (July–August 1977): 3–6.

Guzmán, María G. 'Deciphering Dengue: The Cuban Experience.' *Global Voices of Science* 309, no. 5740 (2005): 1495–7.

Hamilton, Lee. Quoted in Tim Weiner, 'Pope vs. Embargo: Still a Sharp Divide in U.S.,' New York *Times,* 21 January 1998.

Hamilton Friendship Association with Cuba. 'About Us,' http://cuba-canada.org/about (accessed 20 July 2009).

Haney, Patrick J., and Walt Vanderbush. 'The Role of Ethnic Interest Groups in U.S. Foreign Policy: The Case of the Cuban American National Foundation.' *International Studies Quarterly* 43, no. 2 (1999): 341–61.

Harper, Stephen [Canadian Prime Minister]. 'Prime Minister Harper Signals Canada's Renewed Engagement in the Americas.' Speech delivered in San-

tiago, Chile, 17 July 2007. http://www.pm.gc.ca/eng/media.asp
?category=2&id=1759 (accessed 30 July 2008).

Hartz, Louis, ed. *The Founding of New Societies*. New York: Harcourt, Brace
and World 1964.

Hays, Dennis. 'Inspect Cuba for Production of Biological Weapons.' Miami
Herald, 29 July 2002.

Hermanin, Robert. 'Identity, Norms, and National Security: The Soviet
Foreign Policy Revolution and the End of the Cold War.' In Peter J. Katzen-
stein, ed., *The Culture of National Security*. New York: Columbia University
Press 1996.

Hernandez, Francisco 'Pepe.' 'Send U.S. Funds Directly to Cuba's Democratic
Opposition.' Cuban American National Foundation. 15 May 2008.
http://canf1.org/cgibin/artman/search.cgi?action=search&page=1&perpa
ge=5&template=articleLists/categoryIndex.html&categoryNum=33
(accessed 15 May 2008).

Hernández, Rafael. 'Cuba and the United States: Political Values and Interests in a Changing International System.' In Jorge Dominguez and Rafael
Hernández, eds., *U.S.-Cuban Relations in the 1990s*. Boulder, Colo.: Westview Press 1989.

Horowitz, Gad. 'Conservatism, Liberalism, and Socialism in Canada: An
Interpretation.' *Canadian Journal of Economics and Political Science* 32, no. 1
(1966): 143–71.

– 'Tories, Socialists, and the Demise of Canada.' *Canadian Dimension* 2, no. 4
(1965): 12–15.

Howland, Sandra. 'UNB Know-How Boosts Cuba's Biomedical Capability.'
University of New Brunswick, News Release: C891 (30 January 2004).
http://www.unb.ca/news/view.cgi?id=442 (accessed 29 July 2008).

Hunt, Michael H. *Ideology and US Foreign Policy*. New Haven, Conn.: Yale
University Press 1987.

Hurlich, Susan. 'The World's First Synthetic Vaccine for Children.'
CubaNow.net. http://www.cubanow.cult.cu/global/loader.php?secc=10
&cont=culture/num10/8.h tm (accessed 7 January 2006).

Industry Canada. 'Canadian Trade by Industry.' Trade Data Online.
http://www.ic.gc.ca/sc_mrkti/tdst/tdo/tdo.php?lang=30&productType=
NAICS (accessed 28 June 2008).

Institute of Biomedical Engineering. 'Research.' University of New
Brunswick. http://www.unb.ca/biomed/ (accessed 29 July 2008).

Jenks, Leland. *Our Cuban Colony: A Study in Sugar*. New York: Arno Press 1970.

Jervis, Robert. *Perception and Misperception in International Politics*. Princeton,
N.J.: Princeton University Press 1976.

Jockel, Joe, and Joel Sokolsky. 'Lloyd Axworthy's Legacy.' *International Journal* 61, no. 1 (2000–1): 2.

Kaiser, Jocelyn. 'Synthetic Vaccine Is a Sweet Victory for Cuban Science.' *Science* 305, no. 5683 (2004): 460.

Katzenstein, Peter. *Cultural Norms and National Security: Police and Military in Postwar Japan*. Ithaca, N.Y.: Cornell University Press 1996.

Keohane, Robert. *International Institutions and State Power*. Boulder, Colo.: Westview Press 1989.

Kilgour, David. 'Canada's Peacekeeping Role: Then and Now.' http://www .david-kilgour.com/mp/Peacekeeping%20U%20of%20A.html, 'Picking up the Peaces.' Speech delivered at the Shell Canada Lecture Theatre, Edmonton, University of Alberta International Week 2004, 26 January 2004 (accessed 20 January 2008).

Kirk, John, and Peter McKenna. *Canada-Cuba Relations: The Other Good Neighbor Policy*. Gainesville, Fla.: University Press of Florida 1997.

Kirk, John, Peter McKenna, and Julia Sagebien. *Back in Business: Canada-Cuba Relations after 50 Years*. Ottawa: FOCAL [Canadian Foundation for the Americas] 1995.

Klepak, Hal. 'Canada, Cuba, and Latin America: A Paradoxical Relationship.' In Robert Wright and Lana Wylie, eds., *Our Place in the Sun: Canada and Cuba in the Castro Era*. Toronto: University of Toronto Press 2009.

Knox, Paul. 'Graham Protests against Cuban Trials.' *Globe and Mail*, 8 April 2003. http://www.theglobeandmail.com/servlet/story/RTGAM .20030408.ucuba0408/BNStory/international/?query=Cuba (accessed 14 April 2003).

– 'PM Uses Cuban TV to Push Trade Links,' *Globe and Mail*, 27 April 1998.

– 'Why Did Washington Goad Cuba?' *Globe and Mail*, 9 April 2003.

Koring, Paul. 'Axworthy, Helms Aide Slug It out on Cuba.' *Globe and Mail*, 7 March 1998.

Kranish, Michael. 'Incubating Biotech: US Charges Highlight Castro's Efforts to Build Industry.' *Boston Globe*, 15 May 2002.

Kratochwil, Friedrich. *Rules, Norms, Decisions*. Cambridge: Cambridge University Press 1989.

Kratochwil, Friedrich, and John Ruggie. 'International Organization: A State of the Art and an Art of the State.' *International Organization* 40, no. 4 (1986): 753–5.

Lane, Charles. 'And a Child Shall Lead Them: Miami's Passionate, Self-defeating Fight for Elian Gonzalez.' *New Republic*, 24 January 2000. http://www.thenewrepublic.com (accessed 19 August 2001).

Latino News Network. 'CANF Deplores Interpol Chief's Acceptance of Cuba

Terrorism Ties – January 22, 2002.' http://www.latnn.com (accessed 20 September 2002).

Lebow, Richard Ned, and Thomas Risse-Kappen, eds. *International Relations Theory and the End of the Cold War*. New York: Columbia University Press 1996.

Lipset, Seymour Martin. *American Exceptionalism: A Double-Edged Sword*. New York: W.W. Norton 1996.

Lobe, Jim. 'Learn from Cuba, Says World Bank.' Inter Press Service (IPS), 1 May 2001. http://www.hartfordhwp.com/archives/43b/185.html (accessed 2 May 2007).

Lopez, Ernesto, et al. 'Development of Cuban biotechnology.' *Journal of Commercial Biotechnology* 9, no. 2 (2002): 147–52.

McFarquhar, Neil. 'U.S. Embargo on Cuba Again Finds Scant Support at U.N.' New York *Times*, 29 October 2009.

McGillivray, Gillian. 'Trading with the "Enemy": Canadian-Cuban Relations in the 1990s.' *Cuba Briefing Paper Series*, no. 15 (December 1997): 1–27.

McKenna, Peter, and John M. Kirk. 'Canada, Cuba Melting the Bilateral Ice?' Halifax *Herald*, 6 November 2002.

– 'Canadian-Cuban Relations: Muddling through the "Special Period."' In Robert Wright and Lana Wylie, eds., *Our Place in the Sun: Canada and Cuba in the Castro Era*. Toronto: University of Toronto Press 2009.

Markus, Hazel, Jeanne Smith, and Richard L. Moreland. 'Role of the Self-Concept in the Perception of Others.' *Journal of Personality and Social Psychology* 49 (1985): 1494–512.

Marquis, Christopher. 'U.S. Accuses Cuba of Trying to Disrupt Antiterrorism Effort.' New York *Times*, 18 September 2002.

Marquis, Christopher, and Eric Schmitt. 'Bush Faces Pressure from Congress to Alter Cuba Policy.' New York *Times*, 19 May 2002.

Martin, Keith [Canadian Reform, Liberal MP]. 'America's Cuban Debacle.' *TV Times*, Ottawa, 15 March 1996. http://www.keithmartin.org/policy /foreign/foreign_cuba.shtml (accessed 17 July 2002).

Marxist-Leninist Daily. 'Cuba Si! Discussion with Deputy Chief of Cuban Embassy.' 26 January 2005. http://www.cpcml.ca/Tmld2005/D35003.htm (accessed 15 May 2008).

Merkle, Daniel. 'Carter Improves with Age.' ABCNews.com, 1 October 1999. http://www.abcnews.go.com/sections/politics/DailyNews/poll990929 .html (accessed 14 April 2003).

Meisler, Stanley. 'U.N. Rebuffs U.S. on Cuba Embargo-Trade: Allies Desert Washington in 59–3 General Assembly Vote That Urges Lifting of Latest

Restrictions. American Interference in Foreign Subsidiaries Is Alleged.' Los Angles *Times*, 25 November 1992.

Miami *Herald*. 'MPs Irate over Cuba Comments: House Speaker's Remarks Assailed.' 11 March 1998.

Miller, Seumas, and Michael J. Selgelid. *Ethical and Philosophical Consideration of the Dual-Use Dilemma in the Biological Sciences*. The Netherlands: Springer 2008.

Minister of Public Works and Government Services Canada. *Canada-United States Accord on Our Shared Border – Update 2000*. Ottawa: Minister of Public Works and Government Services Canada 2000. http://www.dsppsd .pwgsc.gc.ca/Collection/Ci51-95-2000E.pdf (accessed 30 July 2008).

Misztal, Frank, Master Corporal. 'I Am Canadian.' Canadian Peacekeepers Home Page. http://www.peacekeeper.ca/stories3.html#17 (accessed 11 July 2007).

Molinaro, Denis. '"Calculated Diplomacy": John Diefenbaker and the Origins of Canada's Cuba Policy.' In Robert Wright and Lana Wylie, eds., *Our Place in the Sun: Canada and Cuba in the Castro Era*. Toronto: University of Toronto Press 2009.

Molson Canada. 'I Am Canadian.' YouTube. http://www.youtube.com /watch?v=BRI-A3vakVg (accessed 26 January 2008).

Moravcsik, Andrew. 'Taking Preferences Seriously: A Liberal Theory of International Politics.' *International Organization* 51, no. 4 (1997): 513–53.

Morgan, Dan. 'Federal Pay Raise Near House Passage: End to Cuba Travel Curbs Also Backed.' Washington *Post*, 24 July 2002.

Morley, Morris H. *Imperial State and Revolution: The United States and Cuba, 1952–1986*. Cambridge: Cambridge University Press 1987.

Mozer, David. 'Cuba and the September 11, 2001 Attacks.' 'Cuba, U.S. Policy, Travel and Resources.' http://www.ibike.org/cuba/911.htm (accessed 29 July 2008).

Munton, Don, and David Vogt. 'Inside Castro's Cuba: The Revolution and Canada's Embassy in Havana.' In Robert Wright and Lana Wylie, eds., *Our Place in the Sun: Canada and Cuba in the Castro Era*. Toronto: University of Toronto Press 2009.

Nash, Knowlton. *Kennedy and Diefenbaker: Fear and Loathing across the Undefended Border*. Toronto: McClelland and Stewart 1990.

Nature. Editorial. 'Socialism in One Country.' 436, no. 7049 (2005): 303–4.

NBC/Wall Street Journal Poll. 'Elian Gonzalez, April 29–May 1, 2000.' PollingReport.com. www.pollingreport.com/oldnews.htm (accessed 17 August 2001).

Nicol, Heather N., ed. *Canada, the US and Cuba: Helms-Burton and Its After-*

math. Kingston, Ont.: Centre for International Relations, Queen's University, 1999.

Nordlinger, Jay. 'Meet the Diaz-Balarts: A Couple of Castro's "nephews" – in Congress. (Lincoln and Mario Diaz-Balart).' *National Review*, 10 March 2003.

Nova Scotia-Cuba Association. 'About Us,' http://www.nscuba.org /About_Us.html (accessed 20 July 2009).

Nuccio, Richard. 'Cuba: A U.S. Perspective.' In Richard N. Haass, ed., *Trans-Atlantic Tensions*. Washington, D.C.: Brookings Institution Press 1999.

Obama, Barack [U.S. Senator]. 'Barack Obama on the Cuban Embargo, January 20, 2004.' http://www.youtube.com/watch?v=cZ3SVok9g34 (accessed 21 August 2008).

– 'Editorial.' Miami *Herald*, 22 August 2007.

Odum, Howard W. 'Survey Collection: Harris/ 1643, IRSS Study Number: S1643.' Institute for Research in Social Science, University of North Carolina at Chapel Hill. http://www.veblen.irss.unc.edu (accessed 17 August 2001).

Oficina Nacional de Estadísticas República de Cuba. 'Intercambio comercial de mercancías de países seleccionados por aéreas geográficas.' Sector Externo. http://www.one.cu/aec2006/anuariopdf2006/capitulo7 /VII.4.pdf (accessed 1 July 2008).

Onuf, Nicholas. 'Constructivism: A User's Manual.' In Vendulka Kubalkova, Nicholas Onuf, and Paul Kowert, eds., *International Relations in a Constructed World*. Armonk, N.Y.: ME Sharpe 1998.

– *World of Our Making: Rules and Rule in Social Theory and International Relations*. Columbia: University of South Carolina Press 1989.

O'Sullivan, John L. 'On Manifest Destiny.' In J. and H.G., Publishers, 'The Great Nation of Futurity,' *The United States Democratic Review* 6, no. 23 (1839): 426–30. http://www.mtholyoke.edu/acad/intrel/osulliva.htm (accessed 7 March 2003).

Ouellet, André. *Canadian Foreign Policy*. 133rd House of Commons *Debates*, 35th Parliament, 1st sess., 15 March 1994.

Paterson, Thomas G. *Contesting Castro: The United States and the Triumph of the Cuban Revolution*. New York: Oxford University Press 1994.

PBS Online. 'Lloyd Axworthy.' NewsHour, 23 January 1997. http://www .pbs.org/newshour/bb/latin_america/january97/canada_1-23.html (accessed 3 April 2003).

Pearson Peacekeeping Centre. 'Think about Peace.' http://www.think aboutpeace.ca/en/winners_en.html (accessed 21 July 2008).

– 'Welcome.' http://www.peaceoperations.org/ (accessed 21 July 2008).

Perez, Louis A., Jr. *Cuba: Between Reform and Revolution*. Oxford: Oxford University Press 1988.

Pew Global Attitudes Project. 'Global Opinion Trends 2002–2007.' 24 July 2007. http://www.pewglobal.org/reports/pdf/257.pdf (accessed 3 February 2008).

Pillar, Paul R. *Terrorism and U.S. Foreign Policy*. Washington, D.C.: Brookings Institution Press 2001.

'Polling the Nations' (1986–2001). *Cuba*. Matthews, N.C.: Rasmussen Research 2000.

– *Portrait of America*. Matthews, N.C.: Rasmussen Research 2000.

Powell, Colin L. Secretary of State. 'Foreword.' Report on the Commission for Assistance for a Free Cuba. http://www.cafc.gov/documents /organization/67962.pdf (accessed 31 August 2008).

Pratt, Cranford. 'Canada's Development Assistance: Some Lessons from the Last Review.' *International Journal* 49, no. 1 (1993–4): 93–125.

Rice, Condoleezza, Secretary of State, Chair. 'Report of the Commission for Assistance to a Free Cuba.' Report to the President. 10 July 2006. http://www.cafc.gov/documents/organization/68166.pdf (accessed 31 August 2008).

Ritchie, Charles. *Storm Signals: More Undiplomatic Memories, 1962–1971*. Toronto: Macmillan 1983. Quoted in John Kirk and Peter McKenna, *Canada-Cuba Relations: The Other Good Neighbor Policy*. Gainesville, Fla.: University Press of Florida 1997.

Ritter, Archibald R.M. 'Canadian-Cuban Economic Relations: Past, Present, and Prospective.' In Robert Wright and Lana Wylie, eds. *Our Place in the Sun: Canada and Cuba in the Castro Era*. Toronto: University of Toronto Press 2009.

– 'Cuba Project.' Speech delivered to the City University of New York's Queens College and Graduate School, 2001.

Robbins, Carla Anne. 'Dateline Washington: Cuban-American Clout.' *Foreign Policy*, no. 88 (1992): 162–82.

Robertson, Norman. Quoted in John Kirk and Peter McKenna, *Canada-Cuba Relations: The Other Good Neighbor Policy*. Gainesville, Fla.: University Press of Florida 1997.

Robinson, H. Basil. *Diefenbaker's World: A Populist in Foreign Affairs*. Toronto: University of Toronto Press 1989.

Rochlin, James. *Discovering the Americas: The Evolution of Canadian Foreign Policy towards Latin America*. Vancouver: UBC Press 1994.

Roosevelt, Theodore. *The Roosevelt Corollary to the Monroe Doctrine*. Annual Message to Congress, 6 December 1904. http://www.uiowa.edu/~c030162 /Common/Handouts/POTUS/TRoos.html (accessed 21 March 2001).

Root, Elihu. Quoted in Thomas G. Paterson, *Contesting Castro: The United*

States and the Triumph of the Cuban Revolution. New York: Oxford University Press 1994.

Ruggie, John. 'International Structure and International Transformation: Space, Time and Method.' In James N. Rosenau and Ernst-Otto Czempiel, eds., *Global Changes and Theoretical Challenges.* Lexington, Ky.: Lexington Books 1989.

Sallot, Jeff. 'Cuba Policy Gives Ottawa Leverage for Change, PM Says.' *Globe and Mail,* 17 March 1999.

Scanlan, John, and Gilburt Loescher. 'U.S. Foreign Policy, 1959–80: Impact on Refugee Flow from Cuba.' *Annals of the American Academy of Political and Social Science* 467, no. 1 (1983): 116–37.

Schwab, Peter. *Cuba: Confronting the U.S. Embargo.* New York: St Martin's Press 1999.

Sheinin, David. 'Cuba's Long Shadow: The Progressive Church Movement and Canadian-Latin American Relations, 1970–87.' In Robert Wright and Lana Wylie, eds., *Our Place in the Sun: Canada and Cuba in the Castro Era.* Toronto: University of Toronto Press 2009.

Smith, Wayne. *The Closest of Enemies.* New York: W.W. Norton 1987.

Snow, Anita. 'U.S. Diplomat in Cuba Walks an Often Rocky Road as Chief of Mission on Communist Island, June 7, 2002.' Cuban American National Foundation. http://www.canfnet.org/News/archived/020607newsa.htm (accessed 14 April 2003).

Stairs, Denis. 'The Political Culture of Canadian Foreign Policy.' *Canadian Journal of Political Science* 15 (December 1982): 667–90.

Statistics Canada. 'Latin America and the Caribbean: Exports and Imports: December 1996.' Statistics Canada, Merchandise Trade Statistics, May 1997.

Sullivan, Mark. *CRS Report for Congress: Cuba: Issues for the 110th Congress.* Congressional Research Service, 21 August 2007.

Tamayo, Juan O. 'Jonathan Farrar to Replace Michael Parmly as "Ambassador" to Cuba.' Miami *Herald,* 16 May 2008.

Thomas, Hugh. *Cuba: The Pursuit of Freedom.* New York: Harper and Row 1971.

Thorsteinsdóttir, Halla, et al. 'Cuba – Innovation through Synergy.' *Nature Biotechnology* 22 (2004): DC19–DC23.

Twing, Stephen W. *Myths, Models, and U.S. Foreign Policy: The Cultural Shaping of Three Cold Warriors.* Boulder, Colo.: Lynne Rienner Publishers 1998.

United Nations. Press Release GA/9814. 'For Ninth Successive Year, General Assembly Calls for End of United States Embargo against Cuba.' http://www.un.org/News/Press/docs/2000/20001109.ga9814.doc .html (accessed 31 August 2008).

USA Today/Gallup Poll. 'Cuba, Feb. 21–24, 2008.' http://www.polling report.com/cuba.htm (accessed 4 August 2008).

U.S.-Cuba Trade and Economic Council. 'Foreign Investment and Cuba.' http://www.cubatrade.org/ (accessed 1 July 2008).

U.S. Department of State. 'Background Note: Cuba (09/01).' http://www.state.gov/r/pa/bgn/2886.htm (accessed 15 February 2002).

– *Bureau of Public Affairs* 6 (1962). Quoted in Jutta Weldes, 'The Cultural Production of Crisis: U.S. Identity and Missiles in Cuba.' In *Cultures of Insecurity: States, Communities, and the Production of Danger*. Minneapolis: University of Minnesota Press 1999.

– 'Country Reports on Terrorism – State Sponsors of Terror Overview.' Office of the Coordinator for Counterterrorism. Washington, D.C., 28 April 2006. http://www.state.gov/s/ct/rls/crt/2005/64337.htm (accessed 29 May 2008).

– 'Cuba: U.S. Policy Now and in the Future – Remarks by Michael Rannaberger, Coordinator for Cuban Affairs, before the Governor's Cuba Advisory Group.' Miami, 28 February 1997. http://www.state.gov/www/regions/wha/970228_ranneberger.html (accessed 9 September 2002).

– 'Cuban Liberty and Democratic Solidarity [Libertad] Act of 1996 Conference Report (Senate – March 05, 1996).' http://www.senate.gov/~dood/press/Speeches/104_96/0303.htm (accessed 28 January 2002).

– 'Cuban Liberty and Democratic Solidarity [Libertad] Act of 1996–PL104–114.' http://www.usinfo.state.gov/regional/ar/us-cuba/libertad.htm (accessed 26 August 2001).

– 'Toward a Democratic Cuba.' Speech by President George W. Bush, Washington, D.C., 13 July 2001. http://www.usinfo.state.gov/regional/ar/us-cuba/ (accessed 20 August 2001).

– *Foreign Relations of the United States, Statement of 11 April 1898*. Washington, D.C.: Government Printing Office 1899.

– 'Patterns of Global Terrorism 1998.' Press Briefing, Washington, D.C., 30 April 1999.

– 'Patterns of Global Terrorism – 2002 Overview of State-Sponsored Terrorism.' Office of the Coordinator for Counterterrorism, Washington, D.C., 30 April 2003. http://www.state.gov/s/ct/rls/crt/2002/html/19988.htm (accessed 15 March 2008).

– 'Secretary of State Madeleine K. Albright and Canadian Foreign Minister Axworthy: Remarks in Press Briefing. Ottawa, Canada, March 10, 1998.' http://www.secretary.state.gov/www/statements/1998/980310a.html (accessed 22 February 2002).

U.S. Department of State. Office of the Historian. 'National Security Affairs; Foreign Economic Policy.' U.S. Department of State 1 (1950).

U.S. Government Printing Office. 'Remarks Announcing Sanctions against Cuba following the Downing of Brothers to the Rescue Airplanes.' *Weekly*

Compilation of Presidential Documents, 26 February 1996. http://www.frweb
gate4.access.gpo.gov (accessed 15 April 2002).

U.S. House of Representatives. *Cuban Liberty and Democratic Solidarity Act of
1996*. Report 104–168, sec. 201, 1 March 1996.

– 'Shoot-Down of the Brothers to the Rescue Planes, Hearing before the
Subcommittee on Crime of the Committee on the Judiciary.' 106th Cong.,
1st sess., 19 July 1999. http://www.commdocs.house.gov/committees
/judiciary/hju63608.000/hju63608_ 0.htm (accessed 21 August
2002).

U.S. Interests Section, Havana, Cuba. 'Basic Policy: To Support Peaceful
Change from Within (January 1998).' Embassy of the United States of
America. http://www.usembassy.state.gov/havana/wwwh0012.html
(accessed 24 March 2003).

U.S. Library of Congress. 'Cuba' [search term used to obtain list of bills introduced in 110th Congress]. http://www.thomas.loc.gov/cgi-bin/thomas
(accessed 28 July 2008).

'U.S. Policy: Balancing Strategic and Humanitarian Concerns.' *Congressional
Digest* (March 1999).

U.S. Senate. 'America's Free Trade Act (January 22, 2001).' Library of Congress. http://www.thomas.loc.gov/cgibin/query/D?c107:11:./temp
/~c107usOUxu (accessed 22 March 2001).

U.S. Trade and Economic Council. 'Foreign Investment and Cuba.'
http://www.cubatrade.org (accessed 5 January 2003).

Vanderbush, Walt. 'Exiles and the Marketing of U.S. Policy.' *Foreign Policy
Analysis* 5 (2009): 287–306.

Vaughan, Christopher A. 'Cartoon Cuba: Race, Gender and Political Opinion
Leadership in *Judge*, 1898.' *African Journalism Studies* 24, no. 2 (2003):
195–217.

Vertzberger, Yaacov Y.I. *The World in Their Minds: Information Processing, Cognition, and Perception in Foreign Policy Decisionmaking*. Stanford, Calif.: Stanford University Press 1990.

Wallace, Bruce. 'I Think He Is Changing.' *Maclean's* 111, no. 19 (1998).

– 'Jean and Fidel.' *Maclean's* 3, no. 19 (1998).

Weber, Cynthia. *Faking It: U.S. Hegemony in a 'Post-Phallic' Era*. Minneapolis:
University of Minnesota Press 1999.

Weissert, Will. 'Cuban Activists Briefed on Human Rights, March 7, 2007.'
Cubanet. http://www.cubanet.org/CNews/y07/mar07/16e7.htm
(accessed 28 July 2008).

Wendt, Alexander. 'The Agent-Structure Problem in International Relations
Theory.' *International Organization* 41, no. 3 (1987): 335–70.

– 'Anarchy Is What States Make of It: The Social Construction of Power Poli-
tics.' *International Organization* 46 (spring 1992): 391–425.
– *Social Theory of International Politics*. Cambridge: Cambridge University
Press 1999.
White House. Office of the Press Secretary. 'Fact Sheet: Commission for the
Assistance of a Free Cuba.' http://www.whitehouse.gov/news/releases
/2003/12/20031208-8.html (accessed 31 August 2008).
Wiarda, Howard J. *American Foreign Policy: Actors and Processes*. New York:
HarperCollins College Publishers 1999.
Wilson, Woodrow. 'The Ideals of America.' Speech delivered 26 December
1901. Quoted in David Hollinger and Charles Capper, eds., *The Liberal
Intellectual Tradition*. New York: Oxford University Press 2001.
World Health Organization. 'Cuba: Mortality and Burden of Disease.' World
Health Organization Country Profiles. http://www.who.int/countries
/cub/en/ (accessed 12 December 2005).
World Values Survey. '1999–2001 World Values Survey.' Institute for Social
Research, the University of Michigan. http://www.worldvaluessurvey.org/
(accessed 2 February 2008).
Wright, Cynthia. 'Between Nation and Empire: The Fair Play for Cuba Com-
mittees and the Making of Canada-Cuba Solidarity in the Early 1960s.' In
Robert Wright and Lana Wylie, eds., *Our Place in the Sun: Canada and Cuba
in the Castro Era*. Toronto: University of Toronto Press 2009.
Wright, Robert. 'Northern Ice: Jean Chrétien and the Failure of Constructive
Engagement in Cuba.' In Robert Wright and Lana Wylie, eds., *Our Place in
the Sun: Canada and Cuba in the Castro Era*. Toronto: University of Toronto
Press 2009.
– *Three Nights In Havana: Pierre Trudeau, Fidel Castro and the Cold War World*.
Toronto: HarperCollins 2007.
Wright, Robert, and Lana Wylie, eds. *Our Place in the Sun: Canada and Cuba in
the Castro Era*. Toronto: University of Toronto Press 2009.
Wylie, Lana. 'Ambassador MD: The Role of Health and Biotechnology in
Cuban Foreign Policy.' In Robert Wright and Lana Wylie, eds., *Our Place in
the Sun: Canada and Cuba in the Castro Era*. Toronto: University of Toronto
Press 2009.
– 'Perceptions and Foreign Policy: A Comparative Study of Canadian and
American Policy toward Cuba.' *Canadian Foreign Policy* 11, no. 3 (2004).
Yee, Chen May. 'Cutting-edge Biotech in Old-world Cuba.' *Christian Science
Monitor*, 17 April 2003. http://www.csmonitor.com/2003/0417/p14s03-
stct.html (accessed 28 July 2008).
Zehr, Leonard. 'Biotech Builds on Cuban Innovation, May 2, 2001.' Cubanet.
http://www.cubanet.org/CNews?y01/may01?02e8.hm (accessed 8
December 2005).

Index